eurostat
Statistical books

Eurostat regional yearbook 2011

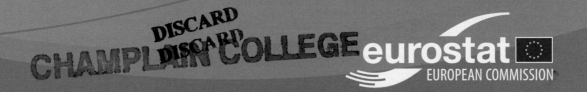

eurostat
EUROPEAN COMMISSION

Europe Direct is a service to help you find answers to your questions about the European Union.

Freephone number (*):

00 800 6 7 8 9 10 11

(*) Certain mobile telephone operators do not allow access to 00 800 numbers or these calls may be billed.

More information on the European Union is available on the Internet (http://europa.eu).

Cataloguing data can be found at the end of this publication.

Luxembourg: Publications Office of the European Union, 2011

ISBN 978-92-79-20366-4
ISSN 1830-9674
doi:10.2785/1392
Cat. No: KS-HA-11-001-EN-C

Theme: General and regional statistics
Collection: Statistical books

Foreword

The *Eurostat regional yearbook* provides an overview of key statistics available for the regions of Europe. A close look at many of the very relevant social, economic and environmental indicators will quickly reveal that national figures do not show the full picture of what is happening in Europe in many, and perhaps most, cases. Very different developments are often visible if one looks at smaller geographical scales. Thus the *Eurostat regional yearbook* is a valuable supplement to *Europe in figures — Eurostat yearbook*, which concentrates exclusively on statistics on a national scale. On this occasion I would like to draw your attention to a recent publication of the European Commission, *Investing in Europe's future — Fifth report on economic, social and territorial cohesion*,  which puts many of the statistics shown in the *Eurostat regional yearbook* into a European policy context: pa.eu/regional_policy/sources/docoffic/official/reports/cohesion5/pdf/5cr_en.pdf

The system of so-called NUTS (nomenclature of territorial units for statistics) on which the regional statistics are based has strong implications beyond the direct field of statistics. Its definition of regions is used more and more in other areas, and thus contributes to shaping the perception of European citizens in their identification with a certain regional structure. The NUTS system thus contributes to the gradual creation of a common European concept of regions.

In 2011, for the first time, you can find the content of this book updated online in 'Statistics explained'. As usual, the latest and most complete versions of all the data can be downloaded from the Eurostat website.

Eurostat is the statistical office of the European Union. Working together with national statistical authorities in the European statistical system, we produce official statistics, which meet the highest possible standards of quality.

I wish you an enjoyable reading experience!

Walter Radermacher
Director-General, Eurostat
Chief Statistician of the European Union

Abstract

Statistical information is an important tool for understanding and quantifying the impact of political decisions on the citizens in a specific territory or region. The *Eurostat regional yearbook 2011* gives a detailed picture of a large number of statistical fields in the 27 Member States of the European Union, as well as in EFTA and candidate countries. The text of each chapter has been written by specialists in statistics and is accompanied by maps, figures and tables. A broad set of regional indicators are presented for the following 16 subjects: population, labour market, labour cost, education, health, European cities, gross domestic product, household accounts, structural business statistics, information society, tourism, land cover and land use, coastal regions, transport, science, technology and innovation and last but not least, a study on trends in densely and thinly populated areas.

Editor-in-chief

Teodóra Brandmüller

Eurostat, Head of section, Unit E.4, Regional statistics and geographical information

Editor

Åsa Önnerfors

Eurostat, Unit E.4, Regional statistics and geographical information

Map production

Abaco Srl, coordinated by César de Diego Diez, Åsa Önnerfors, Daniela Scirankova and Atanas Trifonov

Eurostat, Unit E.4, Regional statistics and geographical information

Dissemination

Isabelle Fiasse

Eurostat, Unit D.4, Dissemination

Contact details

Eurostat

Bâtiment Joseph Bech

5, rue Alphonse Weicker

2721 LUXEMBOURG

E-mail: estat-user-support@ec.europa.eu

For more information please consult

Internet: http://ec.europa.eu/eurostat

Data extracted

February–April 2011

Acknowledgements

The editor-in-chief and the editor of the *Eurostat regional yearbook 2011* would like to thank all of the colleagues who contributed. We would particularly like to thank those who were involved in each specific chapter:

- **Population**: Veronica Corsini, Giampaolo Lanzieri, Monica Marcu and Gabriela Senchea Badea (Eurostat, Unit F.1, Population)
- **Labour market**: Lourdes Prado Ureña and Daniela Scirankova (Eurostat, Unit E.4, Regional statistics and geographical information)
- **Labour cost:** Simone Casali (Eurostat, Unit F.2, Labour market)
- **Education**: Marta Beck-Domzalska, Sorin-Florin Gheorghiu, Dominique Groenez, Sylvain Jouhette, Emmanuel Kailis and Paolo Turchetti (Eurostat, Unit F.4, Education, science and culture)
- **Health**: Marta Carvalhido, Elodie Cayotte and Jean-Marc Schaefer (Eurostat, Unit F.5, Health and food safety; Crime)
- **European cities**: Teodóra Brandmüller (Eurostat, Unit E.4, Regional statistics and geographical information)
- **Gross domestic product**: Andreas Krüger (Eurostat, Unit C.2, National accounts — Production)
- **Household accounts**: Andreas Krüger (Eurostat, Unit C.2, National accounts — Production)
- **Structural business statistics**: Aleksandra Stawińska (Eurostat, Unit G.2, Structural business statistics)
- **Information society**: Anna Lööf and Albrecht Wirthmann (Eurostat, Unit F.6, Information society and tourism statistics)
- **Tourism**: Christophe Demunter and Sylvie Villaume (Eurostat, Unit F.6, Information society and tourism statistics)
- **Land cover and land use:** Paolo Dominici, Marjo Kasanko, Laura Martino and Alessandra Palmieri (Eurostat, Unit E.1, Farms, agro-environment and rural development)
- **Coastal regions**: Isabelle Collet (Eurostat, Unit E.4, Regional statistics and geographical information)
- **Transport**: Anastassia Vakalopoulou (Eurostat, Unit E.6, Transport)
- **Science, technology and innovation**: Ilcho Bechev, Daniela Silvia Crintea, Bernard Félix, Dominique Groenez and Reni Petkova (Eurostat, Unit F.4, Education, science and culture)
- **Trends in densely and thinly populated areas:** Lewis Dijkstra and Angela Winkelhorst (Directorate-General for Regional Policy, Unit C.3, Economic and quantitative analysis; additionality)

We are also very grateful to:

- the **Directorate-General for Translation of the European Commission**, particularly the German, English and French translation units and the Editing Unit;
- the **Publications Office of the European Union**, and in particular Nadine Joffé in Unit B.1, Cross-media publishing and the proofreaders in Unit B.2, Editorial services.

Contents

Foreword 3
Acknowledgements 5

INTRODUCTION 13

Statistics on regions and cities 14
Core content and news in the 2011 edition 14
Coverage 16
The NUTS classification 16
'Statistics explained' 16
Eurostat online data codes 17
More regional information 17

1 POPULATION 19

Introduction 20
Main statistical findings 20
    Population size and density 20
    Population change in 2008 20
    Demographic ageing: the situation today 27
    Conclusion 27
Data sources and availability 31
Context 31

2 LABOUR MARKET 33

Introduction 34
Main statistical findings 34
    Employment 34
    Unemployment 36
    Long-term unemployment 36
    Youth unemployment 40
    Disparities in regional labour markets 44
Data sources and availability 44
    Definitions 44
Context 46

3 LABOUR COST 49

Introduction 50
Main statistical findings 50
    Hourly labour costs 50
    Hours actually worked 50
    Structure of labour costs 50
Data sources and availability 52
Context 55

4 EDUCATION...57

Introduction 58
Main statistical findings 58
   Students in tertiary education 58
   Students aged 17 in education...58
   Participation of four-year-olds in education...58
   Students in upper-secondary and post-secondary non-tertiary education 61
   Tertiary educational attainment 61
   Early leavers from education and training 61
Data sources and availability 66
Context 66

5 HEALTH..69

Introduction 70
Main statistical findings 70
   Causes of death — malignant neoplasms...70
   Combined malignant neoplasms of the larynx, trachea, bronchus and lung 70
   Breast cancer 70
   Malignant neoplasms of the prostate 74
   Hospital discharges...74
   Malignant neoplasms of the trachea, bronchus and lung...74
   Breast cancer 74
   Conclusion 74
Data sources and availability 78
Context 78

6 EUROPEAN CITIES 81

Introduction 82
Main statistical findings 82
   Why cities matter 82
   The urban labour force 82
   Students in higher education...82
   Perception of poverty 86
   Perception of air pollution..86
Data sources and availability 86
Context 91

7 GROSS DOMESTIC PRODUCT 93

Introduction 94
Main statistical findings 94
   Regional GDP per inhabitant in 2008..94
   Major regional differences even within countries themselves 94
   Dynamic catch-up process in the new Member States 96
   Different trends within countries themselves 97

Convergence makes progress...97
Data sources and availability...99
   What is regional gross domestic product?...99
   Purchasing power parities and international volume comparisons................................99
   Dispersion of regional per-inhabitant GDP..101
Context..101

8 HOUSEHOLD ACCOUNTS 103

Introduction...104
Main statistical findings...104
   Private household income..104
   Results for 2008..104
   Disposable income..106
   Dynamic development on the edges of the EU..107
Data sources and availability...110
Context..110

9 STRUCTURAL BUSINESS STATISTICS 113

Introduction...114
Main statistical findings...114
   Regional specialisation...114
   Business concentration...119
Data sources and availability...120
Context..123

10 INFORMATION SOCIETY 125

Introduction...126
Main statistical findings...126
   Access to information and communication technologies...126
   E-commerce by individuals...128
   Regular use of the Internet...129
   Conclusions...133
Data sources and availability...135
Context..135

11 TOURISM 139

Introduction...140
Main statistical findings...140
   Tourism in the EU-27: trends and facts..140
   Top 20 tourist regions in the EU-27..140
   Number of overnight stays..140
   Trends in tourism over the period 2004–09...140
   Overnight stays in campsites...141
   Top 20 tourist regions in the EU-27 visited by foreign tourists..................................141
   Share of inbound tourism..141

Domestic tourism: most popular regions 146

Average length of stay: hotel versus campsites 146

Top 20 regions by accommodation capacity 151

Accommodation capacity in hotels 151

Conclusion 151

Data sources and availability 154

Context 154

12 LAND COVER AND LAND USE 157

Introduction 158

Main statistical findings 158

Artificial areas 158

More than 8.8 % of EU land used for residential, commercial and industrial purposes 158

Cropland covers Europe evenly 161

Grasslands maintain Europe's livestock farming 161

Forests and woodlands dominate the European landscape 161

European landscapes are diverse 161

Conclusions 166

Data sources and availability 166

Glossary 166

Context 167

13 COASTAL REGIONS 169

Introduction 170

Main statistical findings 170

EU coastal regions bordering the maritime basins 170

Population of the EU coastal regions 170

The EU population living along maritime basins 170

Structure of the EU coastal regions' population by maritime basins 170

The EU coastal regions population by maritime basins and urban–rural typology 170

Change in EU coastal regions' population 173

Share of women in the population of EU coastal regions 175

Active population of the EU coastal regions 179

Share of women in the active population of EU coastal regions 179

Unemployment in EU coastal regions 179

Female unemployment in EU coastal regions 179

Data sources and availability 179

Context 180

14 TRANSPORT 185

Introduction 186

Main statistical findings 186

Stock of passenger cars, buses and coaches 186

Stock of road freight vehicles 187

   Air transport 187

   Maritime transport 193

Data sources and availability 199

15 SCIENCE, TECHNOLOGY AND INNOVATION 201

Introduction 202

Main statistical findings 202

   Research and development 202

   Human resources in science and technology 202

   Patents 207

Data sources and availability 208

Context 211

16 TRENDS IN DENSELY AND THINLY POPULATED AREAS 215

Introduction 216

Main statistical findings 216

   Severe material deprivation 216

   At-risk-of-poverty 216

   Access to primary healthcare 216

   Broadband Internet connection 217

   Crime, violence and vandalism 218

   Data sources and availability 219

Context 223

ANNEX 1 — NUTS (Nomenclature of territorial units for statistics) 225

   European Union: NUTS 2 regions 225

   EFTA countries: Statistical regions at level 2 228

   Candidate countries: Statistical regions at level 2 229

ANNEX 2 — Cities participating in the Urban Audit data collection 230

   European Union: Urban Audit cities 230

   EFTA countries: Urban Audit cities 234

   Candidate countries: Urban Audit cities 235

Introduction

Statistics on regions and cities

Eurostat, the statistical office of the European Union, is responsible for collecting and disseminating data at European level, primarily from the 27 Member States of the European Union, but also from the EFTA and candidate countries, at both national and regional levels. The aim of this publication, the *Eurostat regional yearbook 2011*, is to give a flavour of some of the statistics on regions and cities that Eurostat collects and to present the most recent figures for each statistical subject.

The countries within the European Union are often compared with each other, but in reality it is very difficult to compare a small country like Malta, which has around 400 000 inhabitants, or Luxembourg, which has around 500 000 inhabitants, with Germany, the country which has the biggest population in the EU, more than 80 million inhabitants. Comparing regional data that are as detailed as possible is often more meaningful and it also highlights the disparities — or evenness — within the countries themselves. Most statistics in this publication are based on NUTS 2 regions, but this year we have also introduced some maps based on NUTS 3 regions, the lowest available NUTS level, whenever data for this level are available.

A problem with regional statistics and city statistics is that the volume of data inevitably gets very large (there are as many as 1 303 NUTS 3 regions for the EU-27) and there has to be some kind of sorting principle to make the data comprehensible. Statistical maps are excellent for presenting large amounts of statistical data in a user-friendly way. That is why this year's *Eurostat regional yearbook*, like previous editions, contains many thematic maps in which the data are sorted into different statistical classes represented by colour shades on the maps. Some chapters also make use of graphs and tables to present the data, selected and sorted according to principles designed to make the results more apparent.

Europe 2020 is the EU's new growth strategy for the coming decade and is the successor to the Lisbon strategy. The overall target of Europe 2020 is that Europe should become a smart, sustainable and inclusive economy and it sets out a number of specific, measurable statistical targets. The aim is to reach the objectives on employment, innovation, education, social inclusion and climate/energy by the year 2020. The Europe 2020 targets are mentioned explicitly in many of the chapters of this publication and you can study the strategy in more detail on the European Commission website, at: http://ec.europa.eu/europe2020/index_en.htm

You will also find quick access to the Europe 2020 'Headline indicators' on the Eurostat website at: http://epp.eurostat.ec.europa.eu/portal/page/portal/europe_2020_indicators/headline_indicators

Please note that the latest available reference year is not identical across the publication. Each section aims at showing the latest data available, as is frequently the case in statistical publications. In the light of the financial crisis, which had for certain subjects of the publication severe implications in the observed years, it is important to keep in mind the reference year with respect to the overall economic and social events. The following table gives an overview of the latest available reference year for each chapter.

Chapter number	Subject	Latest available reference year
1	Population	2008
2	Labour market	2009
3	Labour cost	2008
4	Education	2009
5	Health	2008
6	European cities	2008
7	Gross domestic product	2008
8	Household accounts	2008
9	Structural business statistics	2008
10	Information society	2010
11	Tourism	2009
12	Land cover and land use	2009
13	Coastal regions	2009
14	Transport	2009
15	Science, technology and innovation	2008
16	Trends in densely and thinly populated areas	2009

Eurostat may have more recent data than shown in the publication. It can be found directly on the Eurostat website. The data codes below all maps, tables and figures in the publication will help you locate the indicator on the Eurostat website.

Core content and news in the 2011 edition

The aim of the publication is to cover as many subjects for which Eurostat collects regional data as possible, and as a result new subjects are constantly introduced. The 2011 edition contains 16 chapters covering a mix of core subjects and new topics. The first chapter on **population** presents the latest figures on some of the basic demographic indicators, such as population density, population change, fertility rates and life expectancy for both men and women. Four out of eight maps in this chapter present statistics by NUTS 3 regions, which gives an even more detailed picture compared to higher regional levels. It is also worth noting that this chapter has the best coverage of the EFTA and candidate countries. The population chapter is in a way the basis for all other statistical subjects, since they depend on the composition of the population.

The second chapter on the **labour market**, based on data from the EU Labour Force Survey (EU-LFS), examines the regional employment and unemployment patterns with a special focus on female participation in the labour market and on the two most severe forms of unemployment, long-term unemployment and youth unemployment. The next chapter is about **labour cost,** based on the Labour Cost Survey (LCS), and shows statistics on NUTS 1 regions for indicators like 'hourly labour costs' and 'hours actually worked'.

Education is crucial to the future economic and social success of the European Union and the fourth chapter shows us the state of play regarding enrolment in education and educational attainment in the countries examined here. The next chapter deals with another topic important to each one of us, namely **health**. Cancer (malignant neoplasm) is on average the second most common cause of death in the European Union and in some countries it is the leading cause of death. The health chapter this year focuses on the death rates for the three most prevalent cancer forms and on the number of hospital discharges of inpatients per 100 000 inhabitants for these types of cancer.

Around 68 % of the European Union's population lives in an urban area, so this is also a topic close to many of us. The chapter on **European cities** shows some of the indicators related to the Europe 2020 goals and it also presents two indicators from the Urban Audit perception survey.

The next three chapters are all economy-related, dealing with, namely, **gross domestic product, household accounts** and **structural business statistics**. Economy is in a sense also the basis of all other chapters and the basis for realising the political goals set out in the Europe 2020 strategy. The results this year are especially interesting as we are now beginning to see statistical evidence of the financial crisis that hit Europe and the rest of the world at the end of the first decade of 2000.

The chapter on the **information society** describes the use of information and communication technologies (ICT) among private persons and households in the European regions. The analysis in this chapter concentrates on the development of broadband connections, Internet access and regular use of Internet, etc., during the most recent two-year period, from 2008 to 2010. **Tourism** is another important economic activity for many regions in Europe, with wide social, cultural and environmental implications. Besides maps for NUTS 2 regions, this edition includes more detailed results on accommodation capacity by NUTS 3 regions. **Land cover and land use** is a topic new to this publication and we are very proud to have the subject represented for the

first time. 'Land cover' describes the biophysical coverage of land (e.g. crops, grass, broad-leaved forest or built-up area) whereas 'land use' indicates the socioeconomic use of land (e.g. agriculture, forestry, recreation or residential use). Both these aspects are essential for monitoring a wide range of environmental and socioeconomic trends, linked to sustainable use of resources as well as climate change and biodiversity. For the second year in a row, we also have a chapter about **coastal regions**, defined as regions (on NUTS level 3) having either a coastline or more than half of their population living within 50 km of the sea. This chapter examines the specific conditions in these NUTS 3 regions and their connection to maritime basins.

Transport statistics are crucial for monitoring and — in the longer term — improving regional accessibility. The transport chapter this year focuses on the following topics: road passenger transport (motorisation rate and shares of public transport vehicles) and stocks of road freight vehicles. It also contains four tables on passenger and freight transport ranked by the top 20 air- and seaport regions in Europe.

The next statistical topic, **science, technology and innovation** is — alongside statistics on education and the information society — a key element for achieving the ambitious goals set out in the Europe 2020 strategy concerning 'smart growth', i.e. to develop a European economy based on knowledge and innovation. This chapter presents the most recent figures on research and development (R & D) and human resources in science and technology (HRST) as well as patent statistics, the latter for the first time in this publication, broken down by NUTS 3 regions.

The last chapter in the *Eurostat regional yearbook 2011* is a study of **trends in densely and thinly populated areas**, another subject which is presented here for the first time. This chapter is based on a classification of areas by degree of urbanisation as defined in the Labour Force Survey, but here the definition has been applied to another statistical area, namely the data collection called EU-SILC (EU-Statistics on Income and Living Conditions). Statistics on five crucial social issues are presented: severe material deprivation; at-risk-of-poverty; access to primary healthcare; broadband Internet connection; and perception of problems with crime, violence and vandalism in the close neighbourhood. All these issues are broken down by degree of urbanisation (densely, intermediate or thinly populated areas) in each country and illustrated by a series of interesting graphs. In contrast to the other topics, this chapter only contains one statistical map, which illustrates the degree of urbanisation concept geographically.

Coverage

The *Eurostat regional yearbook 2011* contains statistics on the 27 Member States of the European Union and, where available, data are also shown for the EFTA countries (Iceland, Liechtenstein, Norway and Switzerland) and the candidate countries (Montenegro, Croatia, the former Yugoslav Republic of Macedonia (¹) and Turkey). Iceland is, from 27 July 2010, in fact both an EFTA and a candidate country, but here it is sorted under the EFTA countries. Montenegro has been a new candidate country since 17 December 2010.

The NUTS classification

NUTS (the nomenclature of territorial units for statistics) is a regional classification for the 27 Member States of the European Union providing a harmonised hierarchy of regions on three geographical levels. The NUTS classification subdivides each Member State into a number of NUTS 1 regions, each of which is in turn subdivided into a number of NUTS 2 regions and so on. If available, administrative structures are used for the different NUTS levels. Where there is no administrative layer for a given level, artificial regions are created by aggregating smaller administrative regions.

The NUTS regulation (Regulation (EC) No 1059/2003 of the European Parliament and of the Council) was adopted in May 2003 and entered into force in July 2003; it has since been amended twice and also supplemented twice with new Member States in 2004 (10 new Member States) and 2008 (two new Member States, Bulgaria and Romania). The second regular amendment (EU No 31/2011) was adopted in January 2011 and will enter into force from 1 January 2012.

These are the principles for determining the NUTS regions in the Member States.

Principle 1: The NUTS regulation defines the following minimum and maximum population thresholds for the size of the NUTS regions.

Level	Minimum	Maximum
NUTS 1	3 million	7 million
NUTS 2	800 000	3 million
NUTS 3	150 000	800 000

Principle 2: NUTS favours administrative divisions (normative criterion).

For practical reasons the NUTS classification is based on the administrative divisions applied in the Member States. That generally comprises two main regional levels; the additional third level is created by aggregating administrative units.

Principle 3: NUTS favours general geographical units.

General geographical units are normally more suitable for any given indicator than geographical units specific to certain fields of activity.

Regions have also been defined and agreed with the EFTA and candidate countries; these regions are called 'statistical regions' and follow exactly the same rules as the NUTS regions in the European Union, except that there is no legal base.

It should be noted that some Member States have a relatively small population and are therefore not divided into more than one NUTS 2 region. Thus, for these countries, the NUTS 2 value is identical to the national value. Following the latest revision of the NUTS classification in 2006, this now applies to six Member States: Estonia, Cyprus, Latvia, Lithuania, Luxembourg and Malta. It also applies to the statistical regions at level 2 in the EFTA countries Iceland and Liechtenstein and in the candidate countries Montenegro and the former Yugoslav Republic of Macedonia. In each of these cases, the whole country consists of one single level 2 NUTS region or statistical region.

A folding map inside the cover accompanies this publication. It shows all NUTS 2 regions in the 27 Member States of the European Union (EU-27) and the corresponding level 2 statistical regions in the EFTA and candidate countries, and it also has a full list of codes and names of these regions. The map is intended to help readers to locate the name and NUTS code of a specific region on the other statistical maps in the publication. More information on the NUTS classification can be found here: http://epp.eurostat.ec.europa.eu/portal/page/portal/nuts_nomenclature/introduction

'Statistics explained'

All the chapters in the *Eurostat regional yearbook* have, for the past couple of years, also been included as articles in '**Statistics explained**', Eurostat's user-friendly guide to European statistics, which you will find on the Eurostat website. 'Statistics explained' is a wiki-based system, with an approach somewhat similar to Wikipedia, which presents statistical topics in an easy-to-understand way. Together, the articles make up an encyclopaedia of European statistics, which is completed by a statistical glossary clarifying the terms used. In addition, numerous links are provided to the latest data and metadata, as well as further information, making 'Statistics explained' a portal for regular and occasional users alike.

(¹) The name of the former Yugoslav Republic of Macedonia is shown in tables as FYR of Macedonia. This does not prejudge in any way the definitive nomenclature for this country, which is to be agreed following the conclusion of negotiations currently taking place on this subject at the United Nations.

In May 2011, 'Statistics explained' contained more than 1 000 articles and glossary items, and its content is regularly expanded and its user-friendliness increased. From next year (2012) onwards, 'Statistics explained' will be used as a tool for producing new content for the *Eurostat regional yearbook*. This is already the case for another important Eurostat publication, namely *Europe in figures — Eurostat yearbook*, which is the most comprehensive selection of Eurostat data at national level. This means that the latest text on each topic both for the *Eurostat yearbook* and for the *Eurostat regional yearbook* will be available in 'Statistics explained' earlier than in the printed versions, and in this way, the most recent results will be made available to our users without the inevitable delays that are part and parcel of making high-quality printed publications. The German and French versions of the two publications will only be available in 'Statistics explained' and not as printed publications from this year (2011) onwards. The increased possibilities for user-friendliness and searchability in the German and French versions offered by 'Statistics explained' were considered more important to spend time and effort on, compared to the very limited number of printed copies disseminated in these two languages. 'Statistics explained' can be accessed via a link on the right-hand side of the Eurostat website or directly at: http://epp.eurostat.ec.europa.eu/statistics_explained

Eurostat online data codes

Under each table, figure or map in all Eurostat publications you will find hyperlinks with Eurostat online data codes, allowing easy access to the most recent data on the Eurostat website. The online data codes lead either to a two- or three-dimensional table in the TGM (table, graph, map) interface or to an open dataset which contains more dimensions and longer time series in the Data Explorer interface ([2]). In the *Eurostat regional yearbook*, these online data codes are given as part of the source below each table, figure and map.

In the PDF version of this publication, the reader is led directly to the freshest data when clicking on the hyperlinks for Eurostat online data codes. Readers of the printed version can access the freshest data by typing a standardised hyperlink into a web browser, for example:

http://ec.europa.eu/eurostat/product?code=<data_code>&mode=view, where <data_code> is to be replaced by the online data code in question. The data codes can also be fed into the 'search' function of the Eurostat website.

More regional information

In the subject area 'Regions and cities' under the heading 'General and regional statistics' on the Eurostat website, you will find statistics on both 'Regions' and 'Urban Audit' (city statistics), containing more dimensions and longer time series than those presented in this publication.

It is also possible to download the Excel files that contain the specific data used to produce the maps and other illustrations for each chapter in this publication. These you will also find on the Eurostat website under the product page of the *Eurostat regional yearbook*.

The yearly updated Eurostat publication *European regional and urban statistics — Reference guide* contains a complete listing of the content of the regional and urban databases. It can be downloaded free of charge from the Eurostat website, just like all other Eurostat publications.

We hope that you will find the 2011 edition of the *Eurostat regional yearbook* both interesting and useful. Any feedback on the content is always welcome.

([2]) There are two types of online data codes: (1) tables (accessed using the TGM interface) with eight-character codes, which consist of three or five letters — the first of which is 't' — followed by five or three digits, e.g. tps00001 and tsdph220; and (2) databases (accessed using the Data Explorer interface), which have codes that use an underscore '_' within the syntax of the code, e.g. nama_gdp_c

Population

1

Introduction

Demographic trends vary across the EU's regions, with certain phenomena making a stronger impact in some regions than in others. This chapter describes the regional pattern of demographic phenomena in 2008, at NUTS 3 level across the EU-27 and by level 3 statistical region for EFTA and candidate countries. However, due to data availability constraints, several demographic indicators were analysed at NUTS 2 regional level.

Main statistical findings

Population size and density

On 1 January 2009, 499.7 million people inhabited the 27 Member States of the European Union. The population density at EU-27 level in 2008 was estimated at 116 inhabitants per km².

Map 1.1 shows the population density in 2008. Generally, the NUTS 3 regions that include the capital city of the country, and in most cases the regions in their immediate vicinity, are among the most densely populated.

The NUTS 3 region of Paris was by far the most densely populated (21 022 inhabitants per km²), followed by Inner London West (10 094) and Inner London East (9 049). Population densities above 5 000 per km² were observed, in decreasing order, in the following NUTS 3 regions: Hauts-de-Seine (France), Bucureşti (Romania), Bruxelles-Capitale/Brussel-Hoofdstad (Belgium), Seine-Saint-Denis and Val-de-Marne (France), Melilla (Spain) and Basel-Stadt (Switzerland).

The least densely populated level 3 statistical region within the territory covered in 2008 was Landsbyggd (Iceland) with 1.2 inhabitants per km². Within the EU-27, the least densely populated NUTS 3 region was Guyane (France) with 2.7 inhabitants per km².

Population change in 2008

Population change in a given reference year is the difference between the population size on 1 January of the following year and on 1 January of the given reference year. Changes in the size of population are the result of the number of births and deaths and of the number of people migrating inward and outward. Population change therefore consists of two components: 'natural change' (the difference between live births and deaths) and 'net migration and statistical adjustment' (see 'Data sources and availability').

Maps 1.2, 1.3 and 1.4 present population change and these two components in 2008, by NUTS 3 regions. For comparability, population change and its two components are presented as crude rates per 1 000 inhabitants, i.e. relative to the size of the average population of the region (see 'Data sources and availability').

The maps show how the population change varies across regions from growth to decline (Map 1.2) due to positive or negative natural change (Map 1.3) and positive or negative net migration and statistical adjustment (Map 1.4).

The current demographic situation in the EU-27 confirms a trend of continuing growth, which has been unbroken since 1960. The population of the EU-27 grew by 4.1 per 1 000 inhabitants in 2008, due to a natural increase (see 'Data sources and availability') of 1.2 per 1 000 inhabitants and net migration ([1]) of 2.9 per 1 000 inhabitants. Although the population of the EU-27 as a whole increased in 2008, this population change was unevenly distributed across the Member States. In 2008, the population increased in 20 EU Member States and declined in the other seven.

The population decline was seen in most of the north-eastern and eastern and part of the south-eastern NUTS 3 regions. The countries with regions most affected by this trend in 2008 were Bulgaria, Germany, Hungary, Romania, Poland, Estonia, Latvia, Lithuania and Croatia, where the population declined in most of their NUTS 3 regions and outpaced the population growth observed in their other regions. A decline in population was also evident in the northern parts of Sweden, in the Finnish region of Itä-Suomi, in many regions of Greece and Portugal and in several regions of Turkey. On the other hand, the population grew in Cyprus, Luxembourg and Malta, and in Montenegro, the former Yugoslav Republic of Macedonia and, to a greater extent, in Turkey.

In nearly all western and south-western regions of the EU, the population increased during 2008. This is particularly evident in Ireland and in almost every region of the United Kingdom, in Italy, Spain, France, including the French overseas departments, and in the Spanish and Portuguese islands in the Atlantic Ocean. Positive population changes were also recorded in Austria, Switzerland, Belgium, Luxembourg and the Netherlands.

The picture provided by Map 1.2 can be sharpened by analysing the two components of population change, i.e. natural change and net migration ([1]).

Map 1.3 shows that, in many regions of the EU, more people died than were born in 2008. The resulting negative natural population change is widespread and affects almost half the regions in the EU. A positive natural change in population can be identified across Ireland, the central parts of the United Kingdom, most regions in France, Belgium, Luxembourg, the Netherlands, Switzerland, Iceland,

([1]) Including statistical adjustments.

Map 1.1: Population density, by NUTS 3 regions, 2008 (¹)
(inhabitants per km²)

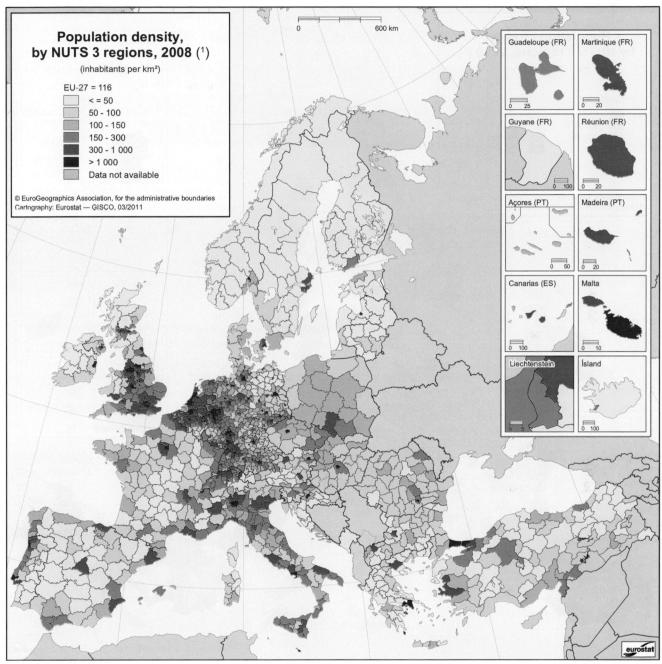

**Population density,
by NUTS 3 regions, 2008 (¹)**

(inhabitants per km²)

EU-27 = 116

- <= 50
- 50 - 100
- 100 - 150
- 150 - 300
- 300 - 1 000
- > 1 000
- Data not available

© EuroGeographics Association, for the administrative boundaries
Cartography: Eurostat — GISCO, 03/2011

Guadeloupe (FR)   Martinique (FR)

Guyane (FR)   Réunion (FR)

Açores (PT)   Madeira (PT)

Canarias (ES)   Malta

Liechtenstein   Ísland

(¹) Population density is calculated as ratio between (annual average) population and surface (land) area. Land area is a country's total area, excluding area under inland water. Bulgaria, Denmark, Germany, France, Cyprus, Poland and Portugal, total area has been used instead of land area; Poland, by NUTS 2 regions, United Kingdom; 2007.

Source: Eurostat (online data code: demo_r_d3dens).

Map 1.2: Population change, by NUTS 3 regions, 2008 (¹)
(per 1 000 inhabitants)

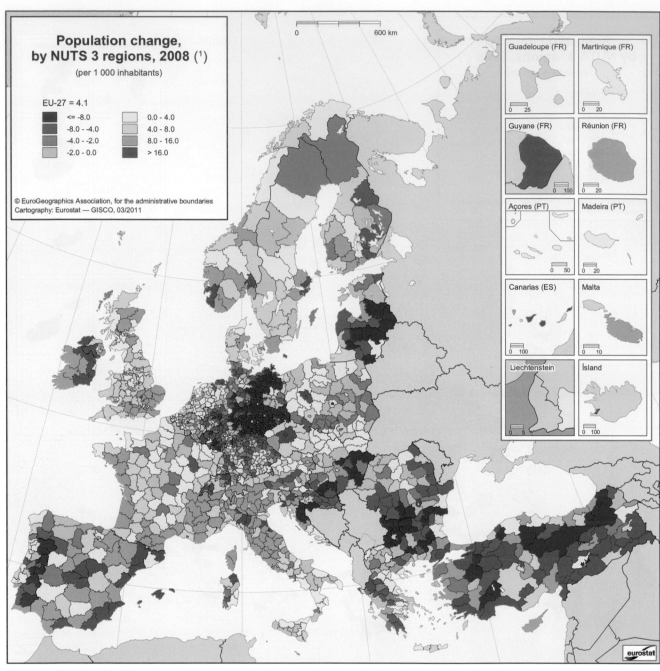

(¹) Belgium and United Kingdom, 2007.

Source: Eurostat (online data code: demo_r_gind3).

Map 1.3: Natural population change, by NUTS 3 regions, 2008 (¹)
(per 1 000 inhabitants)

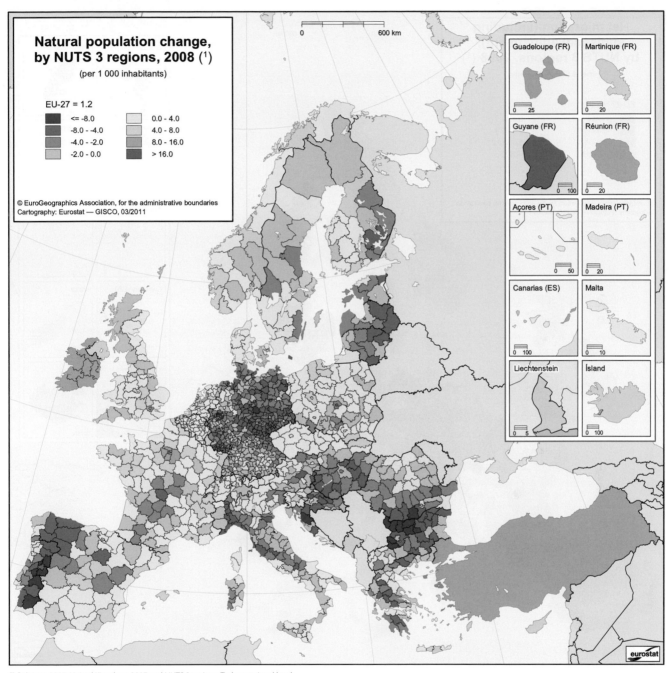

Natural population change, by NUTS 3 regions, 2008 (¹)
(per 1 000 inhabitants)

EU-27 = 1.2

<= -8.0	0.0 - 4.0
-8.0 - -4.0	4.0 - 8.0
-4.0 - -2.0	8.0 - 16.0
-2.0 - 0.0	> 16.0

© EuroGeographics Association, for the administrative boundaries
Cartography: Eurostat — GISCO, 03/2011

Guadeloupe (FR)   Martinique (FR)
Guyane (FR)   Réunion (FR)
Açores (PT)   Madeira (PT)
Canarias (ES)   Malta
Liechtenstein   Ísland

(¹) Belgium, 2007; United Kingdom, 2007 and NUTS 2 regions; Turkey, national level.

Source: Eurostat (online data code: demo_r_gind3 and demo_gind).

Map 1.4: Net migration (including statistical adjustment), by NUTS 3 regions, 2008 (¹)
(per 1 000 inhabitants)

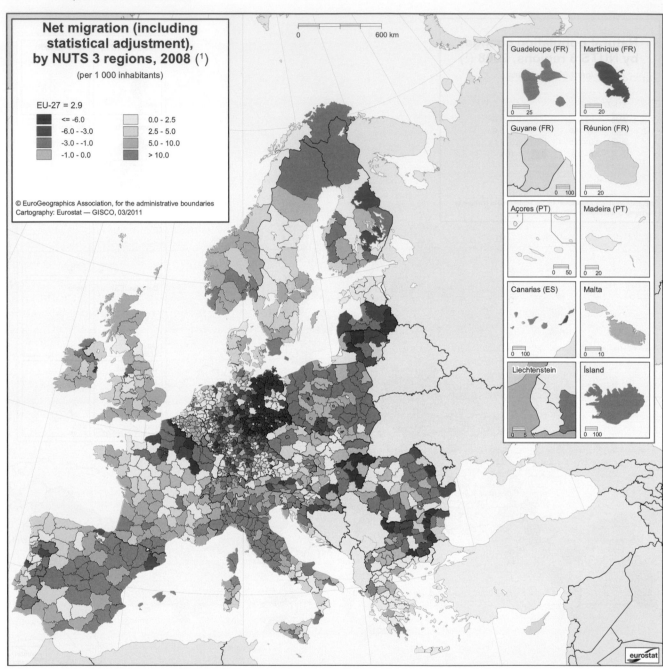

Net migration (including statistical adjustment), by NUTS 3 regions, 2008 (¹)
(per 1 000 inhabitants)

EU-27 = 2.9

- <= -6.0
- -6.0 - -3.0
- -3.0 - -1.0
- -1.0 - 0.0
- 0.0 - 2.5
- 2.5 - 5.0
- 5.0 - 10.0
- > 10.0

© EuroGeographics Association, for the administrative boundaries
Cartography: Eurostat — GISCO, 03/2011

Guadeloupe (FR)   Martinique (FR)   Guyane (FR)   Réunion (FR)   Açores (PT)   Madeira (PT)   Canarias (ES)   Malta   Liechtenstein   Ísland

(¹) Belgium, 2007; United Kingdom, 2007 and NUTS 2 regions; Turkey, national level.

Source: Eurostat (online data code: demo_r_gind3 and demo_gind).

Liechtenstein and Denmark and most regions of Norway. In all these regions, there were more live births than deaths in 2008.

Deaths outnumbered births in most regions of Germany, in Hungary, Croatia, Romania and Bulgaria and also in the Baltic States in the north and Greece and Italy in the south. Other countries showed a more balanced pattern overall.

One major reason for the slowdown in the natural growth of the population is that the EU's inhabitants are having fewer children than they used to. At aggregate level, in the 27 countries that form the EU today, the **total fertility rate** has declined from around 2.5 live births per woman in the early 1960s to 1.60 for the period 2006–08. (For the definition of total fertility rate, see 'Data sources and availability'.)

At national level, over the period 2006–08, a total fertility rate lower than 1.5 children per woman was observed in 17 of the 27 Member States. In the developed parts of the world today, a total fertility rate of around 2.1 live births per woman is considered to be the replacement rate, i.e. the level at which the population would remain stable in the long run if there were no inward or outward migration. Between 2006 and 2008 practically all of the EU, EFTA and candidate countries, with the exception of Turkey and Iceland, were still well below this replacement rate.

Map 1.5 shows the variation in the total fertility rate by NUTS 2 regions. Among the 317 NUTS 2 regions covered in this analysis, over the period 2006–08 the total fertility rate ranged, on average, from one child per woman in Asturias in Spain to 3.7 children in the French overseas department of Guyane.

Life expectancy at birth has risen by about 10 years over the last 50 years, due to improved socioeconomic and environmental conditions and better medical treatment and care.

Maps 1.6 and 1.7 give a picture of the average male and female life expectancy at birth over the period 2006–08 for the NUTS 2 regions. The two maps are directly comparable thanks to the common colour patterns used to classify male and female life expectancy.

In every region, women live longer than men. At EU-27 level, life expectancy at birth averaged 82.2 years for women and 76.1 for men, giving a gender gap of 6.1 years.

The regional data revealed marked differences between the lowest and highest values for females and males. The lowest values were 76.0 years for females (Vest and Nord-Vest regions of Romania and the Yugoiztochen and Severozapaden regions of Bulgaria) and 65.5 years for males (Lithuania). The highest values for life expectancy at birth were 86.0 years for females and 80.2 years for males, both recorded in the Ticino region of Switzerland.

Map 1.6 shows that life expectancy at birth for males is less than or equal to 74 years mostly in the eastern part of the EU-27, covering all regions of the Baltic States, Poland, Slovakia, Hungary, Romania, Bulgaria, the former Yugoslav Republic of Macedonia and Montenegro and a few regions of the Czech Republic, Portugal and Croatia, whereas values higher than 80 years were observed in Åland (Finland) and Ticino (Switzerland). Map 1.7 depicts the regional distribution of life expectancy at birth for females, with values less than or equal to 78 years mainly in the eastern part of Europe, including all regions of Latvia, Lithuania, Romania, Bulgaria, the former Yugoslav Republic of Macedonia and Montenegro, and in most regions of Hungary. Values higher than 84 years were observed in a large number of regions of Spain, France and Italy, in the Salzburg region of Austria and in Switzerland and Liechtenstein.

The smallest gender gap was 3.4 years in the Åland region of Finland, while the largest was 11.8 years in Lithuania.

The third determinant of population change (after fertility and mortality) is **net migration.** As many countries in the EU are currently at a point in the demographic development where natural population change is close to being balanced or negative, net migration is becoming more significant for maintaining the size of the population. Moreover, migration contributes indirectly to natural growth, given that migrants have children. Migrants are also usually younger and have not yet reached the age at which the probability of dying is higher.

Map 1.4 shows net migration (including statistical adjustment) in 2008 by NUTS 3 region across the EU-27, EFTA and candidate countries.

In some EU-27 regions, negative natural change has been offset by positive net migration. This is most striking in the Kerkyra and Ioannina regions of Greece, in the northern and central regions of Italy and in Pest (Hungary), Pieriga (Latvia), La Palma (Spain), Wiener Umland/Nordteil (Austria) and Landes (France). The opposite situation, where positive natural change is cancelled out by negative net migration, is much rarer, but is noticeable in the Miasto Poznań and Miasto Kraków regions of Poland, in the Osttirol and Lungau regions of Austria, in the Ardennes region of France and in the Würzburg Landkreis and Mainz Kreisfreie Stadt regions of Germany.

Four cross-border regions where more people have left than arrived (negative net migration) can be identified on Map 1.4:

- the Nordic countries, covering Iceland, northern regions of Norway and Sweden and western and eastern regions of Finland;
- north-western and central Europe, encompassing a few regions in Ireland, the United Kingdom, the Netherlands, most regions of Germany, north-eastern regions of France and the southern regions of Austria;

Map 1.5: Total fertility rate, by NUTS 2 regions, average 2006–08 (¹)
(live births per woman)

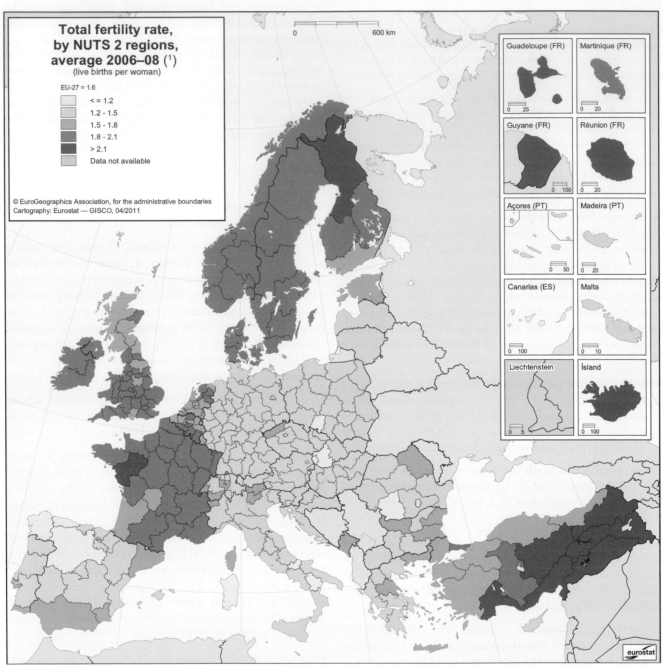

Total fertility rate, by NUTS 2 regions, average 2006–08 (¹)
(live births per woman)

EU-27 = 1.6

- <= 1.2
- 1.2 - 1.5
- 1.5 - 1.8
- 1.8 - 2.1
- > 2.1
- Data not available

© EuroGeographics Association, for the administrative boundaries
Cartography: Eurostat — GISCO, 04/2011

Guadeloupe (FR)   Martinique (FR)
Guyane (FR)   Réunion (FR)
Açores (PT)   Madeira (PT)
Canarias (ES)   Malta
Liechtenstein   Ísland

(¹) Ireland and United Kingdom, 2006–07; Denmark, 2007–08; Belgium, Eastern Scotland (UKM2) and South Western Scotland (UKM3), 2006; Turkey, 2007; Brandenburg (DE4) and Turkey, by NUTS 1 regions.

Source: Eurostat (online data code: demo_r_frate2).

- eastern Europe, comprising most regions of Latvia, Lithuania, Poland, Slovakia, Hungary, Romania, Bulgaria and the former Yugoslav Republic of Macedonia;

- southern Europe, comprising most regions of Portugal, a few regions in Spain, southern Italy, Greece and several regions of Croatia.

Negative net migration was also observed in Guadeloupe and Martinique amongst the French overseas departments.

There are regions where the two components of population change (natural change and net migration) have both moved in the same direction.

In Luxembourg, Malta, Cyprus, Liechtenstein and Montenegro and in most regions of Ireland, Belgium, the Netherlands, Spain, Slovenia and Norway, a positive natural change was accompanied by positive net migration, hence leading to a cumulated increase in their populations.

Conversely, in a large number of NUTS 3 regions in Germany, Latvia, Lithuania, Poland, Hungary, Romania, Bulgaria, Croatia and the former Yugoslav Republic of Macedonia, both components of population change moved in a negative direction. This cumulated decline led to a marked population loss in 2008.

The analysis of net migration of the NUTS 3 regions that include the capital of the country (²) found the following.

Twenty-four regions showed an increase in their population, due to positive natural change combined with strong positive net migration. This trend is most obvious in the capital regions of the Nordic countries (Oslo in Norway, Höfudborgarsvædi in Iceland, Stockholms län in Sweden, Byen København in Denmark and Uusimaa in Finland), in central Europe (Luxembourg, Arr. de Bruxelles-Capitale/ Arr. van Brussel-Hoofdstad in Belgium, Osrednjeslovenska in Slovenia and Hlavní mesto Praha in the Czech Republic) and in the Madrid region of Spain.

In four regions the negative natural change has been offset by positive net migration, namely Budapest (Hungary), Sofia (stolitsa) (Bulgaria), Bucureşti (Romania) and Vilniaus apskritis (Lithuania).

Five regions recorded a positive population change, despite negative net migration, particularly Inner London and Outer London (United Kingdom), Dublin (Ireland), Paris (France) and Grande Lisboa (Portugal).

The Riga region of Latvia showed a cumulated decline caused by a negative natural change compounded by negative net migration.

Demographic ageing: the situation today

A significant and continuous increase in life expectancy at birth, combined with low fertility rates and the build-up of retirements of the post-World War II baby-boom generation, have led to an ageing population. The **old-age dependency ratio** indicates the relationship between the working-age population and elderly persons.

Map 1.8 shows the old-age dependency ratio calculated for NUTS 2 regions for EU, EFTA and candidate countries. At EU-27 level, the total population aged 65 or over as a proportion of the working-age population was 25.6 %. In other words, on average, every 100 persons of working age were supporting 26 aged 65 or more. At the beginning of 2009, the old-age dependency ratio ranged from 5.4 % in the Van region of Turkey to 43.3 % in Liguria in Italy.

Old-age dependency ratios higher than 30 % were found in 68 regions, mainly in:

- Nordic countries, in regions of Sweden and Finland;

- north-western and central and eastern Europe, comprising regions of the United Kingdom, Belgium, Germany and Bulgaria;

- Mediterranean countries, including regions of France, Spain, Portugal, Italy and Greece.

Conclusion

This chapter highlights selected features of trends in the regional population in the EU-27 Member States, EFTA and candidate countries over the period from 1 January 2006 to 1 January 2009. As far as possible, groups of regions with the same phenomena spreading across national boundaries have been identified.

Although a population decline is evident in several regions, the aggregate EU-27 population nevertheless increased by around 2 million people every year over the period examined. The main driver of population growth is net migration, which counterbalanced the negative natural change in the population in many regions.

The impact of demographic changes within the EU is likely to be of major significance in the decades ahead. Consistently low birth rates and higher life expectancy at birth mark the transition to a much older population, already apparent in several regions.

(²) Some capitals cover more than one NUTS 3 region.

Map 1.6: Life expectancy at birth, males, by NUTS 2 regions, average 2006–08 (¹)
(years)

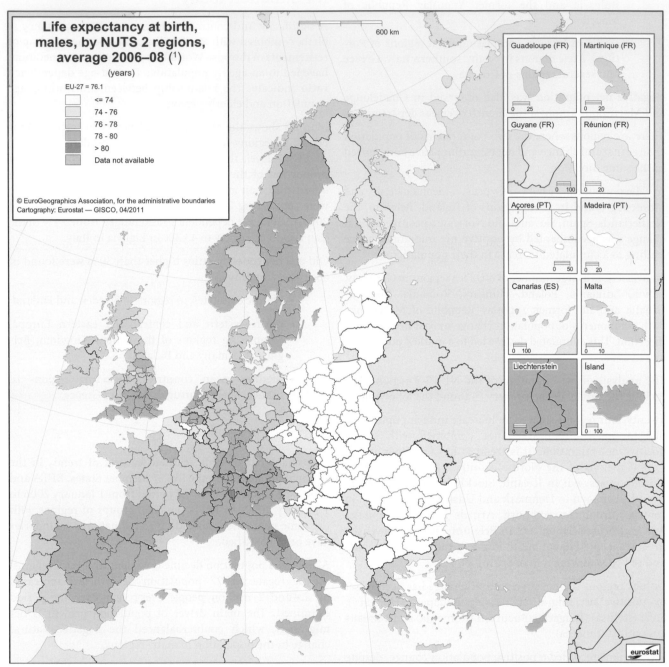

Life expectancy at birth, males, by NUTS 2 regions, average 2006–08 (¹)

(years)

EU-27 = 76.1

- <= 74
- 74 - 76
- 76 - 78
- 78 - 80
- > 80
- Data not available

© EuroGeographics Association, for the administrative boundaries
Cartography: Eurostat — GISCO, 04/2011

Guadeloupe (FR)   Martinique (FR)   Guyane (FR)   Réunion (FR)   Açores (PT)   Madeira (PT)   Canarias (ES)   Malta   Liechtenstein   Ísland

(¹) Belgium, United Kingdom, Norway, Ciudad Autónoma de Melilla (ES64) and Guadeloupe (FR91), 2006–07; Denmark, 2007–08; Ireland, average 2006 and 2008; Guyane (FR93), 2008; Brandenburg (DE4), by NUTS 1 region.

Source: Eurostat (online data code: demo_r_mlifexp).

Map 1.7: Life expectancy at birth, females, by NUTS 2 regions, average 2006–08 (¹)
(years)

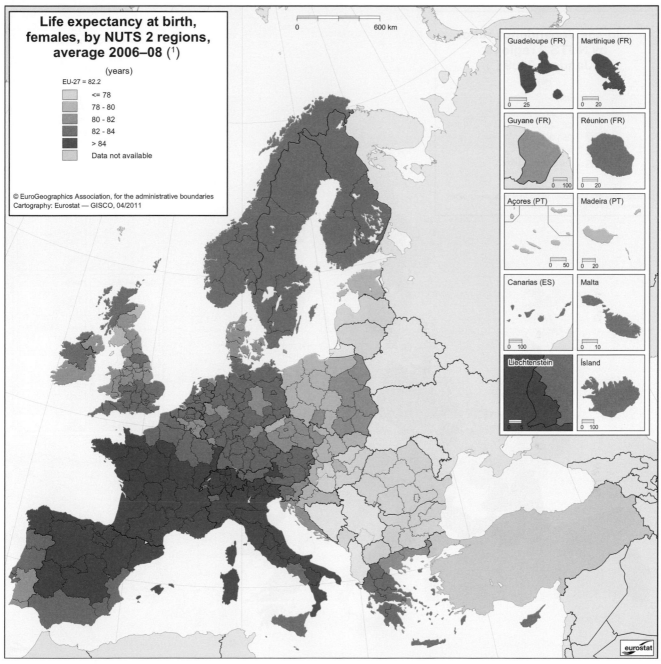

Life expectancy at birth,
females, by NUTS 2 regions,
average 2006–08 (¹)

(years)

EU-27 = 82.2

- <= 78
- 78 - 80
- 80 - 82
- 82 - 84
- > 84
- Data not available

© EuroGeographics Association, for the administrative boundaries
Cartography: Eurostat — GISCO, 04/2011

Guadeloupe (FR)   Martinique (FR)
Guyane (FR)   Réunion (FR)
Açores (PT)   Madeira (PT)
Canarias (ES)   Malta
Liechtenstein   Ísland

(¹) Belgium, United Kingdom, Norway, Ciudad Autónoma de Melilla (ES64) and Guadeloupe (FR91), 2006–07; Denmark, 2007–08; Ireland, average 2006 and 2008;
Guyane (FR93), 2008; Brandenburg (DE4), by NUTS 1 region.

Source: Eurostat (online data code: demo_r_mlifexp).

Map 1.8: Old-age dependency ratio, by NUTS 2 regions, 1 January 2009 (¹)
(%)

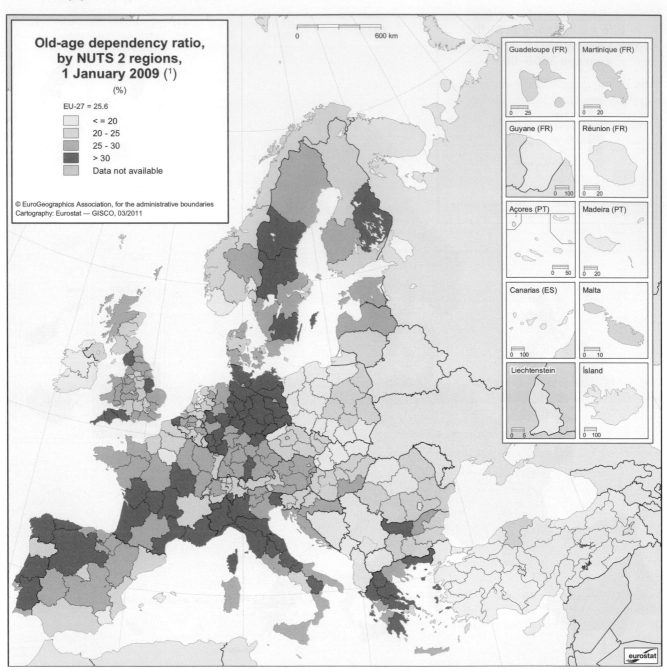

Old-age dependency ratio, by NUTS 2 regions, 1 January 2009 (¹)
(%)

EU-27 = 25.6

- <= 20
- 20 - 25
- 25 - 30
- > 30
- Data not available

© EuroGeographics Association, for the administrative boundaries
Cartography: Eurostat — GISCO, 03/2011

(¹) Belgium and United Kingdom, 1 January 2008.

Source: Eurostat (online data code: demo_r_d2jan).

Data sources and availability

Sources: Eurostat — Population statistics. For further information, please consult the Eurostat website at: http://epp.eurostat.ec.europa.eu/portal/page/portal/population/introduction

Population change is the difference between the size of population at the end and at the beginning of the period.

Population change consists of two components:

- **natural change**, calculated as the difference between live births and deaths; and

- **'net migration including statistical adjustment'**, calculated as the difference between the total change in the population and natural change; the statistics on net migration are therefore affected by all the statistical inaccuracies in the two components of this equation, especially population change. In different countries 'net migration including statistical adjustment' may cover, besides the difference between inward and outward migration, other changes observed in the population figures between 1 January in two consecutive years which cannot be attributed to births, deaths, immigration and emigration.

A 'positive population change' is referred to as population growth. A 'negative population change' is referred to as population decline.

A 'positive natural change', also known as natural increase, occurs when live births outnumber deaths. A 'negative natural change', also known as natural decrease, occurs when live births are less numerous than deaths.

Crude rate of population change is the ratio of the total population change during the year to the average population of the area in question in the same year. This value is expressed per 1 000 inhabitants. The crude rate of natural population change is the ratio of natural population change over a period to the average population of the area in question during the same period. This value is also expressed per 1 000 inhabitants.

Crude rate of net migration (including statistical adjustment) is the ratio of net migration during the year to the average population in the same year. This value is expressed per 1 000 inhabitants. As stated above, the crude rate of net migration is equal to the difference between the crude rate of population change and the crude rate of natural population change (i.e. net migration is considered to be the part of population change not attributable to births and deaths).

Total fertility rate is defined as the average number of children that would be born to a woman during her lifetime if she were to pass through her childbearing years conforming to the age-specific fertility rates that have been measured in a given year.

Life expectancy at birth is the mean number of years that a newborn child can expect to live if subjected throughout his or her life to current mortality conditions.

Population density is the ratio of the (annual average) population of a territory to the surface (land) area of the territory. Land area is a country's total area, excluding the area under inland water.

Old-age dependency ratio is the ratio of the number of elderly persons of an age when they are generally economically inactive (aged 65 and over in this publication) to the number of persons of working age (conventionally 15 to 64 years old).

Context

Demographic trends have a strong impact on the societies of the European Union. Consistently low fertility levels, combined with extended longevity and the fact that the baby boomers are reaching retirement age, are resulting in ageing of the EU population. The number of people of working age is decreasing, while the number of older people is on the rise.

The social and economic changes associated with population ageing are likely to have profound implications for the EU, at both national and regional levels. They stretch across a wide range of policy areas, with an impact on the school-age population, healthcare, participation in the labour force, social protection, social security issues and government finances amongst others.

Labour market

2

Introduction

The serious financial crisis that eventually led to a global decline in economic activity started to become apparent in 2008, but it was in 2009 that European labour markets really felt the full impact, almost reversing the progress made over the previous 10 years.

The aim of this chapter is to analyse the behaviour of European labour markets at a regional level during 2009. As a result of the economic crisis, unemployment soared in the European Union during this year. This increase is evident in all of the Member States, affecting all population groups: male and female, young and old. Nevertheless the scale of the increase varies between countries and even between regions.

It would seem that the targets set in the Lisbon and Europe 2020 strategies (¹) for employment and cohesion are unlikely to be achieved for the moment. Following the goals of the two strategies, this chapter can be divided into three parts: employment, unemployment and cohesion.

The first part provides an overview of employment in the EU regions, focusing on the 20–64 age group, as in Europe 2020, and female employment, as in the Lisbon strategy. The second part will then look at regional unemployment, the change in the unemployment rate over the past five years and two of the main concerns of policymakers: long-term and youth unemployment.

Finally, we take a look at regional cohesion, using tables showing the dispersion of employment and unemployment as indicators of labour market disparities.

Main statistical findings

Employment

The EU-27 employment rate for the 20–64 age group dropped from an average of 70.4 % in 2008 to 69.1 % in 2009, falling for the first time in the past five years and slipping away from the Europe 2020 target, set at 75 %.

(¹) The Lisbon strategy was an action and development plan for the economy of the European Union between 2000 and 2010. Its aim was to make the EU 'the most competitive and dynamic knowledge-based economy in the world, capable of sustainable economic growth with more and better jobs and greater social cohesion' by 2010. It was set out by the European Council in Lisbon in March 2000.

The main targets for 2010 were:
► an overall employment rate of 70 %;
► an employment rate for women of over 60 %;
► an employment rate of 50 % for older workers;
► annual economic growth of around 3 %.

The Europe 2020 strategy has now replaced the outgoing Lisbon Agenda. Made public at the beginning of March 2010, the Europe 2020 strategy is oriented primarily towards 'activating' various aspects of economic growth. It is based on three mutually reinforcing economic growth models and socially oriented priorities: smart growth, sustainable growth and inclusive growth. The target for the labour market in the EU 2020 strategy is: 75 % of 20–64-year-olds to be employed.

Taking into account the 1.3 percentage points fall, it is likely that the situation has remained difficult in 2010. The latest data available at national level for 2010 confirm this. The employment rate for the 20–64 age group in the EU-27 for 2010 was 68.6 %, falling for a second year and showing the impact of the financial crisis.

Map 2.1 presents the distribution of employment rates for the 20–64 age group at NUTS 2 level, with the darkest colour for regions that have already achieved the Europe 2020 target of 75 %.

In 2009, 74 of the 271 NUTS 2 regions in the EU-27 had already achieved the Europe 2020 target, while 62 regions were still 10 percentage points below the overall employment target.

The lowest employment rates were recorded in regions in the south of Spain, the south of Italy, Greece, Poland, Hungary, Bulgaria, Romania and Malta. The overseas regions of France also recorded low employment rates, as did the Belgian regions of Prov. Hainaut and Région de Bruxelles-Capitale/Brussels Hoofdstedelijk Gewest. On the other hand, the northern EU regions, comprising regions in the Netherlands, the United Kingdom, Denmark, Sweden and Finland, recorded relatively high employment rates, and so did a cluster of regions right in the centre of Europe, comprising southern Germany, Austria and the north Italian region of Provincia Autonoma Bolzano/Bozen, the Czech capital region of Praha and the Slovakian capital region of Bratislavský kraj. The margin that separates the lowest and highest regional employment rates in 2009 is still significant, with Campania (Italy) on 44.8 % at the one extreme and Åland (Finland) on 83.9 % at the other.

In the EFTA regions, all employment rates were above 75 %, with the exception of the Swiss region of Ticino, which registered a rate of 72.8 %. In the candidate countries, employment rates ranged from 32.7 % in Sanliurfa (Turkey) to 67.4 % in Sjeverozapadna Hrvatska (Croatia).

The female employment rate in the EU-27 fell in 2009 by 0.5 percentage points to 58.5 %, widening the gap between it and the 60 % Lisbon target. Map 2.2 shows the distribution of female employment rates for the 15–64 age group at NUTS 2 level. There are major differences between Member States, with figures varying from 26.3 % in Campania (Italy) to 75.4 % in Åland (Finland).

There is a strong correlation between the level of female employment and the level of overall employment, with Maps 2.1 and 2.2 following a similar trend. The Lisbon target of 60 % female employment has been met and exceeded in all EFTA regions, in the whole of the Netherlands and Denmark and in some regions in the United Kingdom, Germany, Sweden and Finland. To a lesser extent the 60 % target rate has also been achieved in most regions in France and central Europe, in Estonia, Latvia, Lithuania and Cyprus and in some regions in Portugal. Spain, Italy and Bulgaria each

Map 2.1: Employment rate for the 20–64 age group, by NUTS 2 regions, 2009
(%)

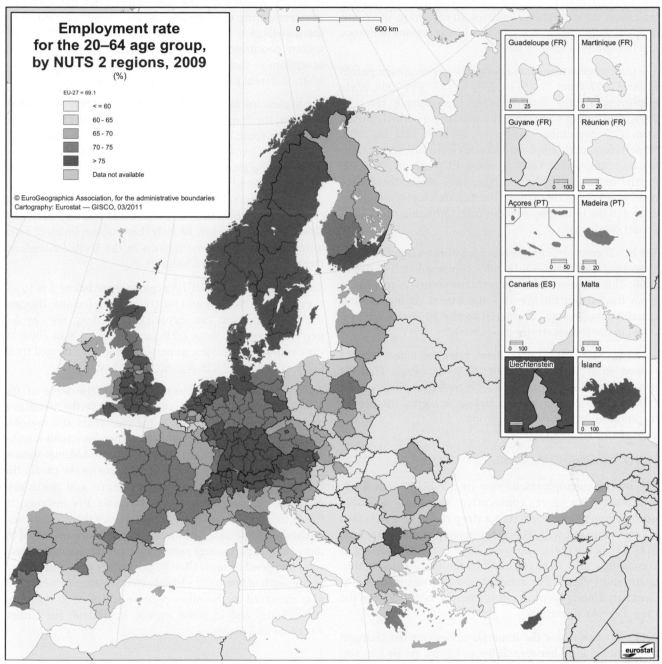

Employment rate
for the 20–64 age group,
by NUTS 2 regions, 2009
(%)

EU-27 = 69.1

- <= 60
- 60 - 65
- 65 - 70
- 70 - 75
- > 75
- Data not available

© EuroGeographics Association, for the administrative boundaries
Cartography: Eurostat — GISCO, 03/2011

0   600 km

Guadeloupe (FR)   Martinique (FR)
0   25   0   20

Guyane (FR)   Réunion (FR)
          0   100   0   20

Açores (PT)   Madeira (PT)
          0   50   0   20

Canarias (ES)   Malta
          0   100   0   10

Liechtenstein   Ísland
0   5   0   100

Source: Eurostat (online data code: lfst_r_lfe2emprt).

have one region (Comunidad de Madrid, Emilia-Romagna and Yugozapaden respectively) up to the 60 % target. On the other hand, female employment rates were quite low in most regions in the candidate countries, in regions in the south of Spain, Italy and Greece, in the overseas regions of France and in regions in eastern Europe.

The male employment rate dropped two percentage points in the EU-27, from 72.7 % in 2008 to 70.7 % in 2009. Male employment rates shrank faster than female rates in 2009, continuing to narrow the gender gap, which closed from 13.7 percentage points in 2008 to 12.2 in 2009. Nonetheless, male employment rates were still higher than female employment rates in most EU regions. In 2009, for the first time in the available time series, there were two NUTS 2 regions where the female employment rate exceeded the male employment rate: Lithuania and Länsi-Suomi (Finland).

The EU-27 employment rate for older workers (aged between 55 and 64) stood at 46.0 % in 2009, compared with 45.6 % in 2008. This increase, of 0.4 percentage points, is surprising given the pattern for overall employment during 2009. It remains low, though, compared to the 50 % rate set as a target in the Lisbon strategy.

At a regional level, employment rates for older workers ranged from a minimum of 26.3 % in Prov. Hainaut (Belgium) to a maximum of 75.7 % in Åland (Finland). In 2009, 148 EU-27 regions had already achieved the Lisbon target rate of 50 % for this age group.

Unemployment

The overall unemployment rate in the EU-27 was 8.9 % in 2009. After four consecutive years of declining unemployment, there was thus a steep rise of 1.9 percentage points compared with 2008. The unemployment rate rose in all 27 Member States between 2008 and 2009. The largest annual increases were recorded in the three Baltic States, Spain and Ireland. The smallest increase was recorded in Germany. Unemployment rates remained fairly stable in the three Benelux countries.

Table 2.1 shows how the unemployment rate has changed at a national level between 2004 and 2009. As we can see, the impact of the economic crisis almost wiped out the decrease in the unemployment rate between 2004 and 2008 in the EU-27. At a national level, the overall performance during this period was an increase in the unemployment rate in most of the countries or a small variation in the rate. Poland, Slovakia and Bulgaria were the only exceptions, with a significant decrease in unemployment if we look at the whole period.

Map 2.3 shows the distribution of unemployment rates by NUTS 3 regions in 2009. They ranged from 1.3 % in Romania to 29.2 % in Spain.

The dispersion between NUTS 3 regions among Member States is quite big, with more than 20 % of the regions returning a two-digit unemployment rate, but a further 20 % presenting unemployment rates below 5 %. However, the distribution of unemployment rates at NUTS 3 level within countries was quite uniform, albeit with some exceptions — Germany, Italy, Greece, France and Poland — where different patterns emerged between regions.

The highest unemployment rates were recorded in the south of Spain, the French overseas departments, the three Baltic States, the south of Italy and Greece and the north-eastern regions of Germany, and in Ireland, Slovakia and some regions in Belgium and Poland. The lowest unemployment rates were found mainly in the Netherlands and a cluster of areas in central Europe comprising regions in Austria, the Czech Republic, the west, centre and south of Germany, Slovenia and the north of Italy. Low unemployment rates were also found in some regions in the United Kingdom, Denmark, Romania and Bulgaria.

Employment rates in EFTA regions were below 5 % in all the regions in Norway and Switzerland. In Iceland, though, the unemployment rate experienced a steep rise, by 4.3 percentage points, from 2.9 % in 2008 to 7.2 % in 2009. In the candidate countries, unemployment rates ranged from 4.2 % to 19.9 %, both in regions in Turkey.

As unemployment has risen sharply in the wake of the economic crisis, it is interesting to analyse the trend and to compare its behaviour over the past years at a regional level. Map 2.4 reflects the change in unemployment rate, by NUTS 2 regions, between 2005 and 2009. Unemployment rates fell significantly over the last five years in all the Polish regions, in regions in the centre and north-east of Germany, in Slovakia and in Bulgaria. For instance, in the Polish regions of Dolnośląskie, Pomorskie, Śląskie and Zachodniopomorskie, the unemployment rate decreased by more than 12 percentage points. By contrast, unemployment rates increased by more than 10 percentage points in regions in the south of Spain. To a lesser extent, unemployment rates also increased in the other regions in Spain, in the three Baltic States and in some regions in Ireland, the United Kingdom and Hungary.

Long-term unemployment

It is worth taking a look at long-term unemployment, as this is one of the policymakers' main concerns. Not only does it affect people's personal lives, it also impacts negatively on social cohesion and may be an obstacle to economic growth as well.

The long-term unemployment share, i.e. the percentage of all unemployed persons who have been looking for a job for more than one year, continued the downward trend which started in 2006. In 2009 the long-term unemployment share

Map 2.2: Female employment rate for 15–64 age group, by NUTS 2 regions, 2009
(%)

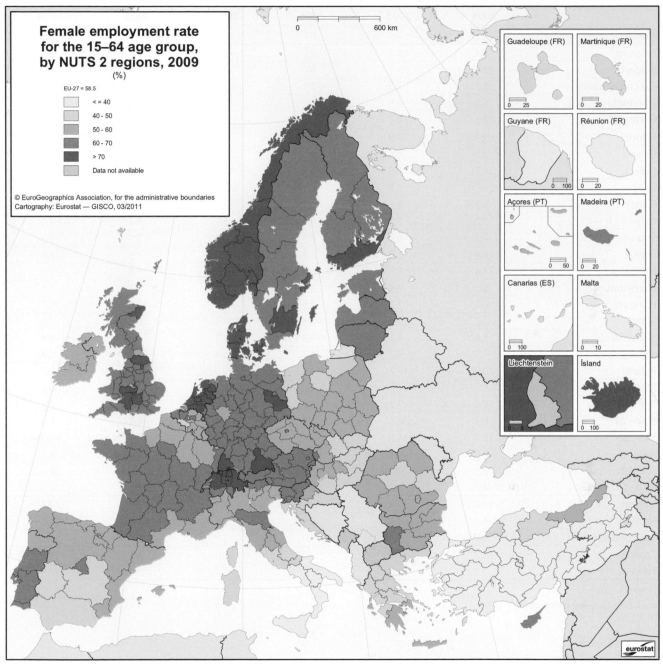

Source: Eurostat (online data code: lfst_r_lfe2emprt).

Table 2.1: Unemployment rate, national level, 2004–09
(%)

	2004	2005	2006	2007	2008	2009
EU-27	9.2	8.9	8.4	7.2	7	8.9
Belgium	8.4	8.4	8.2	7.5	7.0	7.9
Bulgaria	12.0	10.1	9.0	6.9	5.6	6.8
Czech Republic	8.3	7.9	7.1	5.3	4.4	6.7
Denmark	5.5	4.8	:	3.8	3.3	6.0
Germany	10.7	11.1	10.5	8.6	7.5	7.7
Estonia	9.7	7.9	5.9	4.7	5.5	13.8
Ireland	4.5	4.3	4.4	4.6	6.0	11.7
Greece	10.5	9.8	8.9	8.3	7.7	9.5
Spain	11.0	9.2	8.5	8.3	11.3	18.0
France	9.3	9.3	9.3	8.4	7.8	9.5
Italy	8.0	7.7	6.8	6.1	6.7	7.8
Cyprus	4.3	5.3	4.5	3.9	3.7	5.3
Latvia	10.4	8.9	6.8	6.0	7.5	17.1
Lithuania	11.4	8.3	5.6	4.3	5.8	13.7
Luxembourg	8.1	4.5	4.7	4.1	5.1	5.1
Hungary	6.1	7.2	7.5	7.4	7.8	10.0
Malta	7.2	7.3	7.3	6.4	6.0	7.0
Netherlands	4.6	4.7	3.9	3.2	2.8	3.4
Austria	4.9	5.2	4.7	4.4	3.8	4.8
Poland	19.0	17.7	13.9	9.6	7.1	8.2
Portugal	6.7	7.6	7.7	8.0	7.6	9.5
Romania	8.1	7.2	7.3	6.4	5.8	6.9
Slovenia	6.3	6.5	6.0	4.8	4.4	5.9
Slovakia	18.2	16.3	13.4	1 1.1	9.5	12.0
Finland	8.8	8.4	7.7	6.9	6.4	8.2
Sweden	6.5	7.5	7.1	6.2	6.2	8.4
United Kingdom	4.7	4.8	5.4	5.3	5.6	7.6
Iceland	3.0	2.5	2.8	2.3	2.9	7.2
Norway	4.2	4.4	3.4	2.5	2.5	3.1
Switzerland	4.3	4.4	4.0	3.7	3.3	4.1
Croatia	13.7	12.6	:	9.6	8.4	9.1
Turkey	:	:	8.7	8.9	9.7	12.6

: = Data not available.

Source: Eurostat (online data code: lfst_r_lfu3rt).

Map 2.3: Unemployment rate, by NUTS 3 regions, 2009 (¹)
(%)

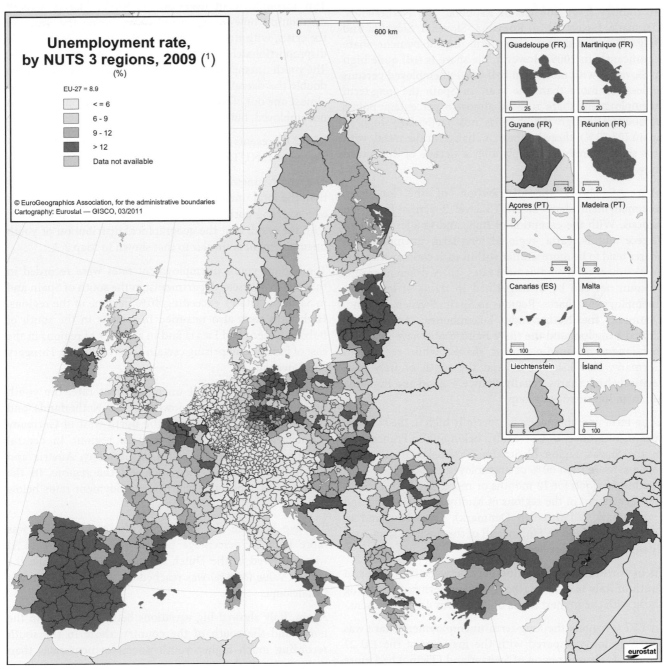

Unemployment rate,
by NUTS 3 regions, 2009 (¹)
(%)

EU-27 = 8.9

<= 6
6 - 9
9 - 12
> 12
Data not available

© EuroGeographics Association, for the administrative boundaries
Cartography: Eurostat — GISCO, 03/2011

Guadeloupe (FR) Martinique (FR)
Guyane (FR) Réunion (FR)
Açores (PT) Madeira (PT)
Canarias (ES) Malta
Liechtenstein Ísland

(¹) Belgium, Bulgaria, Malta, Portugal, Iceland, Norway, Switzerland, Croatia and Turkey, by NUTS 2 regions.

Source: Eurostat (online data code: lfst_r_lfu3rt).

for the EU-27 stood at 33.5 %, which represents a fall of 3.7 percentage points from the 2008 level.

At country level, the Czech Republic, the Netherlands, Denmark, Luxembourg, Romania, Slovenia, Slovakia and Bulgaria reduced their long-term unemployment share significantly in 2009. However, the share is still quite high in Slovakia, with more than half of all unemployed persons jobless for more than one year. In Spain the long-term unemployment share rose by almost 6 percentage points in 2009. Although the share is not particularly high in Spain (23.72 %), there has been a change in the trend, with this share increasing sharply after a decade of downward movement.

Map 2.5 shows the distribution of the long-term unemployment share at NUTS level 2 across European regions. With the exception of Italy, and to a lesser extent Greece and Bulgaria, regional long-term unemployment shares tend to be more similar within each country than the employment or unemployment rates. Three different groups of countries can be distinguished in terms of long-term unemployment shares. Regions in Spain, Sweden, Finland, Denmark, the Netherlands, Luxembourg, Austria, the United Kingdom and the three Baltic States have relatively low long-term unemployment shares, while regions in Germany, Slovakia, Greece and the south of Italy have relatively high shares. Finally, France, Poland and Romania are in an intermediate group.

Long-term unemployment is especially high in the overseas regions of France, in Corse (also belonging to France) and in the Slovak region of Stredné Slovensko. In all these regions, more than 60 % of unemployed persons have been looking for a job for 12 months or more. The lowest values were registered in the regions of Midtjylland, Sjælland and Syddanmark (all three in Denmark), Övre Norrland in Sweden and Åland in Finland, all of them with a long-term unemployment share below 10 %.

As in previous years, the difference between the north and south of Italy is quite marked, the southern regions being those with the highest levels of long-term unemployment.

In EFTA regions the long-term unemployment share was relatively low compared with the majority of the EU-27 regions. Only one region of Switzerland (Ticino) had more than 40 % of unemployed persons looking for a job for more than one year in 2009. Iceland and Norway both registered lower long-term unemployment shares. The 5.85 % share registered in Iceland is the lowest anywhere in Europe.

Finally, there were considerable differences in the long-term unemployment trend across candidate countries. The three regions in Croatia showed quite high shares (all of them above 50 %), whereas most of the regions in Turkey were around 20 %, with just two of its 26 level 2 statistical regions above 30 %.

Youth unemployment

This unemployment overview cannot be closed without mentioning how young people have borne the brunt of the crisis, with unemployment hitting the 15–24-year-olds disproportionately and exceeding 30 % in some countries. The youth unemployment rate in the EU-27 was more than double the overall unemployment rate in 2009. At 19.9 %, almost one out of five young people in the labour force was not employed, but seeking and available for a job.

Map 2.6 presents the regional distribution of youth unemployment at NUTS level 2.

The youth unemployment rate was significantly higher than the total unemployment rate in all countries. There is also a strong correlation between the levels of both rates, with the result that the geographical distribution of youth unemployment is similar to that shown in Map 2.3.

The highest youth unemployment rates were recorded in the French overseas departments, in the south of Spain and in Sardegna (Italy), exceeding 40 % in some of the regions. High rates were also recorded in regions in the south of Italy, in Greece and Latvia and in a cluster of regions in the east of Europe comprising certain areas of Poland, Hungary and Slovakia.

In line with the overall unemployment rate, the youth unemployment rate was lower in the Netherlands and two neighbouring regions in the north-west of Germany (Lüneburg and Weser-Ems) and in regions in central Europe, comprising the south of Germany, Austria and the Italian region of Piemonte. All the regions in the Netherlands registered youth unemployment rates below 10 %.

The gap between the lowest and the highest value was more than 55 percentage points. The lowest rate (4 %) was registered in the Dutch region of Zeeland, while the highest value (59.3 %) was reached on the French island of Guadeloupe.

Again, Italy showed big variations between regions in the north and the south of the country, those in the south recording much higher youth unemployment rates than those in the north.

In EFTA regions the youth unemployment rate was relatively low as compared with the majority of the EU-27 regions, with regional rates ranging from 4.4 % in Ostschweiz (Switzerland) to 15.9 % in Iceland.

On the other hand, most regions in the candidate countries registered rates above the EU-27 average, with values ranging from 10.4 % in the Turkish region of Trabzon to 35.4 % in Središnja i Istočna (Panonska) Hrvatska in Croatia.

Map 2.4: Change in unemployment rate, by NUTS 2 regions, 2009 compared with 2005 (¹)
(Percentage points)

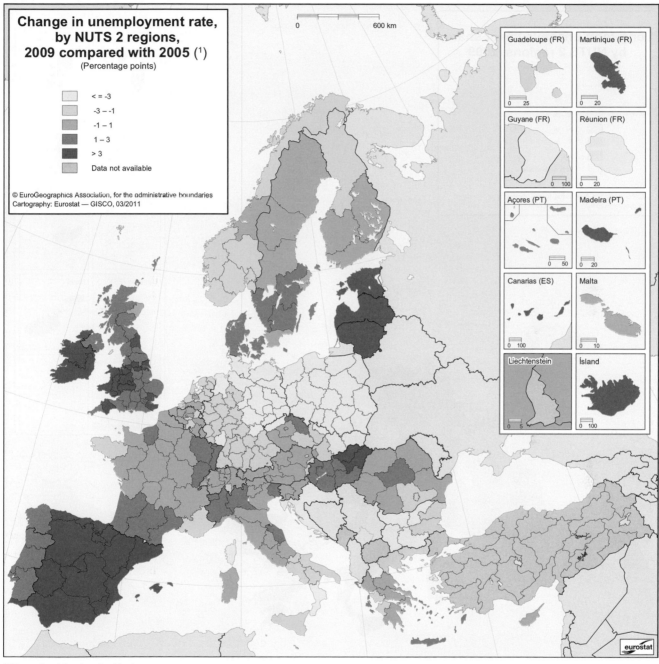

Change in unemployment rate, by NUTS 2 regions, 2009 compared with 2005 (¹)
(Percentage points)

- < = -3
- -3 – -1
- -1 – 1
- 1 – 3
- > 3
- Data not available

© EuroGeographics Association, for the administrative boundaries
Cartography: Eurostat — GISCO, 03/2011

Guadeloupe (FR)   Martinique (FR)
Guyane (FR)   Réunion (FR)
Açores (PT)   Madeira (PT)
Canarias (ES)   Malta
Liechtenstein   Ísland

(¹) Denmark and Croatia, national level.

Source: Eurostat (online data code: lfst_r_lfu3rt).

Map 2.5: Long-term unemployment share, by NUTS 2 regions, 2009
(%)

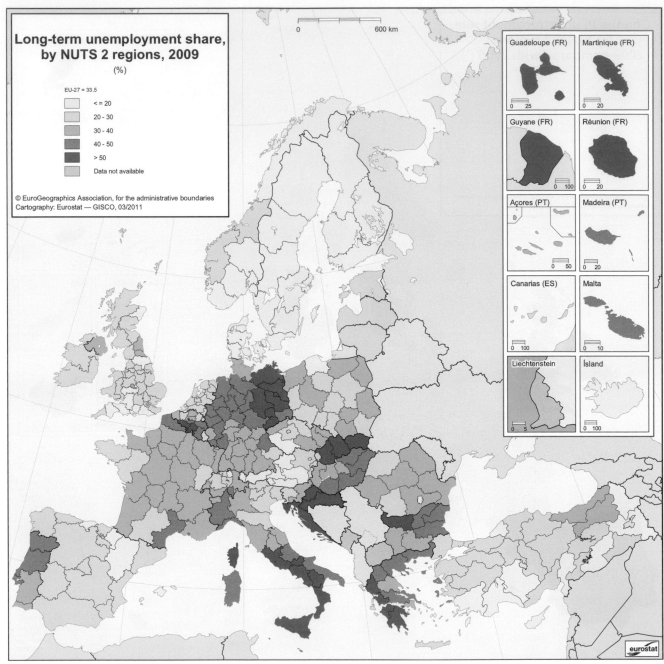

Long-term unemployment share, by NUTS 2 regions, 2009
(%)

EU-27 = 33.5

- <= 20
- 20 - 30
- 30 - 40
- 40 - 50
- > 50
- Data not available

© EuroGeographics Association, for the administrative boundaries
Cartography: Eurostat — GISCO, 03/2011

Guadeloupe (FR)   0 25
Martinique (FR)   0 20
Guyane (FR)   0 100
Réunion (FR)   0 20
Açores (PT)   0 50
Madeira (PT)   0 20
Canarias (ES)   0 100
Malta   0 10
Liechtenstein   0 5
Ísland   0 100

0   600 km

Source: Eurostat (online data code: lfst_r_lfu2ltu).

Map 2.6: Youth unemployment rate (15–24), by NUTS 2 regions, 2009 (%)

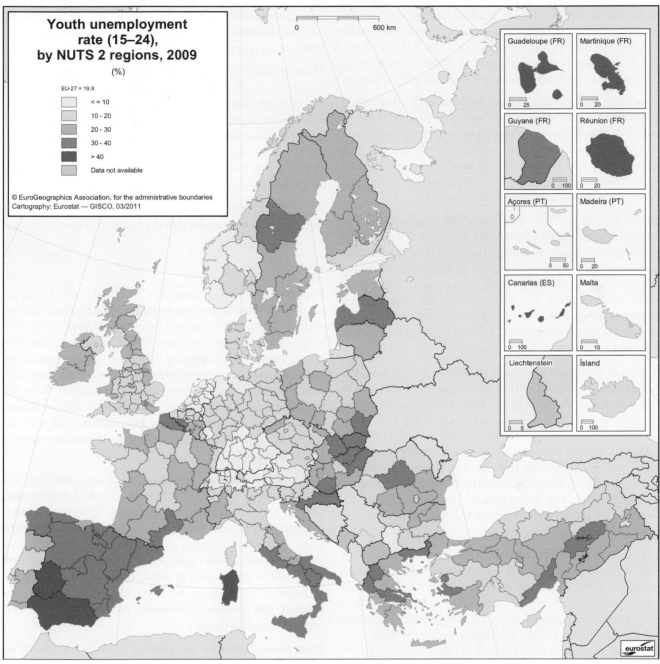

Youth unemployment rate (15–24), by NUTS 2 regions, 2009 (%)

EU-27 = 19.9

- <= 10
- 10 - 20
- 20 - 30
- 30 - 40
- > 40
- Data not available

© EuroGeographics Association, for the administrative boundaries
Cartography: Eurostat — GISCO, 03/2011

Source: Eurostat (online data code: lfst_r_lfu3rt).

Disparities in regional labour markets

The European social cohesion objective seeks to minimise disparities in regional labour markets. It is an easy matter to check whether the employment targets set by the Lisbon and Europe 2020 strategies are going to be fulfilled or not. But analysing only these indicators does not tell us whether regional cohesion is being achieved in meeting those targets.

To analyse how much regions differ from each other within a country or the whole EU-27 we need another kind of indicator. The dispersion of employment and unemployment rates measures the spread of regional rates in a country or in the EU-27, and gives an idea of how much regional rates differ from each other. As the dispersion of these rates declines, so labour market cohesion increases.

Table 2.2 shows the dispersion of employment and unemployment rates for 2007, 2008 and 2009. If we consider previous years' rates, we will see the effect the crisis has had, increasing these rates during 2008 and 2009 and reversing the declining trend which set in five years earlier, in 2003. From 2007 to 2008, the dispersion of employment and unemployment rates in the EU-27 increased by 0.2 and 3.1 percentage points respectively. In 2009 the increases were of 0.5 and 1.9 percentage points respectively.

Although both rates increased in 2009 at EU-27 level, the fact is that dispersion within countries has followed the opposite trend, decreasing for both rates in most of the Member States. This is because there are big differences in the way countries have responded to the crisis. So reactions among regions in the same country have been quite uniform, while reactions among regions in different countries have been comparatively uneven. In most Member States, the dispersion of the employment rate seems to be quite stable, whereas the unemployment rate is more likely to vary.

The country with the highest dispersion for both rates was Italy, with 17.4% for employment and 42% for unemployment. There are marked differences in regional labour market performance between the north and south of Italy, as shown on Maps 2.1 and 2.3. Belgium also registered a high dispersion for the unemployment rate, with 51%. Denmark had the lowest dispersion rates, followed by the Netherlands.

Data sources and availability

The source for regional labour market information down to NUTS level 2 is the EU Labour Force Survey (EU-LFS). This is a quarterly household sample survey conducted in the Member States of the European Union.

The LFS target population is made up of all members of private households aged 15 or over. The survey follows the definitions and recommendations of the International Labour Organisation (ILO). To achieve further harmonisation, the Member States also adhere to common principles when formulating questionnaires.

Most regional results presented here concern NUTS 2 regions, and all regional figures are annual averages of the quarterly surveys, with the exception of employment and unemployment rates. NUTS 3 employment and unemployment data by sex and age are provided by Member States on a voluntary basis. In most cases the source is the LFS, but not always, as there are some cases where estimations and data from registers are used.

For further information about regional labour market statistics, see the metadata on the Eurostat website.

Definitions

Population covers persons aged 15 and over, living in private households (persons living in collective households, such as residential homes, boarding houses, hospitals, religious institutions and workers' hostels, are therefore not included). This category comprises all persons living in the households surveyed during the reference week. The definition also includes persons who are absent from the households for short periods due to studies, holidays, illness, business trips, etc. (but who have maintained a link with the private household). Persons on compulsory military service are not included.

Employed persons are persons aged 15 years and over (16 years and over in Spain, the United Kingdom and Sweden (1995–2001); 15–74 years in Denmark, Estonia, Finland, Hungary, Latvia and Sweden (from 2001 onwards); 16–74 years in Iceland and Norway) who during the reference week performed work, even for just one hour a week, for pay, profit or family gain or were not at work but had a job or business from which they were temporarily absent, for example due to illness, holidays, industrial dispute and education and training.

Unemployed persons are persons aged 15–74 (16–74 in Spain, Sweden (1995–2001), the United Kingdom, Iceland and Norway), who were without work during the reference week, were currently available for work and were either actively seeking work in the past four weeks or had already found a job to start within the next three months.

Employment rate represents employed persons as a percentage of the population.

Old-age employment rate represents employed persons aged 55–64 as a percentage of the population aged 55–64.

Table 2.2: Dispersion of employment and unemployment rates, by NUTS 2 regions, 2007–09
(coefficient of variation)

	Dispersion of employment rates for the age group 15–64			Dispersion of unemployment rates for the age group 15–74		
	2007	2008	2009	2007	2008	2009
EU-27	11.1	1.3	11.8	44.1	47.2	49.1
Belgium	8.6	8.4	8.7	59	60	51
Bulgaria	7.1	7.2	8.1	39	39	31
Czech Republic	4.6	4.0	4.7	42	44	34
Denmark	1.3	1.6	1.8	11	5	7
Germany	4.8	4.8	4.3	44	45	37
Estonia (¹)	–	–	–	–	–	–
Ireland (¹)	–	–	–	–	–	–
Greece	3.5	3.6	3.4	15	19	12
Spain	7.5	8.2	8.8	31	33	27
France	6.5	6.7	6.9	33	36	32
Italy	16.3	17.0	17.4	57	55	42
Cyprus (¹)	–	–	–	–	–	–
Latvia (¹)	–	–	–	–	–	–
Lithuania (¹)	–	–	–	–	–	–
Luxembourg (¹)	–	–	–	–	–	–
Hungary	9.7	10.0	9.7	39	43	31
Malta (¹)	–	–	–	–	–	–
Netherlands	2.2	2.3	2.3	17	16	15
Austria	3.8	3.8	3.3	45	40	31
Poland	4.5	5.1	4.5	14	18	20
Portugal	3.3	3.3	3.3	20	18	18
Romania	4.6	4.3	5.0	28	28	26
Slovenia (¹)	–	–	–	–	–	–
Slovakia	8.3	8.1	8.0	38	41	32
Finland	5.6	5.2	5.3	26	22	18
Sweden	2.4	2.7	3.1	10	13	11
United Kingdom	5.3	5.6	5.9	25	29	24
Norway	2.5	2.3	2.3	14	17	20
Switzerland	3.5	3.7	3.6	22	22	25
Croatia	7.5	7.4	7.8	35	39	38
Turkey	13.1	15.5	15.5	32	28	31

(¹) Estonia, Ireland, Cyprus, Latvia, Lithuania, Luxembourg, Malta and Slovenia comprise only one or two NUTS 2 regions, therefore dispersion rates are not applicable.

Source: Eurostat (online data codes: lfst_r_lmder and lfst_r_lmdur).

Unemployment rate represents unemployed persons as a percentage of the economically active population. The unemployment rate can be broken down further by age and sex. The youth unemployment rate relates to persons aged 15–24.

Long-term unemployment share represents the percentage of total unemployed persons seeking a job for longer than one year.

Dispersion of employment (unemployment) rates is the coefficient of variation of regional employment (unemployment) rates in a country, weighted by the absolute population (active population) of each region.

Context

The results presented in this chapter are related to the Lisbon and Europe 2020 labour market targets and show that 2009 was strongly affected by the worldwide economic crisis, which hit both employment and unemployment and broke the trend of the previous years' strong growth.

The regions' success in dealing with the crisis and the package of measures to be implemented by Member States in the labour market will determine in the years to come not just the nature of the labour market itself, but also the success of regional cohesion.

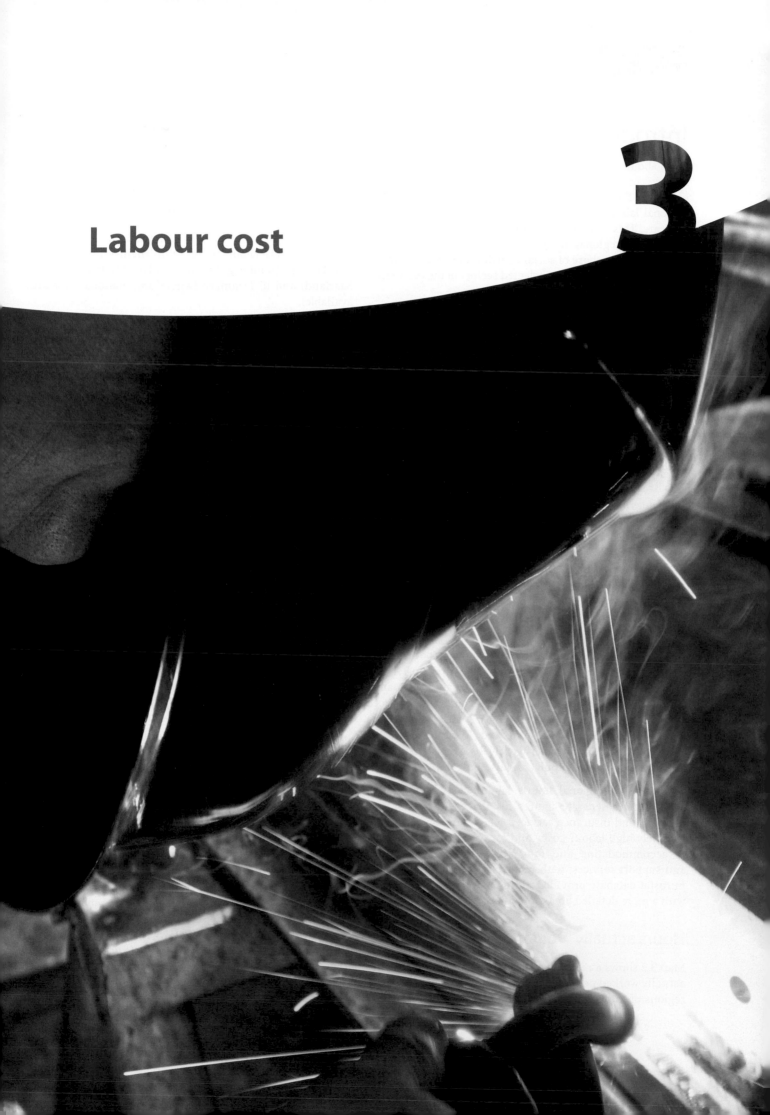

Labour cost

3

Introduction

The Labour Cost Survey (LCS) is one of the key structural surveys in the European Union covering the business economy. Eurostat has collected, processed and published regional labour cost data by economic activity for nearly 25 years. This chapter describes some of the main findings concerning regional hourly labour costs, average hours worked and the share of social contributions in total labour costs paid by employers in selected sectors of the economy.

Main statistical findings

Hourly labour costs

Map 3.1 shows significant regional variations in the cost of labour per hour worked in the business economy in 2008. At EUR 49 per hour, the Île-de-France region surrounding Paris has the highest average labour cost in Europe. This is nearly 25 times higher than Bulgaria, which has the lowest average labour cost at EUR 2 per hour.

The values for the nine regions with the next-highest average labour costs are as follows: EUR 44 per hour in Région de Bruxelles-Capitale/Brussels Hoofdstedelijk Gewest (Belgium), EUR 38 per hour in Norway, EUR 37 per hour in Östra Sverige (Sweden), EUR 36 per hour in Denmark, EUR 35 per hour in Hessen (Germany), EUR 34 per hour in Vlaams Gewest (Belgium) and Hamburg (Germany) and EUR 33 per hour in Région Wallonne (Belgium) and Bassin Parisien (France).

At the other end of the range, the average labour cost is EUR 6 per hour or under in the following 11 regions: Alföld és Észak (Hungary), Region Wschodni (Poland), Lithuania, Latvia, Macroregiunea trei and Macroregiunea patru (both Romania), Yugozapadna I Yuzhna Tsentralna Bulgaria (Bulgaria), Macroregiunea unu and Macroregiunea doi (both Romania), the former Yugoslav Republic of Macedonia and Severna I Iztochna Bulgaria (also Bulgaria).

Figure 3.1 on regional hourly labour costs by economic activity gives separate figures for the energy sector and financial and insurance services, which are known to have relatively high labour costs, and for economic sectors such as accommodation and food services or administrative and support services, with relatively low labour costs. The Eurostat database provides additional data on labour costs with a more detailed breakdown of economic sectors.

Hours actually worked

Map 3.2 shows a regional comparison of the average hours actually worked per year in business in Europe. In 2008, all regions of the United Kingdom, Malta and, in non-EU-27

countries, Norway, the former Yugoslav Republic of Macedonia and Turkey recorded an average number of hours actually worked per employee (in full-time equivalents) per year of over 1 875 hours. The average hours worked per employee were the lowest, at 1 650 or less, in all regions of France, in the three Belgian regions (Région wallonne, Vlaams Gewest and Région de Bruxelles-Capitale/Brussels Hoofdstedelijk Gewest), in Greece's Nisia Aigaiou and Kriti, in seven German regions (Nordrhein-Westfalen, Bayern, Hessen, Hamburg, Bremen, Baden-Württemberg and Saarland) and in Denmark (where only national data are available).

When making comparisons, specific national legislative arrangements and habits concerning working time, which can also vary by economic sector (hotels and restaurants, transport, construction), come into play. The average time worked is also affected by the prevailing economic situation (full order books, short-time working and plant closures). In connection with the Labour Cost Survey, the regional database gives additional information on working time, such as the number of employees and the corresponding total number of hours actually worked and paid, broken down into full-time and part-time workers and in full-time equivalents. These data are also available at two-digit level (divisions) of NACE classification.

Structure of labour costs

Map 3.3 gives an idea of the share of employers' actual social contributions in labour costs in business in European regions in 2008. Comparisons should take into account specific national legislative arrangements and social security models.

The 10 regions with the highest proportions include the regions Bassin Parisien (31.6 %) in France, the Belgian region Vlaams Gewest (29.9 %), Île de France (29.5 %) in France, Région wallonne (29.0 %) in Belgium, Östra Sverige (28.7 %) in Sweden and the former Yugoslav Republic of Macedonia (28.5 %), followed by Région de Bruxelles-Capitale/Brussels Hoofdstedelijk Gewest (28.3 %) in Belgium, the two Swedish regions Södra Sverige (27.9 %) and Norra Sverige (27.6 %) and Nord-Ovest (26.9 %) in Italy.

The 10 regions with the lowest share of employers' actual social contributions in labour costs across Europe include regions in Norway, one Polish region, four regions of the United Kingdom and some smaller EU Member States. The share of employers' actual social contributions in labour costs is lowest in Norway (5.7 %), Denmark (6.9 %) and Luxembourg (11.5 %), followed by three regions in the United Kingdom — Wales (11.9 %), Yorkshire and The Humber (12.1 %) and West Midlands (England) (12.2 %). The region Centralny (12.5 %) in Poland, East of England (12.6 %) in the United Kingdom and Slovenia (12.8 %) also fall within this lower band.

Map 3.1: Hourly labour cost (excluding apprentices), by NUTS 1 regions, 2008 (¹)
(EUR per employee in full-time units in business economy (NACE Rev. 2 B to N))

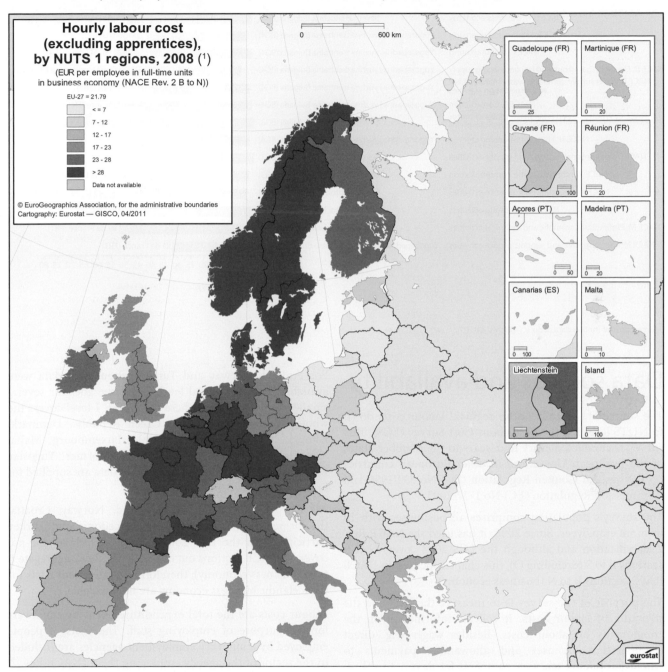

(¹) Turkey, NACE Rev. 1.1 C to K; Finland and Turkey, national level.

Source: Eurostat (online data code: lc_r08cost_r2 and lc_n08cost_r1).

Figure 3.1: Hourly labour costs by economic activity, highest and lowest NUTS 1 region in EU-27, 2008 (¹) (EUR per hour)

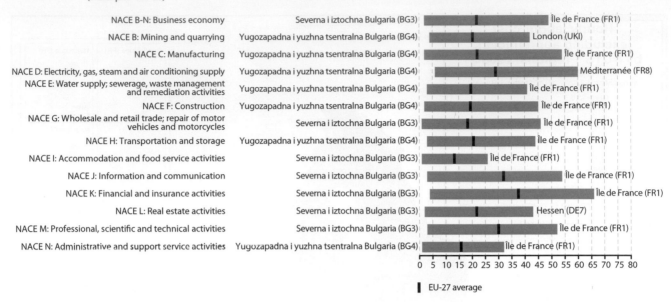

(¹) Finland, national level.

Source: Eurostat (online data code: lc_r08cost_r2).

Data sources and availability

The source of information on regional labour costs down to NUTS level 1 is the EU Labour Cost Survey (LCS). This survey is conducted every four years in the Member States of the European Union and in other European countries on the basis of Council Regulation (EC) No 530/1999 and Commission Regulation (EC) No 1737/2005.

The survey's population comprises all businesses with 10 or more employees. Since 2008, it has used the NACE Rev. 2 classification and although the LCS 2008 covers NACE sections B to S (excluding O), this chapter focuses on NACE Rev. 2 sections B to N (business economy).

The purpose of the survey is to measure the level and the structure of labour costs. It collects information on the components of labour costs. Besides wages (e.g. direct remuneration, bonuses and allowances, payments to employees' saving schemes, payments for days not worked, wages and salaries in kind) these include a multitude of social security contributions payable by the employer (statutory, under collective agreements, contractual or voluntary), together with employers' imputed social contributions (e.g. guaranteed remuneration in the event of sickness or payments to employees leaving the business). Costs of vocational training, taxes and subsidies relating to the employment of staff are also recorded.

At the same time, questions are asked on the number of employees, full-time and part-time workers, full-time equivalents and the number of hours worked and paid.

For Finland, Norway and Turkey, labour cost data were available only at national level. The same goes for several smaller Member States, where the NUTS 1 level covers the whole country: Cyprus, the Czech Republic, Denmark, Estonia, Ireland, Latvia, Lithuania, Luxembourg, Malta, Slovakia, Slovenia, Croatia and the former Yugoslav Republic of Macedonia. No labour cost data are supplied for France's overseas departments.

All EU Member States plus Iceland, Norway, Croatia, the former Yugoslav Republic of Macedonia and Turkey participated in the LCS 2008. However, Iceland did not cover all NACE sections out of the NACE Rev.2 aggregate B to N (business economy); therefore, overall labour costs for the Icelandic business economy are not available.

Labour costs are the total expenditure borne by employers for the purpose of employing staff. The costs of people employed by temporary employment agencies are included in the sector of the agency employing them (NACE Rev. 2: codes 78.1, 78.2 and 78.3), not of the business for which they work.

Besides average labour cost per hour, Eurostat publishes average monthly labour costs and average annual labour costs. The figures are given for full-time workers, part-time workers and apprentices and all workers expressed in full-time equivalents. The total number of employees comprises full-time workers, part-time workers and apprentices. Part-time workers are converted to full-time equivalents on the basis of hours worked. The observations made do not cover apprentices.

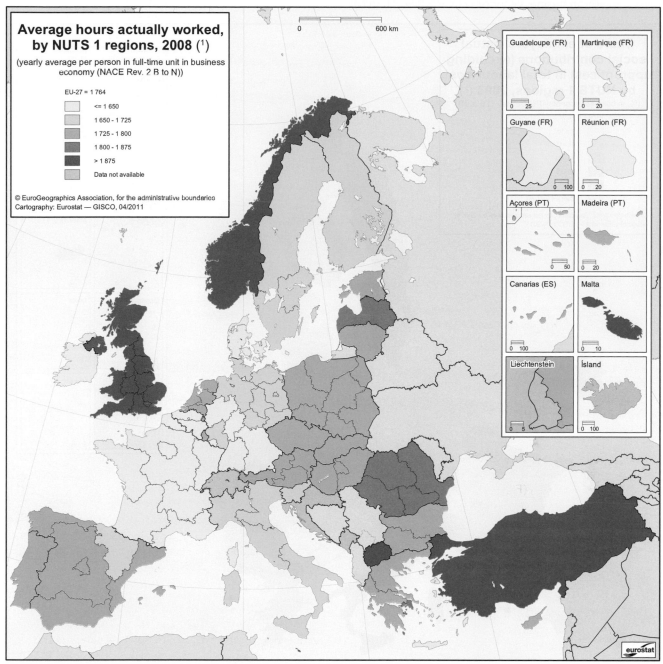

Map 3.2: Average hours actually worked, by NUTS 1 regions, 2008 (¹)
(yearly average per person in full-time unit in business economy (NACE Rev. 2 B to N))

Average hours actually worked, by NUTS 1 regions, 2008 (¹)

(yearly average per person in full-time unit in business economy (NACE Rev. 2 B to N))

EU-27 = 1 764

- <= 1 650
- 1 650 - 1 725
- 1 725 - 1 800
- 1 800 - 1 875
- > 1 875
- Data not available

© EuroGeographics Association, for the administrative boundaries
Cartography: Eurostat — GISCO, 04/2011

Guadeloupe (FR)   Martinique (FR)   Guyane (FR)   Réunion (FR)   Açores (PT)   Madeira (PT)   Canarias (ES)   Malta   Liechtenstein   Ísland

(¹) Turkey, NACE Rev. 1.1 C to K; Finland and Turkey, national level.

Source: Eurostat (online data code: lc_r08num2_r2 and lc_n08num2_r1).

Map 3.3: Share of employers' actual social contributions (excluding apprentices) in total labour cost, by NUTS 1 regions, 2008 (¹)

(%, in business economy (NACE Rev. 2 B to N))

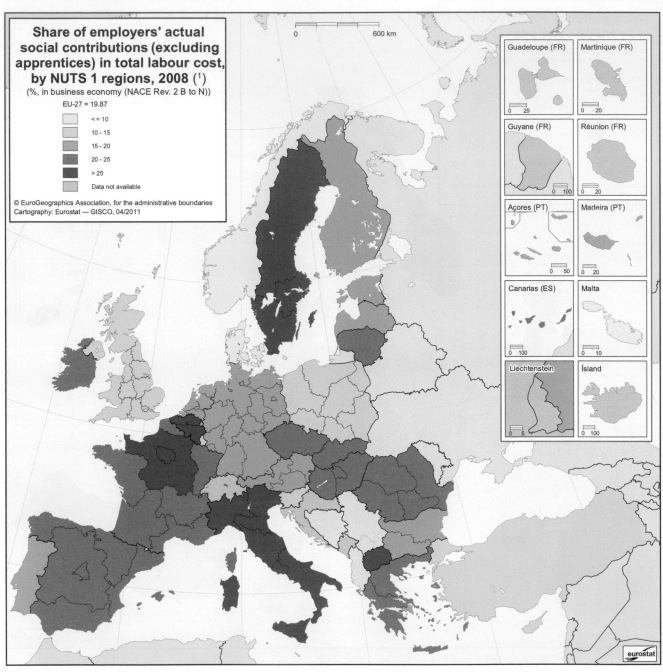

Share of employers' actual social contributions (excluding apprentices) in total labour cost, by NUTS 1 regions, 2008 (¹)

(%, in business economy (NACE Rev. 2 B to N))

EU-27 = 19.87

- <= 10
- 10 - 15
- 15 - 20
- 20 - 25
- > 25
- Data not available

© EuroGeographics Association, for the administrative boundaries
Cartography: Eurostat — GISCO, 04/2011

(¹) Turkey, NACE Rev. 1.1 C to K; Finland and Turkey, national level.

Source: Eurostat (online data code: lc_n08struc_r2 and lc_n08struc_r1).

Employers' actual social contributions are attributed to the period during which the work is done.

Context

Labour costs are a major component of the cost of producing goods and services and correspond to the costs borne by the employer for employing staff. Although labour costs are not the sole deciding factor in choosing where to locate a business, they are a key factor.

It is also important to know whether the regions examined are home to predominantly knowledge-intensive, capital-intensive or labour-intensive industries.

In 2008, the average labour cost across the EU in businesses with 10 or more employees in business economy (i.e. NACE Rev. 2 sections B to N) was EUR 21.8 per hour worked. There are considerable differences between European regions, however, in the level and structure of labour costs.

Education

4

Introduction

Education, vocational training and lifelong learning play a vital role in the economic and social strategies of the European Union.

This chapter takes a look at Eurostat's regional statistics on enrolment in education, educational attainment and participation in lifelong learning, which make it possible to measure progress at regional level and to identify which regions are doing well and which are lagging behind.

Main statistical findings

Students in tertiary education

'Tertiary education' is the level of education offered by universities, vocational universities, institutes of technology and other institutions that award academic degrees or professional certificates. Access to tertiary-level education typically requires successful completion of an upper-secondary and/or post-secondary non-tertiary level programme.

Tertiary-level education can be classified according to the following characteristics:

ISCED level 5A is, for the most part, theoretically based and is intended to provide adequate qualifications for entry into advanced research programmes and professions with high skills requirements. Three-year bachelor and four-to-five-year masters programmes are typical examples in this category.

ISCED level 5B is more practical, technical and employment-oriented.

ISCED level 6 (PhD-like studies) leads to an advanced research qualification.

The tertiary education indicator highlights the mobility of students. In 2009, the number of students in tertiary education in the EU-27 countries stood at nearly 19 million.

Map 4.1 shows the number of students enrolled in tertiary education (ISCED levels 5 and 6) in 2009 (2008/09 academic year) as a percentage of the corresponding regional population aged 20 to 24. This indicator is a function of the number of students in the region and of the number of residents aged 20 to 24 in that region and gives an idea of how attractive the region is to tertiary students. Since it is based on data on the area where students study, and not the area where they come from or live, it is likely that some students are not resident in the region where they are studying. Hence, regions which show high values (e.g. more than 100) for this indicator host big universities or other

tertiary education institutions and, as a consequence, attract large numbers of students from outside the region.

Some of the factors to consider when interpreting this indicator are the age-group structure of the population within regions and the corresponding structure of the tertiary education system between regions. The indicator gives an indication of the concentration or spread of tertiary education institutions across regions.

Students aged 17 in education

Compulsory education and the age when compulsory education ends vary greatly between the EU Member States. In most countries, compulsory education ends at the age of 15 or 16, which is typically at the end of lower-secondary education. By the age of 17, it is possible to have finished secondary education in some countries, whereas in others, pupils may have just started the upper-secondary level (often high school or vocational training leading directly to a labour market qualification). At the age of 17, most young people in the European Union are still in education.

At the age of 17, young people are faced with the choice of whether to remain in education, go into training or look for a job. Even if compulsory education ends before 17, over the last decade young people have become more likely to continue with their education.

Map 4.2 depicts students aged 17 (at all levels of education) as a percentage of the corresponding age group in each region. Almost everywhere in Europe, this indicator gives a result of more than 75 %. This means that, for one reason or another, the younger generations are still in the education system even after the compulsory schooling age.

Participation of four-year-olds in education

Learning begins at birth. The period from birth to the start of primary education is a critical formative stage for the growth and development of children. The learning outcomes and the knowledge and skills acquired during primary education are stronger when children learn and develop appropriately in the years preceding regular schooling.

The purpose of pre-primary education is to prepare children physically, emotionally, socially and mentally to enter grade 1 of primary education, giving them the ability and skills to enter the education system.

The indicator reflects participation in early childhood education by NUTS 2 region, by measuring the percentage of four-year-olds who are in either pre-primary or primary education. By far the majority of four-year-olds attend pre-primary school. A four-year-old child can be enrolled either

Map 4.1: Students in tertiary education, as a percentage of the population aged 20 to 24 years old,
by NUTS 2 regions, 2009 ([1])
(ISCED levels 5 and 6)

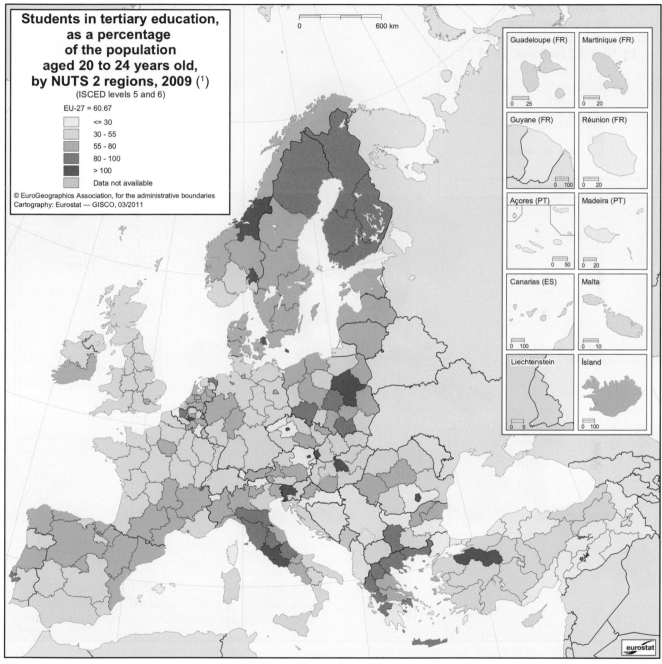

**Students in tertiary education,
as a percentage
of the population
aged 20 to 24 years old,
by NUTS 2 regions, 2009 ([1])**
(ISCED levels 5 and 6)

EU-27 = 60.67

- <= 30
- 30 - 55
- 55 - 80
- 80 - 100
- > 100
- Data not available

© EuroGeographics Association, for the administrative boundaries
Cartography: Eurostat — GISCO, 03/2011

0   600 km

Guadeloupe (FR)   Martinique (FR)
0   25   0   20

Guyane (FR)   Réunion (FR)
0   100   0   20

Açores (PT)   Madeira (PT)
0   50   0   20

Canarias (ES)   Malta
0   100   0   10

Liechtenstein   Ísland
0   5   0   100

eurostat

([1]) Data covers enrolments at regional level in school year 2008/09; Belgium, Greece and United Kingdom, 2008; Switzerland, national level; Germany and United Kingdom, by NUTS 1 regions.

Source: Eurostat (online data code: tgs00094).

Map 4.2: Students aged 17, as a percentage of corresponding age population, by NUTS 2 regions, 2009 (¹)
(ISCED levels 0–6)

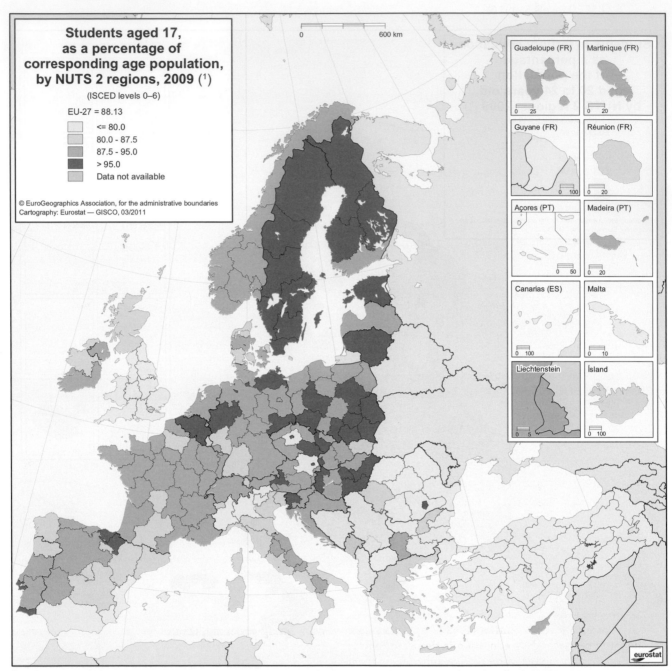

Students aged 17,
as a percentage of
corresponding age population,
by NUTS 2 regions, 2009 (¹)

(ISCED levels 0–6)

EU-27 = 88.13

- <= 80.0
- 80.0 - 87.5
- 87.5 - 95.0
- > 95.0
- Data not available

© EuroGeographics Association, for the administrative boundaries
Cartography: Eurostat — GISCO, 03/2011

(¹) Belgium, Greece and United Kingdom, 2008; Belgium, Greece, Netherlands, Switzerland and Croatia, national level; Germany and United Kingdom, by NUTS 1 regions.

Source: Eurostat (online data code: tgs00091).

in pre-primary or in primary school. The data highlight that most four-year-olds attend pre-primary schools. Ireland and the United Kingdom are the only countries where a significant proportion of four-year-olds are in primary education. At the age of four, most children in the European Union are therefore in pre-primary education, which is generally available from at least three to four years of age in Member States. Enrolment in pre-primary education is often voluntary. Nevertheless, many countries have full participation rates.

As Map 4.3 shows, in countries such as Belgium, Denmark, France, Germany, Iceland, Italy, Luxembourg, Malta, the Netherlands, Norway and Spain, almost all four-year-olds are in education. By contrast, in Croatia, Greece, Ireland, Poland, most regions of Finland, the former Yugoslav Republic of Macedonia, Turkey and Switzerland, fewer than 50 % of four-year-olds are enrolled.

Students in upper-secondary and post-secondary non-tertiary education

At age 16, young people are faced with the choice of whether to remain in education, go into vocational training or seek employment. Over the last decade, young people have become more likely to choose to continue their education at this age.

Map 4.4 shows the percentage of students enrolled in upper-secondary education (ISCED level 3) and post-secondary non-tertiary education (ISCED level 4) as a percentage of the population aged between 15 and 24 years old in the region.

General upper-secondary education provides extensive all-round learning based on the basic education received. The objective is to equip students with sufficient skills and knowledge for them to go on studying. Upper-secondary education usually begins at the end of full-time compulsory education and typically requires nine years or more of full-time education (since the beginning of primary level) for admission. General upper-secondary education includes school programmes which, upon successful completion, typically give access to university-level programmes. Vocational upper-secondary education is designed mainly to introduce students to the world of work and prepare them for further vocational or technical education programmes. Post-secondary non-tertiary education (ISCED level 4) covers programmes which are beyond the boundary of upper-secondary education but are not considered to be tertiary education. Often they are more advanced technical and vocational programmes for teacher training, medical professions, commerce and marketing.

Students generally start upper-secondary education at the age of 15 to 17 and finish it two to four years later. The starting/finishing ages and the age range depend on the national educational programmes. Students can normally

attend upper-secondary education programmes relatively close to where they have grown up. For this indicator, a broad age group has been defined to cover the relatively wide spread in ages, depending on the country.

Tertiary educational attainment

Map 4.5 shows the proportion of the population aged 25 to 64 who have successfully completed university or similar (tertiary-level) education. The demographic profile of a region has some influence on educational attainment, as younger generations tend to achieve higher levels than older generations. In 2009, 58 regions in the EU had more than 32 % of the population with higher education.

These include large cities such as Brussels, London, Paris, Berlin, Leipzig, Dresden, Helsinki, Stockholm, Madrid and Utrecht in the Netherlands. Oslo (Norway), Genève and Zürich (Switzerland) also fall into this category. In EU Member States such as Ireland, Sweden, Finland, the Netherlands, Belgium, Germany and Estonia, educational attainment levels are generally high across the whole country.

The regions with the lowest percentages of people with tertiary education are largely concentrated in the rural areas of nine EU countries, in marked contrast to their larger cities. This is the case in Portugal and Romania in particular, in Turkey and, to a lesser extent, in Croatia, Bulgaria, the Czech Republic, Italy, Greece, Hungary, Poland and Slovakia. It also applies to some islands, such as Sardegna and Sicilia (Italy), Açores and Madeira (Portugal) and Malta.

Early leavers from education and training

The indicator 'Early leavers from education and training' tracks the percentage of individuals aged 18 to 24 who have finished no more than a lower-secondary education, and who are not involved in further education and training.

As Map 4.6 shows, the share of early leavers from education and training varies significantly across the EU-27. Several regions display a percentage below 10 %, which means they have reached the objective set in the EU 2020 strategy. They are situated in Croatia, Slovakia, Poland, Slovenia, the Czech Republic, Luxembourg, Lithuania, Austria and Finland. Higher percentages above 20 % are observed in Spain, Portugal, Malta and the southern regions of Italy (Sud, Isole), as well as in Turkey and Iceland.

These high percentages are not necessarily associated with high unemployment within the age group. Over 70 % of early leavers from education and training are in employment in Malta, Portugal and Iceland. On the other hand, more than 70 % of early leavers from education and training are inactive or unemployed in Slovakia, Hungary and Bulgaria.

Education

Map 4.3: Participations rates of 4-year-olds in education, by NUTS 2 regions, 2009 (¹)
(%, at pre-primary and primary education, ISCED levels 0 and 1)

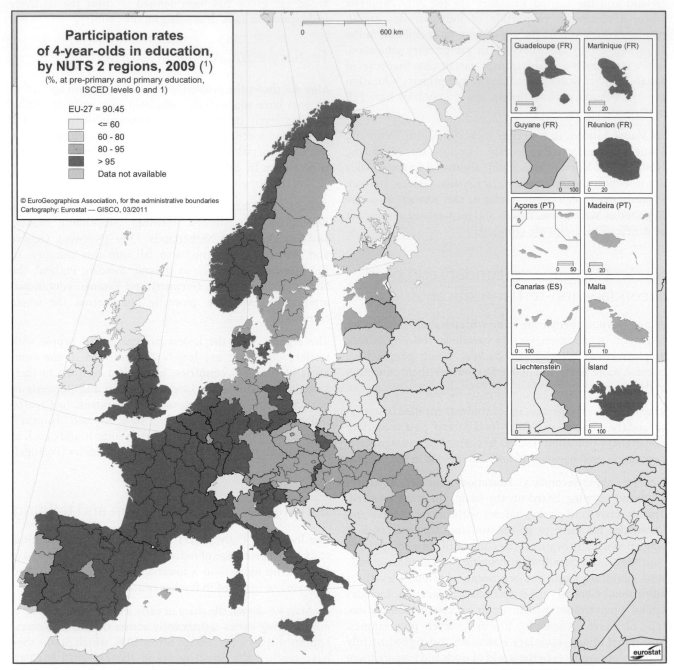

(¹) Belgium, Greece and United Kingdom, 2008; Belgium, Greece, Netherlands, Switzerland and Croatia, national level; Germany and United Kingdom, by NUTS 1 regions.

Source: Eurostat (online data code: tgs00092).

4

Map 4.4: Students at upper secondary and post-secondary non-tertiary education, as a percentage
of the population aged 15 to 24, by NUTS 2 regions, 2009 (^{1})
(ISCED levels 3 and 4)

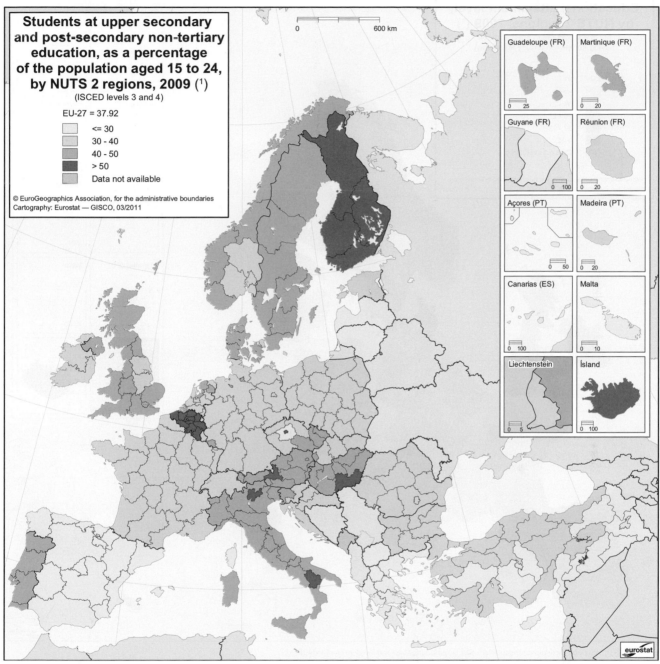

**Students at upper secondary
and post-secondary non-tertiary
education, as a percentage
of the population aged 15 to 24,
by NUTS 2 regions, 2009 (^{1})**
(ISCED levels 3 and 4)

EU-27 = 37.92

- <= 30
- 30 - 40
- 40 - 50
- > 50
- Data not available

© EuroGeographics Association, for the administrative boundaries
Cartography: Eurostat — GISCO, 03/2011

0   600 km

Guadeloupe (FR)   Martinique (FR)
0   25   0   20

Guyane (FR)   Réunion (FR)
        0   100   0   20

Açores (PT)   Madeira (PT)
        0   50   0   20

Canarias (ES)   Malta
0   100   0   10

Liechtenstein   Ísland
0   5   0   100

(^{1}) Data covers enrolments at regional level in school year 2008/09; Belgium, Greece and United Kingdom, 2008; Switzerland, national level; Germany and United Kingdom, by NUTS 1 regions.
Source: Eurostat (online data code: tgs00093).

Map 4.5: Educational attainment level, by NUTS 2 regions, 2009 (¹)
(% of the population aged 25 to 64 having completed tertiary education)

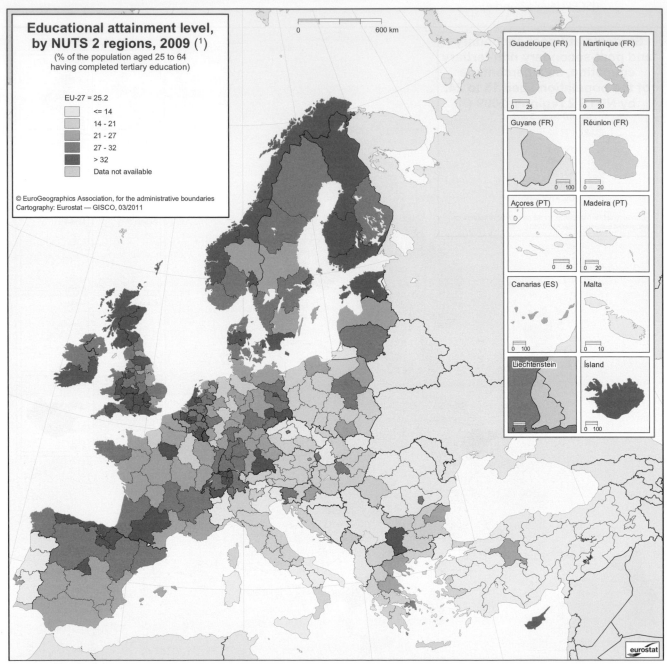

(¹) Corse (FR83), data not reliable due to small sample size; Luxembourg, Malta and Sweden, provisional data.

Source: Eurostat (online data code: edat_lfse_11).

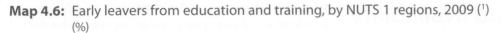
Map 4.6: Early leavers from education and training, by NUTS 1 regions, 2009 (¹)
(%)

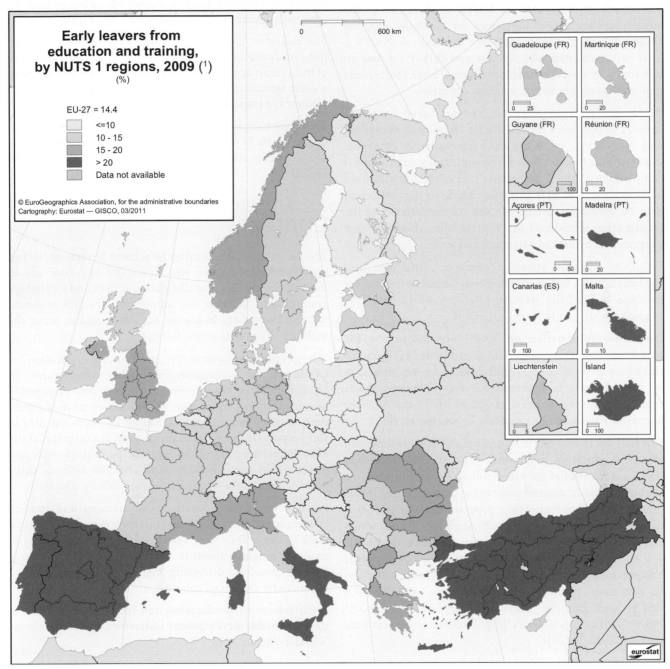

(¹) Slovenia and Croatia, data lack reliability due to small sample size; Luxembourg, Malta and Sweden, provisional data.

Source: Eurostat (online data code: edat_lfse_16).

Data sources and availability

The maps are presented at NUTS level 2, except for educational enrolment indicators for Germany and the United Kingdom, where data are available at NUTS 1 level only. In Switzerland, Croatia and Turkey, no data on enrolment by age are available at regional level. Hence, only national figures are shown for these countries.

As the structure of education systems varies from one country to another, a framework for assembling, compiling and presenting national and international education statistics and indicators is a prerequisite for international comparability. The International Standard Classification of Education (ISCED) provides the basis for collecting data on education. ISCED-97, the current version of the classification introduced in 1997, classifies all educational programmes by field of education and level.

ISCED-97 presents standard concepts, definitions and classifications. A full description is available on the Unesco Institute of Statistics website: http://www.uis.unesco.org/ev.php?ID=3813_201&ID2=DO_TOPIC

Qualitative information on school systems in the EU Member States is organised and disseminated by Eurydice (http://www.eurydice.org/) and covers, for example, age of compulsory school attendance and numerous issues relating to the organisation of school life in the Member States (decision-making, curricula, school hours, etc.).

Statistics on enrolment in education include enrolment in all initial education programmes and all adult education with content similar to initial education programmes or leading to qualifications similar to the corresponding initial programmes. Apprenticeship programmes are included, except those which are entirely work-based and which are not supervised by any formal education authority. The data source used for Maps 4.1 to 4.4 are two specific Eurostat tables which form part of the UOE data collection on education systems. 'UOE' incorporates UIS-UNESCO, OECD and Eurostat data. See: http://circa.europa.eu/Public/irc/dsis/edtcs/library?l=/public/unesco_collection&vm=detailed&sb=Title

Education attainment level is defined as the percentage of people of a given age group (excluding those who did not answer the question 'highest level of education or training attained') having attained a given education level.

The indicator 'Early leavers from education and training' (previously named 'Early school leavers') tracks the percentage of individuals aged 18 to 24 who have finished no more than a lower-secondary education (ISCED levels 0, 1, 2 or 3c), and who are not engaged in further education and training.

These two indicators are a collection of annual series based on the quarterly results of the EU Labour Force Survey (EU-LFS). The educational attainment level reported is based on ISCED-97.

Context

The EU is currently aiming to achieve several goals and benchmarks for higher education. The key aims are to increase the number of mathematics, science and technology graduates, to increase the number of Erasmus students, to raise investment in higher education and to foster the mobility of students across Europe.

The preparation given by pre-primary education is considered the foundation for further development. In December 2008, the European Commission proposed a new benchmark, saying that 95 % of four-year olds should participate in pre-primary education by 2020. The aim of this proposal is to underpin progress on the target set at the 2002 Barcelona Summit to increase participation in pre-primary education to 90 % of all children between three years of age and the beginning of compulsory education.

Early leavers from education and training and tertiary educational attainment are headline indicators for the Europe 2020 strategy. They were selected with other indicators to monitor progress towards a smarter, knowledge-based, greener economy, delivering high levels of employment, productivity and social cohesion.

'Early leavers from education and training' is also one of the **sustainable development indicators**, under the theme 'social inclusion'.

Health

Introduction

Health is one of the issues that matter the most to European citizens. Determining the health status of an entire population is not an easy task and there is no single standard measure to do so. There are some useful indicators, such as average lifespan, the prevalence of preventable diseases or death and the availability of health services. Other widely used indicators are infant mortality rate, due to its association with education, economic development and availability of health services, morbidity and mortality measures. Eurostat compiles and disseminates these indicators at regional, national and European levels.

This section addresses some causes of death by cancer, the major form being combined neoplasms of the larynx, trachea, bronchus and lungs, and two gender-related forms, breast and prostate cancer. It also focuses on hospital discharges for in-patients suffering from those diseases. There is no direct relation between these two data collections.

Main statistical findings

Causes of death — malignant neoplasms

Causes of death data give information on diseases leading directly to death, so they can be used as an indicator to plan health services. In the EU-27, the major cause of death was disease of the circulatory system but in France cancer took the lead, with 3 717 more deaths for the average period 2006–08. In the Netherlands, cancer was also higher than circulatory system diseases, with 661 more deaths in the average period 2007–09.

Looking at the 27 Member States, the three-year average standardised death rate for 2006–08 for all malignant neoplasms show that the highest rates were in Hungary (240.9), Poland (207.7) and the Czech Republic (205.7). The lowest rates were in Cyprus (120.4), Finland (138.6) and Portugal (153.3). Analysing the data by gender, for men, Lithuania and Estonia had the second and third highest rates while Germany had one of the lowest. For women, Ireland has one of the highest rates of malignant neoplasms, in particular of the larynx, trachea, bronchus and lung and breast cancer, while Spain has one of the lowest.

Combined malignant neoplasms of the larynx, trachea, bronchus and lung

The form of cancer with highest death rates in all Member States, for all ages and both sexes, is combined malignant neoplasms of the larynx, trachea, bronchus and lung, with a three-year-average standardised death rate in 2006–08 of 39.6 per 100 000 inhabitants. The highest rates are in Hungary (68.4), Poland (54.9) and the Netherlands (47.3) and the lowest rates are in Cyprus (20.5), Portugal (26.0) and Finland (26.6).

Analysing the data by gender, the 2006–08 three-year-average standardised death rate for all ages for men is 65.8 in the EU-27. The highest rates are in Hungary (114.3), Poland (100.4) and Estonia (90.7). For women, the three-year-average standardised death rate is 18.9 per 100 000 inhabitants in the EU-27. Again, Hungary had the highest rate (35.7) followed by the Netherlands (31.7) and Ireland (28.6). The lowest rates are in Cyprus (7.7), Portugal (8.2) and Lithuania (8.6).

The regions with the highest rates are Eszak-Alfold (80.7), Eszak-Magyarorszag (71.9) and Del-Dunantul (71.7) in Hungary. The lowest rates were found in the French regions of Martinique (13.3), Guadeloupe (13.6) and Guyane (13.8). Analysing the data by gender, the Hungarian regions again had high death rates, followed by the Polish region of Warminsko-Mazurskie (127.0) for men and Flevoland (36.4) for women. The lowest rates for women are the Italian regions of Molise (5.8), Basilicata and Calabria (5.9).

The data can be analysed by age group using the crude death rate. The annual 2008 crude death rate shows that the highest rate was in the age group 80–84 (216.5), followed by 75–79-year-olds, with a rate of 258.3. Some countries, like Latvia, Romania, Slovenia and Slovakia, had higher rates in the age group 70–74. Amongst men, Bulgaria had the highest rate in the younger age group 65–69 (329.5).

Breast cancer

The three-year-average standardised death rate shows that for the EU-27, in all ages and both sexes, breast cancer, together with malignant neoplasms of the colon, was the second largest cause of death by cancer, with 13.3 deaths by 100 000 inhabitants. For women, this was the main cause of death in most Member States, with a rate of 23.9 per 100 000 inhabitants; for men the rate is 0.3. Exceptions are Hungary, the Netherlands and Poland, where this form of cancer is second to malignant neoplasms of the larynx, trachea, bronchus and lung. The highest rates of breast cancer for women are in Ireland (29.7), the Netherlands (28.9) and Hungary (26.7) while Spain (18.4), Portugal (19.6), and Finland (20.9) have the lowest rates.

For women, the most-affected regions are Friesland (35.9) in the Netherlands, Trier in Germany (31.7) and Bucureşti - Ilfov in Romania (31.3). The lowest rates were found in the French Réunion (14.1), Cantabria in Spain (15.2) and Ionia Nisia in Greece (15.3). For men, the region with the highest rate is Ciudad Autonoma de Ceuta (1.1).

An analysis of the 2008 crude death rate for women in the EU-27 by age group shows that breast cancer increases with age and that women over 85 are the most affected, with a rate of 223.8 per 100 000 inhabitants. In this age group, the

Map 5.1: Malignant neoplasms, by NUTS 2 regions, 2006–08 (¹)
(standardised death rate per 100 000 inhabitants)

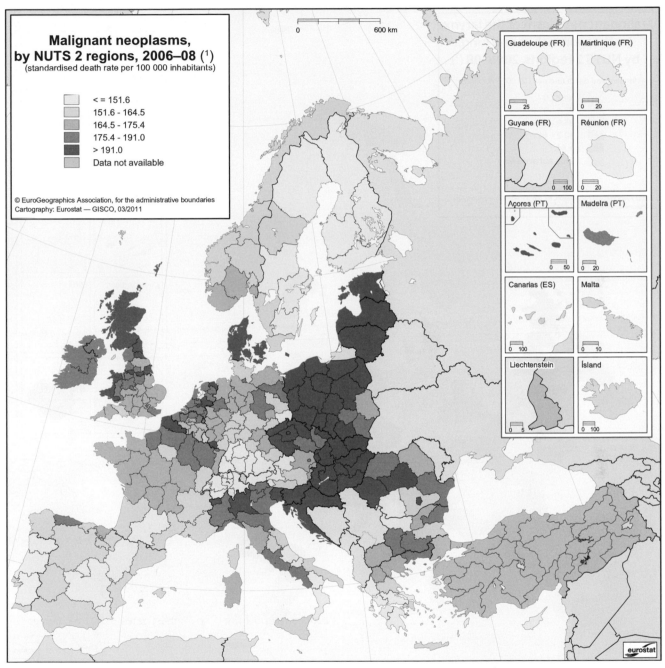

**Malignant neoplasms,
by NUTS 2 regions, 2006–08** (¹)
(standardised death rate per 100 000 inhabitants)

- < = 151.6
- 151.6 - 164.5
- 164.5 - 175.4
- 175.4 - 191.0
- > 191.0
- Data not available

© EuroGeographics Association, for the administrative boundaries
Cartography: Eurostat — GISCO, 03/2011

0   600 km

Guadeloupe (FR)   Martinique (FR)
0   25   0   20

Guyane (FR)   Réunion (FR)
0   100   0   20

Açores (PT)   Madeira (PT)
0   50   0   20

Canarias (ES)   Malta
0   100   0   10

Liechtenstein   Ísland
0   5   0   100

eurostat

(¹) Malta, Sweden and Switzerland, 2005–07; Denmark, England and Wales, 2004–06; Scotland and Northern Ireland, 2002–04; Italy, 2001–03; Belgium, 2000–02;
Denmark, Slovenia and Croatia, national level; Scotland, NUTS 1 level.

Source: Eurostat (online data code: tgs00058).

Map 5.2: Malignant neoplasms of the larynx, trachea, bronchus and lung, by NUTS 2 regions, 2006–08 (¹)
(standardised death rate per 100 000 inhabitants)

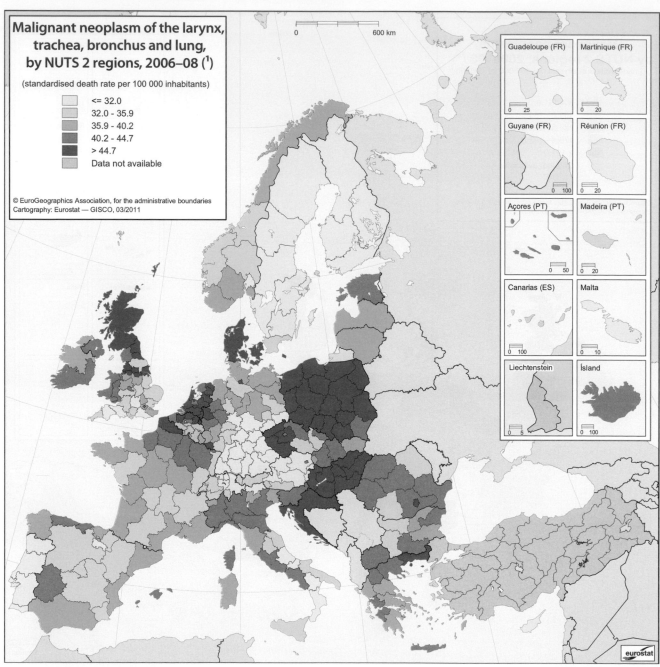

Malignant neoplasm of the larynx, trachea, bronchus and lung, by NUTS 2 regions, 2006–08 (¹)

(standardised death rate per 100 000 inhabitants)

- <= 32.0
- 32.0 - 35.9
- 35.9 - 40.2
- 40.2 - 44.7
- \> 44.7
- Data not available

© EuroGeographics Association, for the administrative boundaries
Cartography: Eurostat — GISCO, 03/2011

(¹) Malta and Sweden, 2005–07; Denmark, England and Wales, 2004–06; Scotland and Northern Ireland, 2002–04; Italy, 2001–03; Belgium, 2000–02;
Denmark, Slovenia and Croatia, national level; Scotland, NUTS 1 level.

Source: Eurostat (online data code: hlth_cd_ysdr1).

Map 5.3: Malignant neoplasm of the breast by NUTS 2 regions, 2006–08 (¹)
(standardised death rate per 100 000 inhabitants in females)

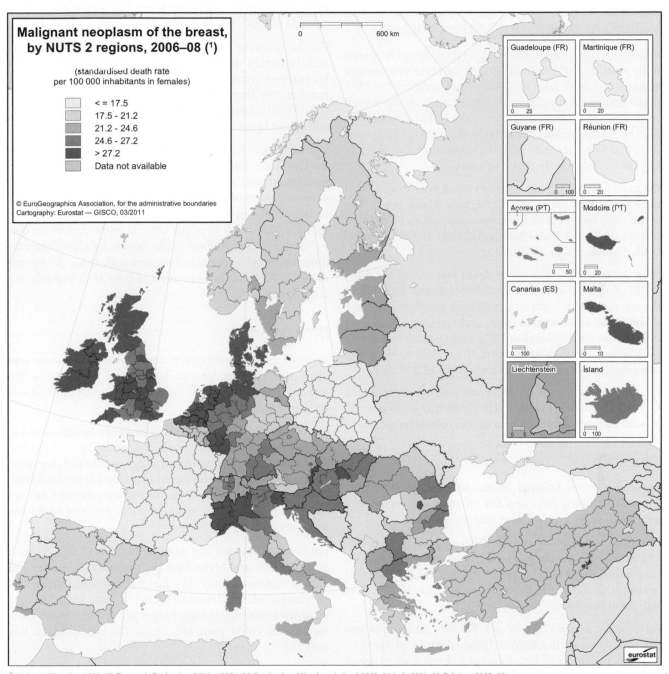

(¹) Malta and Sweden, 2005–07; Denmark, England and Wales, 2004–06; Scotland and Northern Ireland, 2002–04; Italy, 2001–03; Belgium, 2000–02; Denmark, Slovenia and Croatia, national level; Scotland, NUTS 1 level.

Source: Eurostat (online data code: hlth_cd_ysdr1).

highest rates were in Slovenia, Greece and Ireland and the lowest rates were in Romania, Lithuania and Bulgaria.

Malignant neoplasms of the prostate

Another gender-related form of cancer is malignant neoplasm of the prostate. For men in the EU-27, the three-year-average standardised death rate (2006–08) is 21.4, compared to 230.1 for all malignant neoplasms. Prostate cancer is the second most common cause of death for males in EU-27 countries. High rates are found in Lithuania (36.4), Latvia (34.7), Estonia (33.7) and Slovenia (33.2), with the lowest in Romania (15.1), Italy (16.0), Bulgaria (16.9) and Spain (17.6).

The most affected regions are the French Martinique (47.0) and Guadeloupe (41.1) and the Finish Åland (44.2). The lowest rates are found in the Romanian regions of Sud-Vest Oltenia (10.2) and Sud - Muntenia (10.8) and the Spanish Ciudad Autonoma de Melilla (10.5).

From 2000 to 2008, the crude death rate for males in the EU-27 of all ages increased in 2007 (28.3) and 2008 (28.4). The countries with highest rates in 2008 were Estonia (40.5), Latvia (35.5) and Portugal (34.3) and the lowest rates were in Romania (16.6), Slovakia (19.1) and Luxembourg (19.4). Estonia had the highest increase (from 31.7 to 40.5) and Luxembourg saw a marked decrease from 24.8 to 19.4.

The rate of prostate cancer increases with age. People aged 85 + have the highest rates, 657.0, for the EU 27. In general, prostate cancer starts to be a problem around the age of 50.

Hospital discharges

Regional data on hospital discharges of in-patients were not available until 2005 and not all countries are yet in a position to provide this data at subnational level.

Alongside information on the different 'causes of death', data on hospital discharges at national and regional levels are complementary means of estimating the frequency of treatment of some lethal diseases such as specific forms of malignant neoplasm.

On average, around 18 000 per 100 000 inhabitants and per country were discharged from hospitals in the EU-27 in 2008. However, that number hides a wide range of variations between countries, from 9 500 in Malta to over 27 500 in Austria.

A comparison of the number of in-patient discharges at NUTS level 2 indicates that regions in central Europe have the highest number of discharges per 100 000 inhabitants.

Malignant neoplasms of the trachea, bronchus and lung

The above observation on central Europe also applies to combined malignant neoplasms of the trachea, bronchus

and lung. In principle, the area stretching from Germany in the west to Romania in the east and from Croatia in the south to Denmark in the north has higher rates of in-patients per 100 000 inhabitants than other areas of the EU.

For the age group 70–74, Austria reports the highest figures (938 in-patient discharges per 100 000 inhabitants), with Hungary in second place (with 868) and Malta the lowest number (69). There is a similar pattern in the next age group (75–79), with Austria and Malta again recording the highest and lowest figures.

Out of the countries that provide regional data, Germany, the Czech Republic and, to a lesser degree, France show the greatest internal variability. In Bremen (Germany), 400 in-patients per 100 000 inhabitants were discharged, compared to barely 166 in Rheinland-Pfalz. Similarly, the ratio of Praha in the Czech Republic (205) is more than twice that in Stredni Cechy. In France, the figures for Corse are very different from the mainland regions (121, twice the French average). The data for Germany and the Czech Republic are 2006 figures.

Breast cancer

Another major malignancy causing hospital stays and discharges is the gender-associated breast cancer. Again, the rates are highest in central Europe, followed by Finland and the Baltic States.

The population of women aged 40 to 44 can be considered as a 'turning point' for the risk of breast cancer. In all countries, this cohort is the first to record a high number of in-patient discharges. The same phenomenon is found at regional level. For this age group, Austria has the highest rate, with 485 per 100 000 inhabitants, Germany reports 352, and Malta has the lowest with 32.

Looking at the two age groups 70–74 and 75–79, once again Austria and Malta have the highest and lowest rates of all countries, just as they had for combined malignant neoplasms of the trachea, bronchus and lung. Austria recorded a rate of 1 164 discharges per 100 000 inhabitants for persons 70–74 years old, whilst the rate in Malta was only 101.

Germany and Austria also show important regional disparities when aggregating all female age groups. In Germany, Niedersachsen had a rate of 684 in-patient discharges per 100 000 inhabitants, but it was 1 229 in Schleswig-Holstein. In Austria, the difference is even bigger: as compared to Burgenland with only 626, Wien had a rate of 1919. Again, the data for Germany are from 2006.

Conclusion

Information on hospital discharges and causes of death are a prerequisite for monitoring the performance of health policy.

Map 5.4: Malignant neoplasms by NUTS 2 regions, 2008 (¹)
(hospital discharges, in-patients, rate per 100 000 inhabitants)

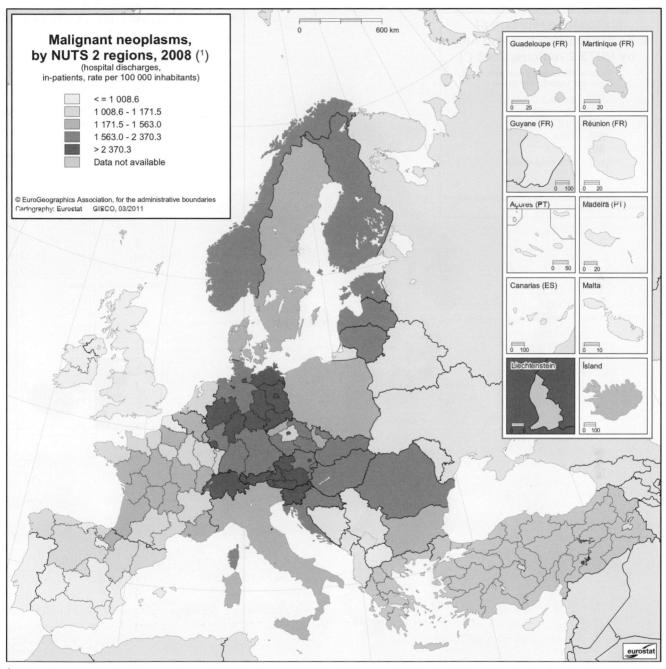

Malignant neoplasms, by NUTS 2 regions, 2008 (¹)
(hospital discharges, in-patients, rate per 100 000 inhabitants)

- < = 1 008.6
- 1 008.6 - 1 171.5
- 1 171.5 - 1 563.0
- 1 563.0 - 2 370.3
- > 2 370.3
- Data not available

© EuroGeographics Association, for the administrative boundaries
Cartography: Eurostat   GISCO, 03/2011

Guadeloupe (FR)   Martinique (FR)
Guyane (FR)   Réunion (FR)
Açores (PT)   Madeira (PT)
Canarias (ES)   Malta
Liechtenstein   Ísland

(¹) Belgium, Denmark, Estonia, Italy, Cyprus, Luxembourg and United Kingdom, 2007; Czech Republic, Germany, Finland, Sweden, Iceland and former Yugoslav Republic of Macedonia, 2006; Portugal, 2005; Belgium, Bulgaria, Denmark, Italy, Hungary, Netherlands, Poland, Portugal, Romania, Slovenia, Slovakia, Finland, Sweden, United Kingdom, Switzerland, Norway and Croatia, national level; Germany, NUTS 1 level.

Source: Eurostat (online data code: hlth_co_disch2t).

Map 5.5: Malignant neoplasm of the trachea, bronchus and lung, by NUTS 2 regions, 2008 (¹)
(hospital discharges, in-patients, rate per 100 000 inhabitants)

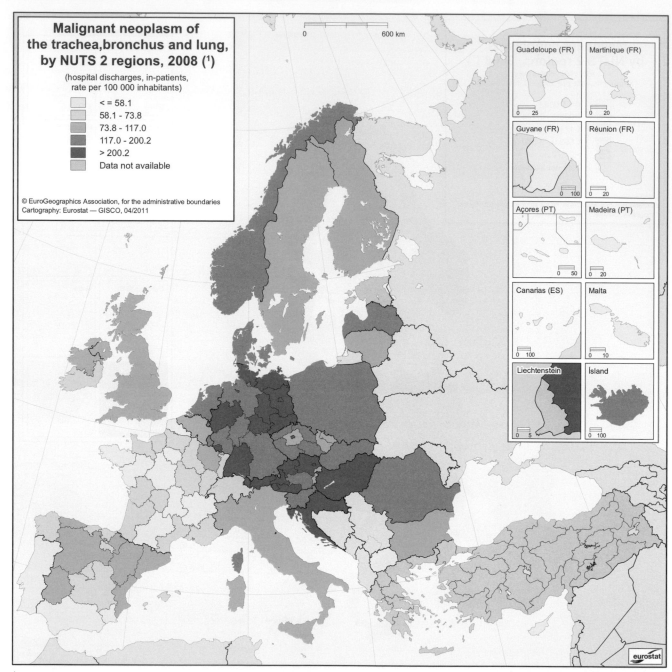

Malignant neoplasm of the trachea,bronchus and lung, by NUTS 2 regions, 2008 (¹)

(hospital discharges, in-patients, rate per 100 000 inhabitants)

- < = 58.1
- 58.1 - 73.8
- 73.8 - 117.0
- 117.0 - 200.2
- > 200.2
- Data not available

© EuroGeographics Association, for the administrative boundaries
Cartography: Eurostat — GISCO, 04/2011

(¹) Belgium, Denmark, Estonia, Italy, Cyprus, Luxembourg and United Kingdom, 2007; Czech Republic, Germany, Finland, Sweden, Iceland and former Yugoslav Republic of Macedonia, 2006; Portugal, 2005; Belgium, Bulgaria, Denmark, Italy, Hungary, Netherlands, Poland, Portugal, Romania, Slovenia, Slovakia, Finland, Sweden, United Kingdom, Switzerland, Norway and Croatia, national level; Germany, NUTS 1 level.

Source: Eurostat (online data code: hlth_co_disch2t).

Map 5.6: Malignant neoplasm of the breast, by NUTS 2 regions, 2008 (¹)
(hospital discharges, in-patients, rate per 100 000 inhabitants in females)

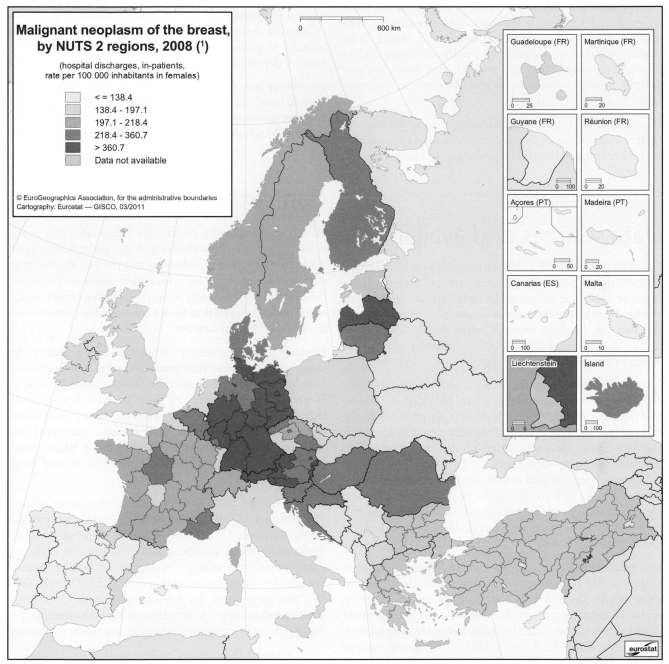

Malignant neoplasm of the breast, by NUTS 2 regions, 2008 (¹)

(hospital discharges, in-patients, rate per 100 000 inhabitants in females)

- < = 138.4
- 138.4 - 197.1
- 197.1 - 218.4
- 218.4 - 360.7
- > 360.7
- Data not available

© EuroGeographics Association, for the administrative boundaries
Cartography: Eurostat — GISCO, 03/2011

0   600 km

Guadeloupe (FR)   Martinique (FR)   0 25   0 20

Guyane (FR)   Réunion (FR)   0 100   0 20

Açores (PT)   Madeira (PT)   0 50   0 20

Canarias (ES)   Malta   0 100   0 10

Liechtenstein   Ísland   0 5   0 100

(¹) Belgium, Denmark, Estonia, Italy, Cyprus, Luxembourg and United Kingdom, 2007; Czech Republic, Germany, Finland, Sweden, Iceland and former Yugoslav Republic of Macedonia, 2006; Portugal, 2005; Belgium, Denmark, Italy, Hungary, Netherlands, Poland, Portugal, Romania, Slovenia, Slovakia, Finland, Sweden, United Kingdom, Switzerland, Norway and Croatia, national level; Germany, NUTS 1 level.

Source: Eurostat (online data code: hlth_co_disch2t).

Regional indicators provide an insight into similarities, particularities and differences across regions in Europe.

There can be big differences between regions in the same country, and regions in different countries may be very similar. A thorough analysis of trends and variations in health indicators at regional level is therefore essential to plan and monitor action and programmes, formulate new policies, develop new strategies and contribute to evidence-based health policymaking.

Eurostat's work on health statistics mainly focuses on further improvements that are needed to make the current data more comparable and complete and to extend regional coverage.

Data sources and availability

Cause of death (COD) statistics are based on information from death certificates. COD statistics record the underlying cause of death, i.e. to quote the definition adopted by the World Health Assembly, 'the disease or injury which initiated the train of morbid events leading directly to death, or the circumstances of the accident or violence which produced the fatal injury'.

In addition to absolute numbers, crude death rates and standardised death rates for COD are provided at national and regional levels. Regional-level data are provided in the form of three-year averages, along with yearly crude death rates for some age groups. The crude death rate (CDR) indicates mortality in relation to the total population. It is expressed per 100 000 inhabitants, i.e. calculated as the number of deaths recorded in the population over a given period divided by the population in the same period and then multiplied by 100 000. Crude death rates are calculated for five-year age groups.

However, the CDR is strongly influenced by the population structure. In a relatively 'old' population there will be more deaths than in a 'young' one because mortality is higher in older age groups. For comparisons, the age effect can be taken into account by using a standard population. The standardised death rate (SDR) is a weighted average of age-specific mortality rates. The weighting factor is the age distribution of a standard reference population. The 'standard European population' defined by the World Health Organisation (WHO) is used for this purpose. Standardised death rates are expressed per 100 000 inhabitants and calculated for the 0–64 age group ('premature death'), 65+ and for all ages. Causes of death are classified into the 65 on the 'European shortlist', which is based on the international statistical classification of diseases and related health problems (ICD) developed and maintained by the WHO.

Hospital discharges are the formal release of a patient from a hospital after a procedure or course of treatment. They occur any time a patient leaves hospital upon completion of treatment, signing out against medical advice, transferring to another healthcare institution or death. A discharge includes in-patients and day cases but excludes transfers to another department within the same institution.

In-patients are patients who are formally admitted (or 'hospitalised') to an institution for treatment and/or care and stay for a minimum of one night or more than 24 hours in the hospital or other institution providing in-patient care.

Context

Health is an important priority for Europeans, who expect to be protected against illness and disease at home, in the workplace and when travelling across the EU. Health issues cut across a range of topics — including consumer protection (food safety issues), safety at work and environmental and social policies — and thus have a considerable impact on the EU's revised Lisbon strategy.

Member States generally have the responsibility for organising and delivering health services and healthcare. The EU has the responsibility to give added value by launching initiatives such as those on cross-border health threats and patient mobility, reducing health inequalities and addressing key health determinants. Gathering and assessing accurate, detailed information on health issues is vital for the EU to effectively design policies and target future action.

On 23 October 2007, the European Commission adopted a new strategy 'Together for health: A strategic approach for the EU 2008–13' to set objectives that will guide future work on health at European level. Within the European Commission, the strategy is supported by the 'Second programme of community action in the field of health 2008–13'. This programme has been adopted with three broad objectives that align future action on health more closely to the objectives of prosperity, solidarity and security, namely:

- improving citizens' health security;
- promoting health to improve prosperity and solidarity;
- generating and disseminating health knowledge.

To monitor progress on these objectives, Regulation (EC) No 1338/2008 of the European Parliament and of the Council on Community statistics on 'public health and health and safety at work' is the legal framework for compiling the required background statistics. It covers causes of death, health status, health determinants and healthcare.

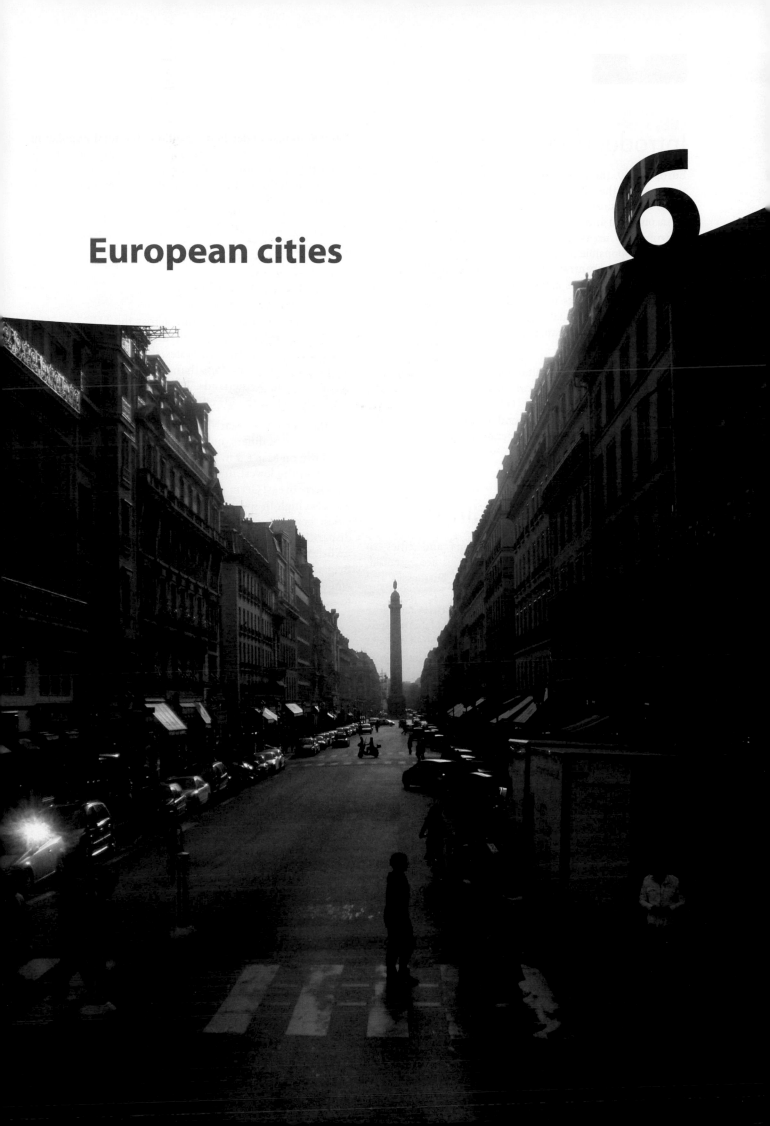

European cities

6

Introduction

Europe 2020, the new strategy for the EU designed as the successor to the Lisbon strategy, targets knowledge-based, green and inclusive growth. One crucial aspect is a better focus on green and socially inclusive growth in urban areas. Metropolitan areas are drivers of economic growth but they are responsible for most greenhouse gas emissions and often have a concentration of social problems. The Europe 2020 strategy requires action to be underpinned by sound and coherent statistics using indicators. The Urban Audit assesses the current situation and monitors developments in Europe's cities. Its ultimate goal is to help cities improve the quality of urban life.

The Urban Audit is the result of joint work by participating cities, the national statistical offices belonging to the European statistical system (ESS) and the European Commission's Directorate-General for Regional Policy. The success of this data collection depends on their contribution and continued support.

Main statistical findings

The European Union needs all regions and cities to contribute for it to achieve its goals. Cities are essential, as they are the home of most work places, businesses and higher education institutions. This chapter presents a few indicators reflecting some of the challenges cities face, like unemployment, creating and keeping a skilful labour force, air pollution and poverty. The indicators presented are just a few examples, just as these are but a few of the challenges.

Why cities matter

Based on the revised urban–rural typology, 68 % of the EU population live in urban areas. The two most populous cities in the EU are London and Paris. Apart from these two megapolises, Europe features a unique polycentric structure of large, medium and small cities (see Map 6.1).

Map 6.1 illustrates the distribution of urban dwellers across cities of different sizes in Europe. Each circle on the map represents an Urban Audit city. At present, the Urban Audit data collection includes more than 300 cities. The size of the circle reflects the number of inhabitants in the core city. Six cities in the Urban Audit have more than 3 million inhabitants: Berlin, Madrid, Paris and London and, in Turkey, Ankara and İstanbul. Another 20 cities have between 1 million and 3 million inhabitants. They are spread all over Europe. There are considerably more smaller cities with between half a million and 1 million inhabitants. There are 80 cities in the next tier, with populations ranging from

250 000 to just under half a million. The total population of all cities in each size category mentioned so far has about the same number of inhabitants, approximately 30 million, underlining the balanced distribution of the urban population in Europe. However, the Urban Audit does not include every city in Europe. Several cities, especially in the smaller size group of fewer than 250 000 inhabitants, are not included.

The urban labour force

The average unemployment rate across the EU-27 in 2008 was 7 %. There are considerable differences in unemployment rates between Member States, the highest being 11.3 % in Spain and the lowest (less than 4 %) in Cyprus, Denmark, Austria and the Netherlands. The distribution of unemployment rates across the EU cities is considerably wider.

As the reference year of the last available data for unemployment differs, our analysis is divided accordingly. As shown on Map 6.2 in 2008, Dutch, Swiss and Norwegian cities had the lowest unemployment rates, and the highest rates were in east German and Belgian cities. Unemployment was also high in several Polish, Portuguese and Romanian cities; here the data refer to the year 2004. The largest disparities between cities within a country were recorded in Belgium, Spain, France and Romania. For example, in Belgium the unemployment rate was below 5 % in Brugge, while in Charleroi it was above 15 %. This underlies the need to examine the territorial aspects of unemployment.

Students in higher education

Whether cities experience a 'brain drain' or a 'brain gain' depends on a number of factors, including their ability to attract students to their colleges and universities. Retaining university and college graduates in the city is the next step to establishing a highly skilled workforce. Map 6.3 shows the number of students in universities and other further education establishments per 1 000 resident population. Almost all participating countries have 'university cities'. Cities where more than 200 students per 1 000 inhabitants are enrolled in higher education are widely dispersed across Europe. However, Poland, Slovakia, the Czech Republic and Portugal have a high concentration of these cities.

Looking at the number of students relative to inhabitants means that large cities have a relatively low indicator value, although many host prestigious and large universities. Warszawa (Poland) and București (Romania) are the only cities with more than 1 million inhabitants where the number of students is above 200 per 1 000 residents. Assessing the absolute number of students in colleges and universities could be an alternative indicator.

Map 6.1: Total resident population in Urban Audit core cities, 2008 (¹)
(inhabitants)

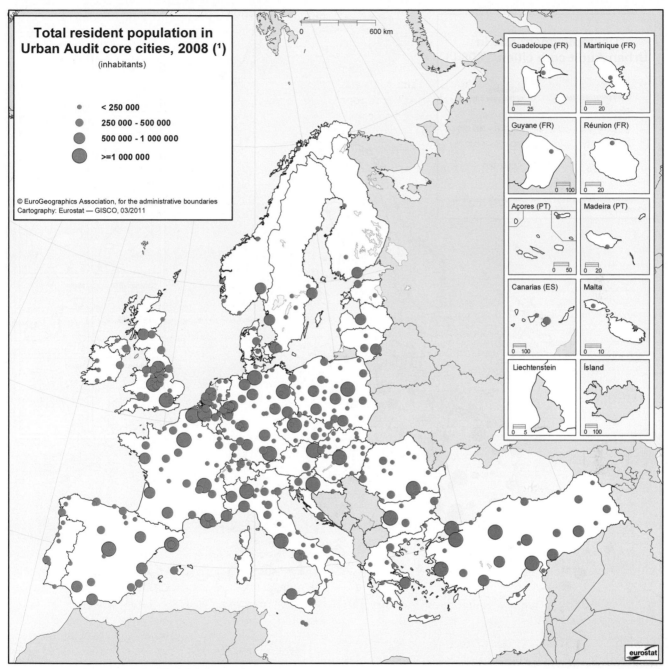

Total resident population in Urban Audit core cities, 2008 (¹)

(inhabitants)

- < 250 000
- 250 000 - 500 000
- 500 000 - 1 000 000
- >=1 000 000

© EuroGeographics Association, for the administrative boundaries
Cartography: Eurostat — GISCO, 03/2011

Guadeloupe (FR)   Martinique (FR)   Guyane (FR)   Réunion (FR)   Açores (PT)   Madeira (PT)   Canarias (ES)   Malta   Liechtenstein   Ísland

(¹) Ireland and France, 2006; Bulgaria, Denmark, Greece and Turkey, 2004; Croatia, 2001.

Source: Eurostat (online data code: urb_icity).

Map 6.2: Unemployment rate in Urban Audit core cities, 2008 (¹)
(%)

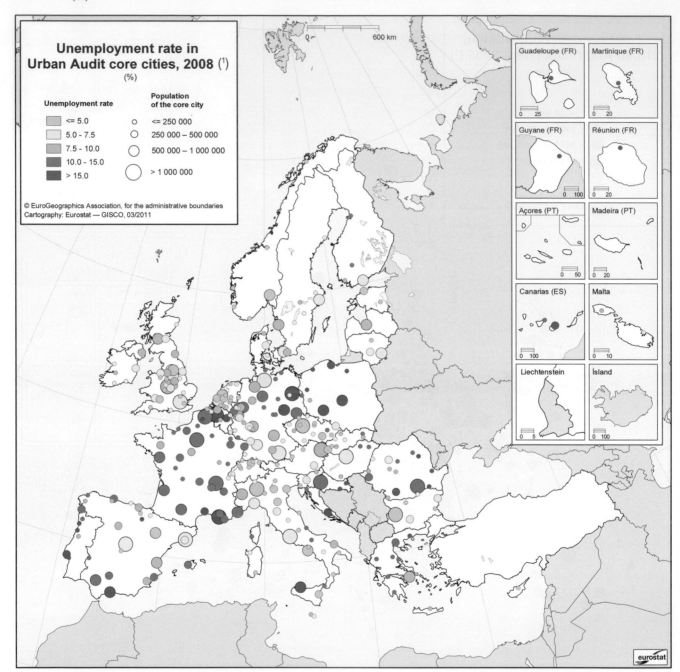

**Unemployment rate in
Urban Audit core cities, 2008 (¹)**
(%)

Unemployment rate	Population of the core city
<= 5.0	○ <= 250 000
5.0 - 7.5	○ 250 000 – 500 000
7.5 - 10.0	○ 500 000 – 1 000 000
10.0 - 15.0	○ > 1 000 000
> 15.0	

© EuroGeographics Association, for the administrative boundaries
Cartography: Eurostat — GISCO, 03/2011

600 km

Guadeloupe (FR)   Martinique (FR)
0   25   0   20

Guyane (FR)   Réunion (FR)
0   100   0   20

Açores (PT)   Madeira (PT)
0   50   0   20

Canarias (ES)   Malta
0   100   0   10

Liechtenstein   Ísland
0   5   0   100

eurostat

(¹) Bulgaria, Denmark, Greece, Italy, Cyprus, Hungary, Poland, Portugal, Romania, Slovenia, Belfast (United Kingdom), Turkey and Croatia 2004; Trento (Italy), 2005; Ireland and France, 2006.

Source: Eurostat (online data code: urb_icity).

Map 6.3: Students in higher education (ISCED levels 5 and 6) in Urban Audit core cities, 2008 (¹)
(students per 1 000 resident population)

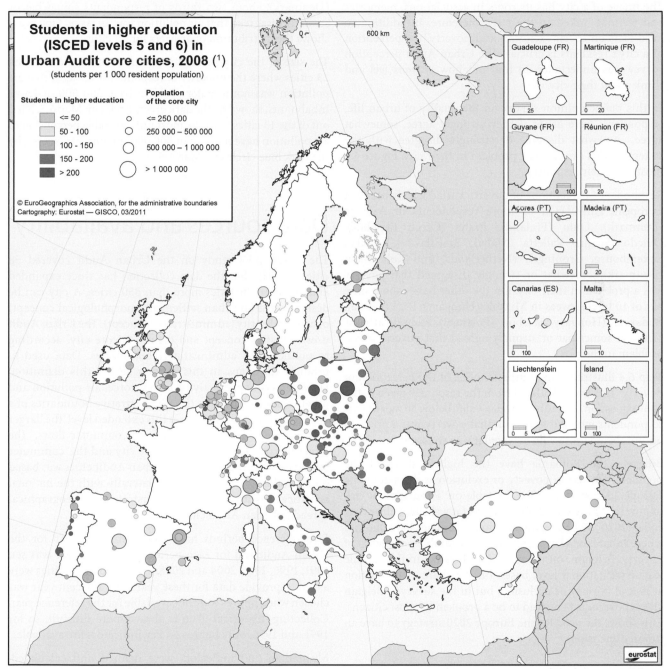

Students in higher education (ISCED levels 5 and 6) in Urban Audit core cities, 2008 (¹)
(students per 1 000 resident population)

Students in higher education
- <= 50
- 50 - 100
- 100 - 150
- 150 - 200
- > 200

Population of the core city
- <= 250 000
- 250 000 – 500 000
- 500 000 – 1 000 000
- > 1 000 000

© EuroGeographics Association, for the administrative boundaries
Cartography: Eurostat — GISCO, 03/2011

(¹) Bulgaria, Denmark, Greece, Spain, Cyprus, Belfast (United Kingdom) and Turkey, 2004; Ireland and Giurgiu (Romania), 2006; Germany and Switzerland, 2007.

Source: Eurostat (online data code: urb_icity).

Perception of poverty

The image of a city has its roots in associations, memories and feelings linked to the city. Therefore, in addition to hard facts on social exclusion and poverty, the perception of a city's residents is crucial. The Urban Audit perception survey was undertaken to find out how citizens feel and think about their city.

In this public opinion survey on the quality of urban life, respondents were asked if they strongly agree, somewhat agree, somewhat disagree or strongly disagree with the statement that poverty is a problem in their city. Figure 6.1 illustrates their responses.

Respondents' perceptions of poverty varied widely between European cities. Half or more respondents in Aalborg (Denmark), Oulu (Finland), Praha (Czech Republic), Oviedo (Spain), Valletta (Malta), Bratislava (Slovakia), Luxembourg, Groningen (Netherlands) and København (Denmark) somewhat or strongly disagreed that poverty was a problem in their city. On the other hand, about nine out of 10 interviewees in Miskolc (Hungary), Riga (Latvia), Budapest (Hungary), Lisboa (Portugal) and Diyarbakir (Turkey) somewhat or strongly agreed that poverty was a problem in their city (¹).

Map 6.4 illustrates the synthetic index of the perception of poverty. This was calculated from the responses given to the above question. A synthetic index value below 50 means that respondents who did not think that poverty was a problem outnumbered those who believed it was an issue.

Bulgaria and Romania have the highest share of the population at risk of poverty or exclusion as defined by the Europe 2020 strategy. (See the table on 'Population at risk of poverty or exclusion' on the Eurostat website, online data code: t2020_50.) Nevertheless, both countries have one city where inhabitants have a relatively favourable perception of poverty. Belgium, on the other hand, ranks in the 'middle league' at national level based on the share of population at risk of poverty or exclusion, but in the surveyed Belgian cities, poverty is perceived to be a problem by most citizens. This shows the need for the Europe 2020 strategy to have an urban dimension.

Perception of air pollution

Air pollution appears to be a problem in most cities, with some exceptions. Respondents in Rostock (Germany), Groningen (Netherlands) and Białystok (Poland) mainly felt that air pollution was not a problem in their city. In Oviedo

(¹) European Commission Directorate-General for Regional Policy, 'Survey on perception of quality of life in 75 European Cities', Publications Office of the European Union, Luxembourg, 2010 (http://ec.europa.eu/regional_policy/sources/docgener/studies/pdf/urban/survey2009_en.pdf).

(Spain), Rennes (France), Newcastle (United Kingdom), Piatra Neamt (Romania), Leipzig (Germany) and Aalborg (Denmark), about two thirds of respondents somewhat or strongly disagreed that air pollution was an issue. Figure 6.2 shows the distribution of answers for all cities.

The size of the city seems to matter. Seventeen out of the 23 cities where the majority of respondents thought that air pollution was not a major problem have 500 000 or fewer inhabitants, shown by the dark green circles on Map 6.5. Nine out of the 13 cities with the most unfavourable perception of air pollution have more than 500 000 inhabitants, shown by the dark blue circles on Map 6.5.

Data sources and availability

The initial pilot study on the Urban Audit covered 58 cities in 1999, but the data collection has since expanded and currently includes more than 350 cities. A city can be designated as an urban settlement (morphological concept) or as a legal entity (administrative concept). The Urban Audit uses the latter concept and defines a 'core city' according to political and administrative boundaries. Data used to produce the maps in this chapter reflect this definition. However, economic activity, labour force, air pollution and other issues clearly cross the administrative boundaries of a city. To capture information at this extended level, the 'larger urban zone' was defined based on commuter flows. The larger urban zone includes the core city and the 'commuter belt' around it. The selection of Urban Audit cities was based on several criteria and agreed bilaterally with the national statistical institutes. Map 6.1 illustrates the geographical spread of Urban Audit cities.

Five reference periods have been defined so far for the Urban Audit and for each period a reference year was set: 1991, 1996, 2001, 2004 and 2008. Where possible, cities were asked to provide data for these years. An adjacent year was chosen when figures were not available for the reference year. Collecting 'historical' data is always more difficult, so for 1991 and 1996, only figures on key indicators are available.

More than 300 indicators were defined and calculated, covering most aspects of quality of life in a city including demography, housing, health, crime, labour market, income disparity, local administration, educational qualifications, environment, climate, travel patterns, information society and cultural infrastructure.

Data availability differs from domain to domain. Data on demography are available for more than 90 % of cities, but data on the environment are available for fewer than half of the cities.

Figure 6.1: Perception of poverty in 75 Urban Audit cities, 2009
(Percentage of respondents who strongly agree, somewhat agree, somewhat
disagree or strongly disagree with the statement that in this city poverty is a problem)

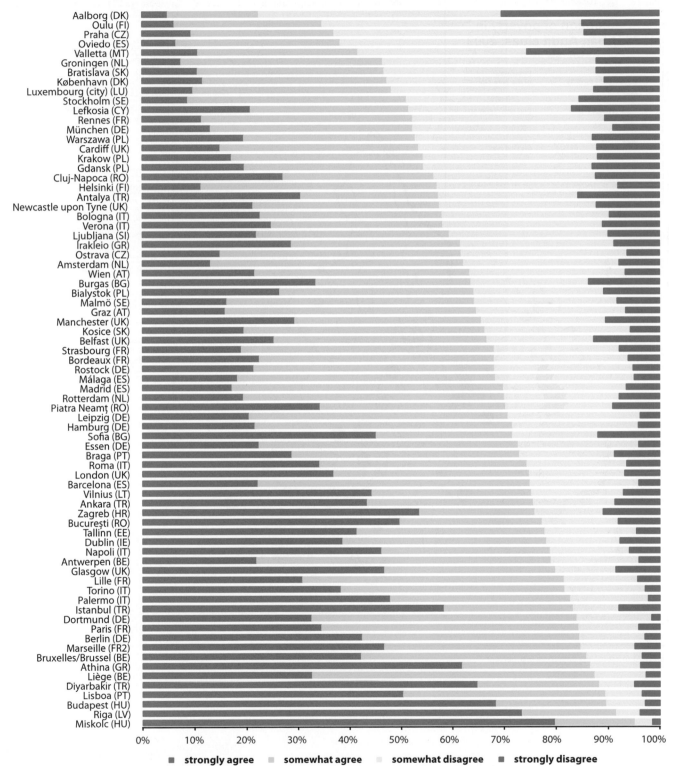

Map 6.4: Perception of poverty in 75 Urban Audit cities, 2009
(synthetic index)

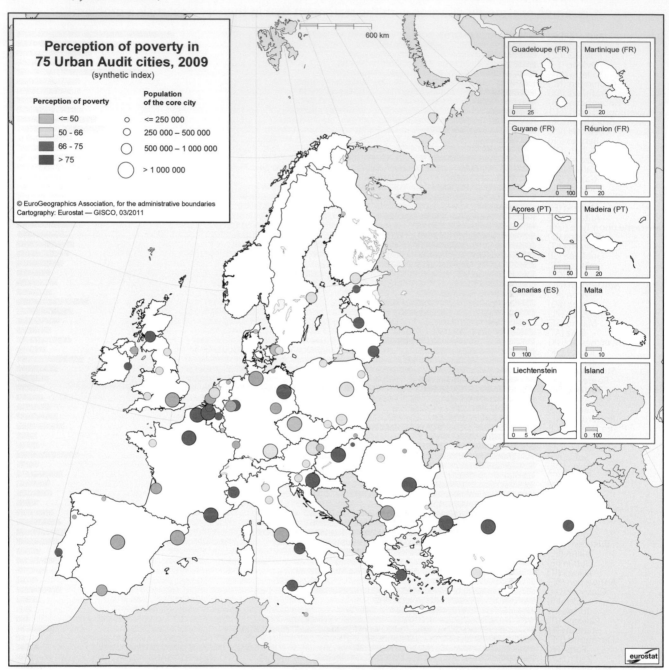

Source: Eurostat (online data code: urb_percep).

Figure 6.2: Perception of air quality in 75 Urban Audit cities, 2009
(Percentage of respondents who strongly agree, somewhat agree, somewhat disagree or strongly disagree with the statement that in this city air pollution is a problem)

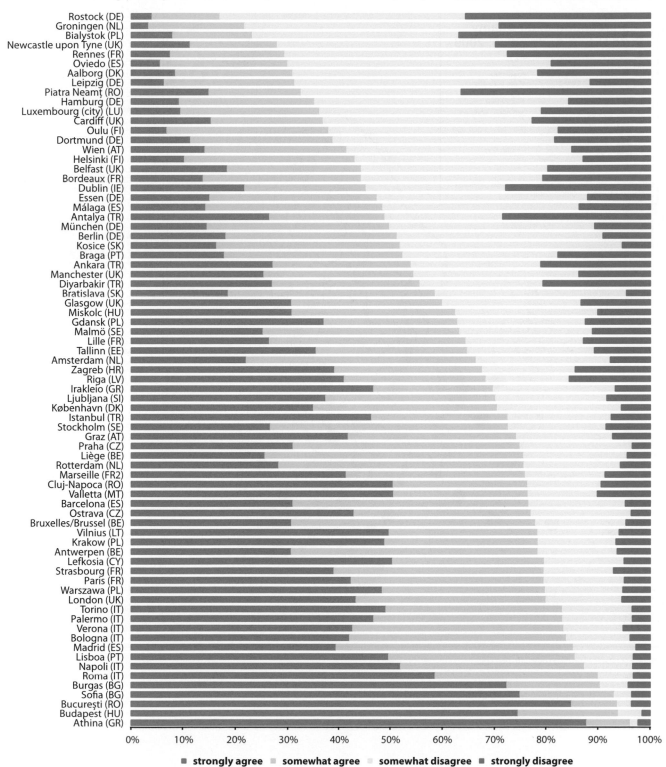

■ **strongly agree** ■ **somewhat agree** ■ **somewhat disagree** ■ **strongly disagree**

Map 6.5: Perception of air quality in 75 Urban Audit cities, 2009
(synthetic index)

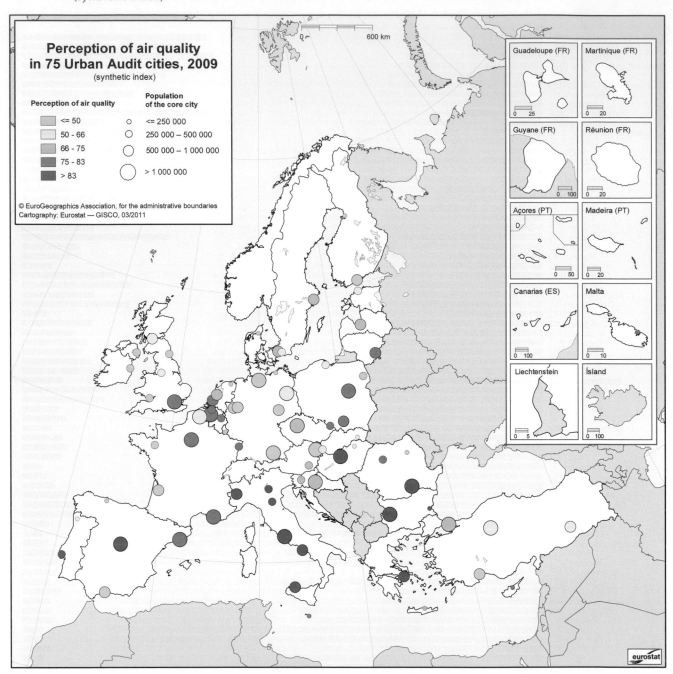

**Perception of air quality
in 75 Urban Audit cities, 2009**
(synthetic index)

Perception of air quality		Population of the core city	
	<= 50	○	<= 250 000
	50 - 66	○	250 000 – 500 000
	66 - 75	○	500 000 – 1 000 000
	75 - 83	○	> 1 000 000
	> 83		

© EuroGeographics Association, for the administrative boundaries
Cartography: Eurostat — GISCO, 03/2011

Guadeloupe (FR)　Martinique (FR)
Guyane (FR)　Réunion (FR)
Açores (PT)　Madeira (PT)
Canarias (ES)　Malta
Liechtenstein　Ísland

Source: Eurostat (online data code: urb_percep).

The Urban Audit perception survey is a useful complement to the statistics. The last survey took place in 2009 and included 75 cities in the EU, Croatia and Turkey. Survey data were collected through telephone interviews of samples of 500 people per city. The synthetic indexes presented on Maps 6.4 and 6.5 were calculated in two steps: first, the difference between the number of those who agree and disagree was divided by the number of respondents. Then the index was standardised at a value between 0 and 100. The higher the index value, the greater the level of agreement in the city. Values below 50 suggest that more than half of the respondents disagreed.

Context

Cities are focal points of consumption of energy and materials. They are hubs of transport networks, bringing together polluters and protectors of the environment, skilled workers and unemployed, the homeless and the wealthy, culture and crime. Are they on course to reach the targets set by 2020? Eurostat invites everyone to come to their own conclusions and to see where they stand by looking at the figures in the Urban Audit data collection available on the Eurostat website.

Gross domestic product

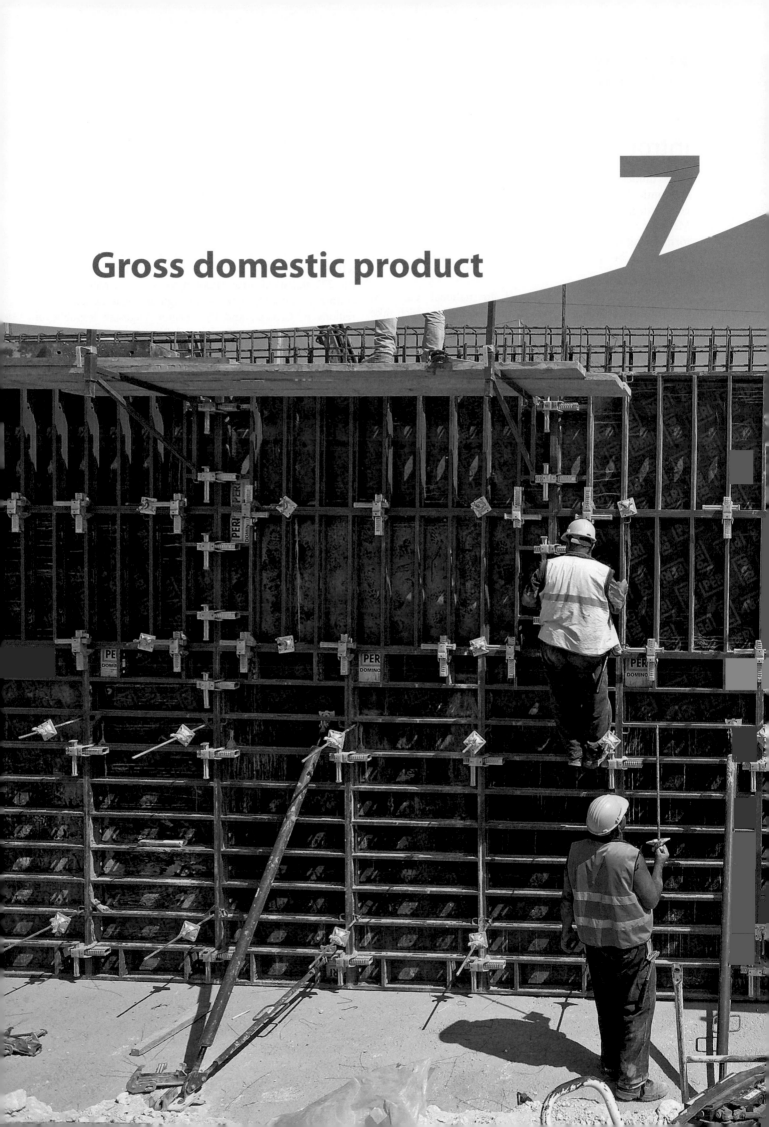

Introduction

Gross domestic product (GDP) is a key measure of a nation's economic development and growth. This chapter considers economic growth across the regions of the European Union Member States and candidate countries Croatia and the former Yugoslav Republic of Macedonia. It finds that the differences between Member States are quite large, but decreasing.

Economic activity is expressed in national currency, converted by purchasing power parities (PPPs), which take account of different price levels between Member States, allowing for a more accurate comparison. Thanks to PPPs, GDP is converted into an artificial common currency, called purchasing power standards (PPS). This makes it possible to compare purchasing power in countries that use different national currencies.

Finally, the chapter considers the level of economic dynamism in the regions of Member States and candidate countries, and finds that new Member States are continuing to catch up at a relatively strong rate.

Main statistical findings

Regional GDP per inhabitant in 2008

Map 7.1 shows per-inhabitant GDP (as a percentage of the EU-27 average of 25 100 PPS) for the European Union, Croatia, the former Yugoslav Republic of Macedonia and Turkey, which has, after a lengthy interruption, again provided data (for the reference years 2004–06) in line with the European system of accounts (ESA95) Data Transmission Programme.

The regions with the highest per-inhabitant GDP are in southern Germany, the south of the UK, northern Italy and Belgium, Luxembourg, the Netherlands, Austria, Ireland and Scandinavia. The regions around certain capitals, Madrid, Paris, Praha and Bratislava, also fall into this category. The weaker regions are concentrated in the southern, south-western and south-eastern periphery of the Union, in eastern Germany and the new Member States, Croatia, the former Yugoslav Republic of Macedonia and Turkey.

Detailed analysis of the data in this chapter does not cover Turkey, since the data available consists of a time series that only goes up to 2006, i.e. two reference years less than for other countries.

Within the EU, per-inhabitant GDP ranges from 28 % of the EU-27 average (6 500 PPS) in Severozapaden in Bulgaria to 343 % (85 800 PPS) in the capital region of Inner London in the UK.

The factor between the two ends of the distribution is therefore 13.2:1. Luxembourg at 280 % (70 000 PPS) and Brussels at 216 % (54 100 PPS) are in positions two and three, followed by Groningen (Netherlands) at 198 % (49 700 PPS), Hamburg at 188 % (47 100 PPS) and Praha at 173 % (43 200 PPS) in positions four, five and six. Praha (Czech Republic) thus remains the region with the highest per-inhabitant GDP in the new Member States; Bratislavský kraj (Slovakia) follows with 167 % (41 800 PPS) in ninth position among the 275 statistical areas (known as NUTS 2 regions of the countries examined here — 271 regions in the EU plus three regions in Croatia, and the former Yugoslav Republic of Macedonia). However, Praha and Bratislavský kraj must be regarded as exceptions as regards regions in the new Member States that joined in 2004. The next most prosperous regions in the new Member States are a long way behind: Bucureşti - Ilfov in Romania at 113 % (28 300 PPS) in position 74, Zahodna Slovenija (Slovenia) at 109 % (27 300 PPS) in position 87, Közép-Magyarország (Hungary) at 107 % (26 800 PPS) in position 96 and Cyprus at 97 % (24 400 PPS) in position 129.

With the exception of four other regions (Mazowieckie in Poland, Sjeverozapadna Hrvatska in Croatia, Malta and Vzhodna Slovenija in Slovenia), all the other regions of the new Member States, Croatia and the former Yugoslav Republic of Macedonia have a per-inhabitant GDP in PPS of less than 75 % of the EU-27 average.

As a result, in 2008, GDP in 67 regions was less than 75 % of the EU-27 average. Some 24.4 % of the population of the EU, Croatia and the former Yugoslav Republic of Macedonia lives in these 67 regions. Only a quarter of these regions are in EU-15 countries, while three quarters are in new Member States, Croatia and the former Yugoslav Republic of Macedonia.

At the upper end of the spectrum, 40 regions have per-inhabitant GDP of more than 125 % of the EU-27 average; these regions are home to 19.4 % of the population. Regions with a per-inhabitant GDP of between 75 % and 125 % of the EU-27 average are home to 56 %, and thus a clear majority of the population of the 29 countries under consideration (EU-27, Croatia and the former Yugoslav Republic of Macedonia). Some 9.3 % of the population live in the 27 regions whose per-inhabitant GDP is less than 50 % of the EU-27 average. With the exception of the French overseas department of Guyane, all these regions are located in the new Member States, Croatia or the former Yugoslav Republic of Macedonia.

Major regional differences even within countries themselves

There are also substantial regional differences within countries themselves, as Figure 7.1 shows. In 2008, the highest per-inhabitant GDP was more than twice the lowest in 13

Map 7.1: Gross domestic product (GDP) per inhabitant, in purchasing power standard (PPS), by NUTS 2 regions, 2008 (¹)
(in percentage of EU-27 = 100)

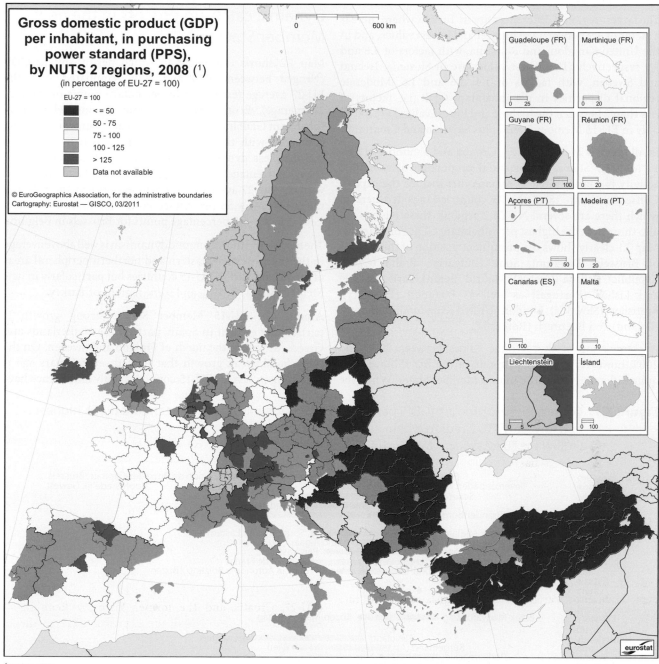

Gross domestic product (GDP) per inhabitant, in purchasing power standard (PPS), by NUTS 2 regions, 2008 (¹)
(in percentage of EU-27 = 100)

EU-27 = 100

- <= 50
- 50 - 75
- 75 - 100
- 100 - 125
- > 125
- Data not available

© EuroGeographics Association, for the administrative boundaries
Cartography: Eurostat — GISCO, 03/2011

Guadeloupe (FR)   Martinique (FR)
Guyane (FR)   Réunion (FR)
Açores (PT)   Madeira (PT)
Canarias (ES)   Malta
Liechtenstein   Ísland

(¹) Turkey, 2006.

Source: Eurostat (online data code: nama_r_e2gdp).

of the 23 countries examined here with several NUTS 2 regions. This group includes seven of the nine new Member States/candidate countries, but only six of the 14 EU-15 Member States.

The largest regional differences are in Turkey, where there is a factor of 4.9 between the highest and lowest values, and in the United Kingdom and Romania, with factors of 4.8 and 3.9 respectively. The lowest values are in Slovenia, Ireland and Sweden, with factors of 1.4, 1.6 and 1.6. Moderate regional disparities in per-inhabitant GDP (i.e. factors of less than 2 between the highest and lowest values) are found only in EU-15 Member States, plus Slovenia and Croatia.

In all the new Member States, Croatia and a number of EU-15 Member States, a substantial proportion of economic activity is concentrated in regions that include the capital. Consequently, in 18 of the 23 countries included here in which there are several NUTS 2 regions, these regions are also those with the highest per-inhabitant GDP. For example, Map 7.1 clearly shows the prominent position of the regions of Brussels (Belgium), Sofia (Bulgaria), Praha (Czech Republic), Athina (Greece), Madrid (Spain), Paris (France) and Lisboa (Portugal) as well as Budapest (Hungary), Bratislava (Slovakia), London (United Kingdom), Warszawa (Poland) and București (Romania).

A comparison of the extreme values between 2000 and 2008, however, shows that trends in the EU-15 have been quite different from those in new Member States. While the gap between the regional extreme values in the new Member States and Croatia is growing in most cases, it is shrinking in one out of every two EU-15 countries.

Dynamic catch-up process in the new Member States

Map 7.2 shows the extent to which per-inhabitant GDP changed between 2000 and 2008, compared with the EU-27 average (expressed in percentage points of the EU-27 average). Economically dynamic regions, whose per-inhabitant GDP increased by more than 3 percentage points compared with the EU average, are shown in green. By contrast, less dynamic regions (those with a fall of more than 3 percentage points in per-inhabitant GDP compared with the EU-27 average) are shown in orange and red. The range is from + 58 percentage points for Bratislavský kraj (Slovakia) to – 40 percentage points for Brussels in Belgium.

The map shows that economic dynamism is well above average in the south-western, eastern and northern peripheral areas of the EU, not just in EU-15 countries but particularly in new Member States, Croatia and some regions of Turkey.

Among the EU-15 Member States, strong growth is particularly evident in Spain, parts of the Netherlands and Greece, as well as the north of Finland and Sweden. On the other hand, weak growth that started several years ago is persisting in several EU-15 countries. Italy and France have

Figure 7.1: Gross domestic product (GDP) per inhabitant, in purchasing power standard (PPS), highest and lowest NUTS 2 region within each country, 2008 ([1])
(in % of the EU-27 average, EU-27 = 100)

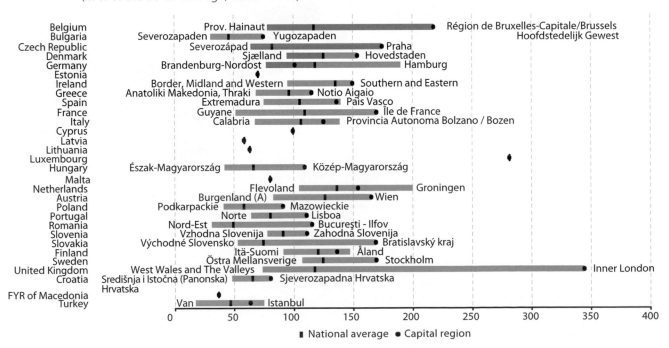

([1]) Turkey, 2006.

Source: Eurostat (online data code: nama_r_e2gdp).

been particularly badly hit. Not a single region achieved the EU-27 average growth rate during the eight-year period 2000–08. Performance has also been weak in a number of regions of Germany, Portugal, Sweden and the UK. Ireland is a special case. Due to the economic and financial crisis, both NUTS 2 regions fell back to the levels of 2001, i.e. by 15 percentage points, during the year 2008.

Of the new Member States, apart from the very dynamic capital regions, the Baltic States, Romania, Slovakia, the Czech Republic and most regions of Poland have seen growth markedly above the average. Croatia and the former Yugoslav Republic of Macedonia also reveal above-average economic growth for the eight-year period 2000–08.

Closer analysis of the most dynamic regions shows that 41 EU-27 regions have outperformed the EU average by more than 10 percentage points; of these, 24 are in new Member States.

The 10 fastest-growing regions are spread over nine EU Member States. Among these 10, there are five capital regions in new Member States. The three regions in EU-15 countries in this top-10 group (Luxembourg, Groningen in the Netherlands and Inner London) can all be considered special cases.

The non-capital region with the strongest growth in the new Member States was Vest (Romania), where per-inhabitant GDP (in PPS) increased by 23.8 percentage points compared to the EU-27 average between 2000 and 2008.

At the lower end of the distribution curve, there is a clear concentration: of the 34 regions in which per-inhabitant GDP fell by more than 10 percentage points below the EU-27 average, 13 are in Italy, six in France, five in the UK and four in Germany.

Closer examination of the new Member States yields the pleasing result that, between 2000 and 2008, only one region (Malta with– 5.8 percentage points) fell back, compared with the EU-27 average.

The catch-up process in new Member States was of the order of 1.7 percentage points per year between 2000 and 2008, compared to the EU average. Per-inhabitant GDP (in PPS) in these 12 Member States thus rose from 45 % of the EU-27 average in 2000 to almost 59 % in 2008. In 2008, performance was particularly strong, with 2.7 percentage points. This can be explained partly by the fact that the economic and financial crisis struck first in the EU-15 Member States, some of which, like Ireland, Italy and Denmark, were already in recession in 2008. On the other hand, among new Member States, only Estonia and Latvia already had negative volume growth rates in 2008, and the full effects of the crisis became apparent only in 2009. The initial data available on certain Member States for 2009 and 2010 would suggest that the recession affected rural regions and areas lagging behind in terms of economic development less severely than regions with a high per-inhabitant GDP, or with a high level of dependence on exports or tourism.

Different trends within countries themselves

A more detailed analysis of trends within countries between 2000 and 2008 shows that the economic development of regions within a country can be almost as diverse as between regions in different countries.

The largest differences were seen in the Netherlands, Romania, Slovakia and the United Kingdom, where there were performance differences of more than 40 percentage points relative to the EU average for the per-inhabitant GDP of the fastest- and slowest-growing regions. The countries with the smallest differences between regions were Ireland, Slovenia, Denmark and Finland, with regional performance differences of between 2 and 9 percentage points.

In both new Member States and EU-15 countries, significantly diverging regional trends were the result mainly of dynamic growth in capital regions. However, as the values for Slovenia (6 percentage points) and Poland (14 percentage points) show, the data available do not confirm the assumption that major regional growth disparities are a typical feature of new Member States.

The data also show that the regions with the lowest levels of per-inhabitant GDP made significant progress. Between 2000 and 2008, Nord-Est and Sud - Muntenia (both in Romania) caught up by 11 and 18 percentage points and Yuzhen tsentralen (Bulgaria) by 9 percentage points compared to the EU-27 average.

Convergence makes progress

This section addresses the question of whether convergence among the regions of the EU-27 has made progress over the eight-year period 2000–08. Regional convergence of per-inhabitant GDP (in PPS) can be assessed in various ways on the basis of data supplied to Eurostat by national statistical institutes.

The simplest approach is to measure the gap between the highest and lowest values. By this method, the gap closed from a factor of 17.2 in 2000 to 13.2 in 2008. The main reason for this clear convergence was faster economic growth in Bulgaria and Romania. However, as this approach looks only at the extreme values, it is clear that the majority of shifts between regions are not taken into account.

A much more accurate evaluation of regional convergence is afforded by the dispersion of regional GDP calculated by Eurostat for the EU-27 and Croatia since 2007 (for details of the method see below, 'Data sources and availability', 'Dispersion of regional per-inhabitant GDP'). This takes account of divergences from the national average in all NUTS 2 regions for each country in turn, weighted by the regional population. Figure 7.2 compares the values of dispersion at regional level NUTS 2 for 2000 and 2008; the order of countries follows the values ranked in 2008. In the

Map 7.2: Change of gross domestic product (GDP) per inhabitant, in purchasing power standard (PPS), by NUTS 2 regions, 2008 as compared with 2000 (^{1}) (in percentage points of the average EU-27)

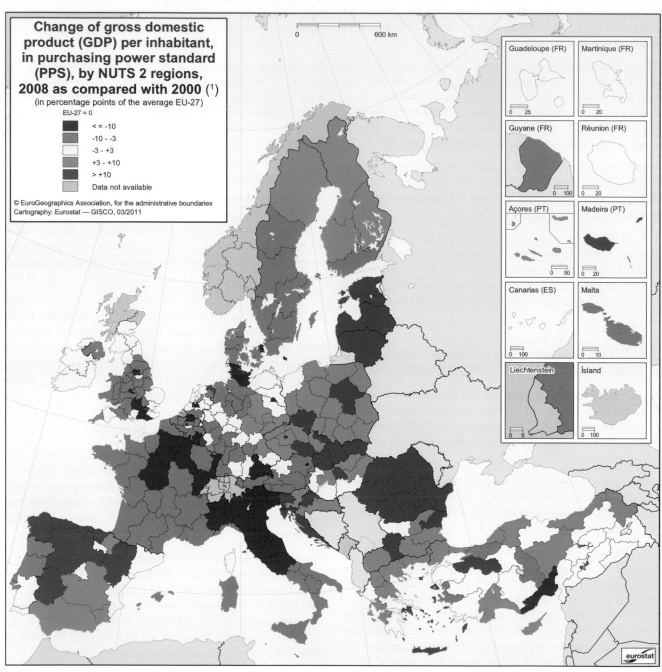

(^{1}) Denmark, Eurostat estimate; Turkey, 2006 as compared with 2000; Croatia, 2008 as compared with 2001.

Source: Eurostat (online data code: nama_r_e2gdp).

first instance, a downward trend is apparent, i.e. a decrease in regional dispersion for the EU-27 as a whole. An examination of the trend in individual countries reveals clear differences between certain groups of Member States. First, most of the EU-15 countries have lower dispersion than the new Member States. In addition, values in the EU-15 countries are generally decreasing, whereas they are increasing considerably in some of the new Member States. It is thus evident that the economic catching-up process in new Member States has so far gone hand-in-hand with increasing regional disparities.

The approach most often used at present involves classifying the regions according to their per-inhabitant GDP (in PPS) in relation to the average of the EU-27. This enables calculation of the proportion of the population living in more or less prosperous regions, and how this proportion has changed over time.

Table 7.1 shows clear progress in economic convergence between regions over the eight-year period 2000–08 for the EU-27, Croatia and the former Yugoslav Republic of Macedonia: the proportion of the population living in regions where per-inhabitant GDP is less than 75 % of the EU-27 average fell from 28.1 % to 24.4 %. At the same time, the proportion of the population living in regions where this value is greater than 125 % fell from 24.3 % to 19.4 %. These shifts at the top and bottom ends of the distribution meant that the proportion of the population in the midrange (per inhabitant GDP of 75–125 %) increased sharply from 47.6 % to 56.2 %. This corresponds to an increase of around 51 million inhabitants.

A comparison between the data for 2000 and 2008 reveals that eight regions managed to pass the 75 % threshold in the course of this period. These were two regions in Greece, as well as one region each in Spain, France, Poland, Romania, Slovenia and Croatia. These regions are home to 19.6 million people, or around 3.9 % of the population of the 29 countries examined here. At the same time, however, GDP in one Italian and one UK region, covering a total of 6 million inhabitants, i.e. approx. 1.2 % of the EU population, again fell below the 75 % threshold. Taking both developments into account, as a result of economic development between the years 2000 and 2008, the population living in regions with a GDP of more than 75 % of the EU-27 average grew by 13.6 million people.

A more detailed analysis shows that, in addition, many regions with a GDP of less than 50 % of the EU-27 average have made quite substantial progress. Between 2000 and 2008, the population living in these regions fell by almost a third, from 14.8 % to 9.3 % of the 29 countries examined here, i.e. by over 25 million. At the same time, only one region (the French overseas department of Guyane) fell back below the 50 % threshold.

Moreover, an examination of the 10 weakest regions as at 2000, where 4.8 % of the population lived at that time, shows that this group made strong progress. Per-inhabitant GDP in

these regions rose, from 22.6 % to 36.4 % of the EU-27 average between 2000 and 2008. This shows the strong catch-up process under way in Bulgaria and Romania.

Data sources and availability

What is regional gross domestic product?

The economic development of a region is, as a rule, expressed in terms of its gross domestic product (GDP). This indicator is also frequently used as a basis for comparisons between regions.

But what exactly does it mean, and how can comparability be established between regions of different sizes and with different currencies?

A meaningful comparison can be made only by comparing the regional GDP with the population of the region in question. This is where the distinction between place of work and place of residence becomes significant. GDP measures the economic output achieved within national or regional boundaries, regardless of whether this was attributable to resident or non-resident employed persons. The use of GDP per inhabitant is, therefore, only straightforward if all employed persons involved in generating GDP are also residents of the region in question.

In areas with a high proportion of commuters, regional GDP per inhabitant can be extremely high, particularly in economic centres such as London (United Kingdom) or Wien (Austria), Hamburg (Germany), Praha (Czech Republic) or Luxembourg, and relatively low in the surrounding regions, even if households' primary income in these regions is very high. Regional GDP per inhabitant should, therefore, not be equated with regional primary income.

Regional GDP is calculated in the currency of the country in question. To make GDP comparable between countries, it is converted into euro, using the official average exchange rate for the given calendar year. However, exchange rates do not reflect all the differences in price levels between countries. To compensate for this, GDP is converted using conversion factors, known as purchasing power parities (PPPs), to an artificial common currency, called purchasing power standard (PPS). This makes it possible to compare the purchasing power of different national currencies.

Purchasing power parities and international volume comparisons

International differences in GDP values, even after conversion via exchange rates to a common currency, cannot be attributed solely to differing volumes of goods and services. The 'level of prices' component is also a major contributing factor. Exchange rates reflect many factors

Figure 7.2: Dispersion of regional GDP per inhabitant, in PPS, NUTS level 2, 2000 and 2008 (¹)
(%)

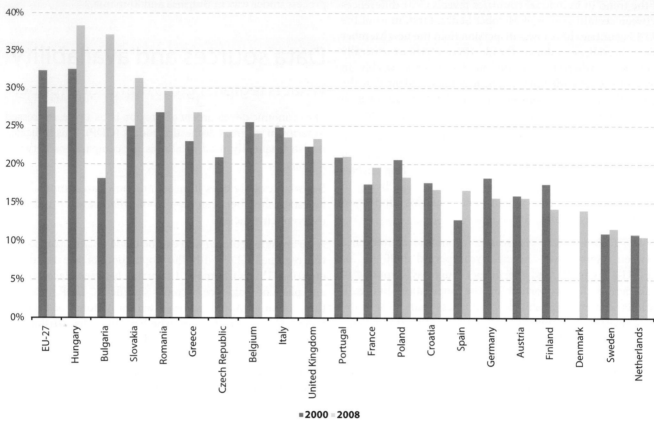

■ **2000** ■ **2008**

(¹) Regional dispersion is not applicable for Estonia, Ireland, Cyprus, Latvia, Lithuania, Luxembourg, Malta and Slovenia; Croatia, 2001 and 2008.

Source: Eurostat (online data code: nama_r_e0digdp).

Table 7.1: Proportions of resident population of EU-27, Croatia and former Yugoslav Republic of Macedonia in economically stronger and weaker regions

Percentage of population of EU-27, Croatia and FYR of Macedonia resident in regions with a GDP per inhabitant of	2000	2008
> 125 % of EU-27 = 100	24.3	19.4
> 110 % to 125 % of EU-27 = 100	15.5	16.0
> 90 % to 110 % of EU-27 = 100	21.5	24.7
> 75 % to 90 % of EU-27 = 100	10.5	15.5
less than 75 % of EU-27 = 100	28.1	24.4
of which: less than 50 % of EU-27 = 100	14.8	9.3

Source: Eurostat (nama_r_e2gdp).

relating to supply and demand in the currency markets, such as international trade, inflation forecasts and interest rate differentials. Conversions via exchange rates are, therefore, of only limited use for international comparisons. To obtain a more accurate comparison, it is essential to use special conversion rates which remove the effect of price-level differences between countries. Purchasing power parities are currency conversion rates of this kind, converting economic data expressed in national currencies into an artificial common currency, called purchasing power standard (PPS). PPPs are, therefore, used to convert the GDP and other economic aggregates (e.g. consumption expenditure on certain product groups) of various countries into comparable volumes of expenditure, expressed in PPS.

With the introduction of the euro, prices can now, for the first time, be compared directly between countries in the euro area. However, the euro has different purchasing power in different countries within the euro area, depending on the national price level. PPPs must, therefore, also continue to be used to calculate pure volume aggregates in PPS for Member States within the euro area.

In their simplest form, PPPs are a set of price ratios, which show the relationship between the prices in national currency of the same good or service in different countries (e.g. a loaf of bread costs EUR 1.87 in France, EUR 1.68 in Germany, GBP 1.45 in the UK, etc.). A basket of comparable goods and services is used for price surveys. These are selected so as to represent the whole range of goods and services, taking account of different consumption structures in different countries. The simple price ratios at product level are aggregated to PPPs for product groups, then for overall consumption and, finally, for GDP. To have a reference value for the calculation of the PPPs, a country is usually chosen and used as the reference country, and set to 1. For the European Union, the selection of a single country as a base seemed inappropriate. Therefore, the PPS is the artificial common reference currency unit used in the EU to express the volume of economic aggregates for the purpose of spatial comparisons in real terms.

Unfortunately, for reasons of cost, it will not be possible in the foreseeable future to calculate regional currency conversion rates. If such regional PPPs were available, the GDP in PPS for numerous peripheral or rural regions of the EU would probably be higher than that calculated using the national PPPs.

Calculating in PPS instead of euros can lead to differences in the ranking of regions. For example, in 2008, the Swedish region of Östra Mellansverige was recorded as having a per-inhabitant GDP of EUR 30 800, ranking above the Italian region of Marche, with EUR 26 700. However, in PPS, Marche, at PPS 26 500 per inhabitant, is ahead of Östra Mellansverige, at PPS 26 200.

In terms of distribution, the use of PPS rather than the euro has a levelling effect, as regions with a very high per-inhabitant GDP also generally have relatively high price levels. This reduces the range of per-inhabitant GDP in the NUTS 2 regions in the EU from around EUR 85 300 to around PPS 79 300.

Per-inhabitant GDP in PPS is the key variable for determining the eligibility of NUTS 2 regions under the European Union's structural policy.

Dispersion of regional per-inhabitant GDP

Since 2007, Eurostat has calculated a new, derived indicator which records the differences between regional per-inhabitant GDP and the national average, and makes them comparable between countries. This dispersion indicator is calculated at NUTS 2 and at NUTS 3 levels. The figures used by Eurostat are based on GDP in purchasing power standards (PPS).

For a given country, the dispersion 'D' of the regional GDP of the level 2 regions is defined as the sum of the absolute differences between regional and national GDP per inhabitant, weighted on the basis of the regional share of population and expressed in percent of the national GDP per inhabitant:

$$D = 100 \frac{1}{Y} \sum_{i=1}^{n} | (y_i - Y) | (p_i / P)$$

In the above equation:

- y_i is the regional per-inhabitant GDP of region i;
- Y is the national average per-inhabitant GDP;
- p_i is the population of region i;
- P is the population of the country;
- n is the number of regions of the country.

The value of the dispersion of GDP per inhabitant is zero if the values of regional GDP per inhabitant are identical in all regions of the country or economic area (such as the EU or the euro area), and it will show, all other things being equal, an increase if the differences in per-inhabitant GDP between the regions grow. A value of 30 % therefore means that the GDP of all regions of a given country, weighted on the basis of the regional population, differs from the national value by an average of 30 %.

Context

GDP is an important indicator of economic activity and growth in a region. It is used to make comparisons between Member States of the EU and is crucial in determining a wide range of policies, such as the extent to which a Member State should contribute to the EU budget.

Three-year averages of GDP, for example, are particularly important, because they are used to decide which regions are eligible to receive support from the European Union's Structural Funds.

Household accounts

8

Introduction

One of the primary aims of regional statistics is to measure the wealth of regions. This is of particular relevance as a basis for policy measures which aim to provide support for less well-off regions.

The indicator most frequently used to measure the wealth of a region is regional gross domestic product (GDP), usually expressed in purchasing power standard (PPS) per inhabitant to make the data comparable between regions of differing size and purchasing power.

GDP is the total value of goods and services produced in a region by the people employed in that region, minus the necessary inputs. However, owing to a multitude of interregional flows and state interventions, the GDP generated in a given region often does not tally with the income actually available to the inhabitants of the region. This chapter takes a look at household incomes in the regions of the European Union and at how much of this is available after income distribution mechanisms have had an effect.

Main statistical findings

Private household income

In market economies with state redistribution mechanisms, a distinction is made between two stages of income distribution. The primary distribution of income shows the income of private households generated directly from market transactions, i.e. the purchase and sale of factors of production and goods.

These include in particular the compensation of employees, i.e. income from the sale of labour as a factor of production. Private households can also receive income on assets, particularly interest, dividends from equity shares and rents. Then there is income from operating surpluses and self-employment. Interest and rents payable are recorded as negative items for households in the initial distribution stage. The balance of all these transactions is known as the primary income of private households.

Primary income is the point of departure for the secondary distribution of income, which means the state redistribution mechanism. All social benefits and transfers other than in kind (i.e. monetary transfers) are now added to primary income. From their income, households have to pay tax on income and wealth, pay their social contributions and effect transfers. The balance remaining after these transactions have been carried out is called the **disposable income** of private households.

For an analysis of household income, a decision must first be made about the unit in which data are to be expressed if comparisons between regions are to be meaningful.

For the purposes of making comparisons between regions, regional GDP is generally expressed in PPS, so that meaningful volume comparisons can be made. The same process should therefore be applied to the income parameters of private households. These are converted using specific purchasing power standards for final consumption expenditure, called purchasing power consumption standards (PPCS).

Results for 2008

Primary income

Map 8.1 gives an overview of primary income in the NUTS 2 regions of the 24 countries examined here. Centres of wealth are clearly evident in southern England, north-eastern Scotland, Paris, northern Italy, Austria, Madrid and north-eastern Spain, Vlaams Gewest (Belgium), the western Netherlands, Stockholm (Sweden) and Nordrhein-Westfalen, Hamburg and its surroundings, Hessen, Baden-Wurttemberg and Bayern (Germany). Also, there is a clear north–south divide in Italy and a west–east divide in Germany, whereas in France income distribution is relatively uniform between regions. The United Kingdom, too, has a north–south divide, albeit less marked than the divides in Italy and Germany.

In the new Member States, most of the regions with relatively high primary incomes are capital regions, in particular Bratislava in Slovakia (112 % of the EU-27 average) and Praha in the Czech Republic (95 %). Zahodna Slovenija and Vzhodna Slovenija (Slovenia) and Bucureşti - Ilfov (Romania) also have primary incomes higher than 75 % of the EU average. All the regions of the Czech Republic, apart from Praha, and 15 other regions in the new Member States have primary incomes of private households between 50 % and 75 % of the EU average. The figure is below 50 % in the remaining regions of the new Member States.

The regional values range from 3 600 PPCS per inhabitant in Severozapaden (Bulgaria) to 35 900 PPCS in the UK region of Inner London. The 10 regions with the highest income per inhabitant include four regions in Germany, three in the UK and one each in Belgium, France and Sweden. This concentration of regions with the highest incomes in the United Kingdom and Germany is also evident when the ranking is extended to the top 30 regions: this group contains 11 German and six UK regions, along with three regions each in Belgium, Italy and Austria, two in the Netherlands, and one each in France and Sweden.

It is no surprise that the 30 regions at the tail end of the ranking are all located in the new Member States; they comprise 12 of the 16 Polish regions, all six Bulgarian regions, seven of the eight Romanian regions, four Hungarian regions and one Slovakian region. In 2008, the highest and lowest primary incomes in the EU regions differed by a factor of 9.8. Seven years earlier, in 2000, this factor had been 14.3. It follows that the gap between the opposite ends of the distribution

Map 8.1: Primary income of private households per inhabitant (in PPCS), by NUTS 2 regions, 2008 ([1])
(% of EU-27 = 100)

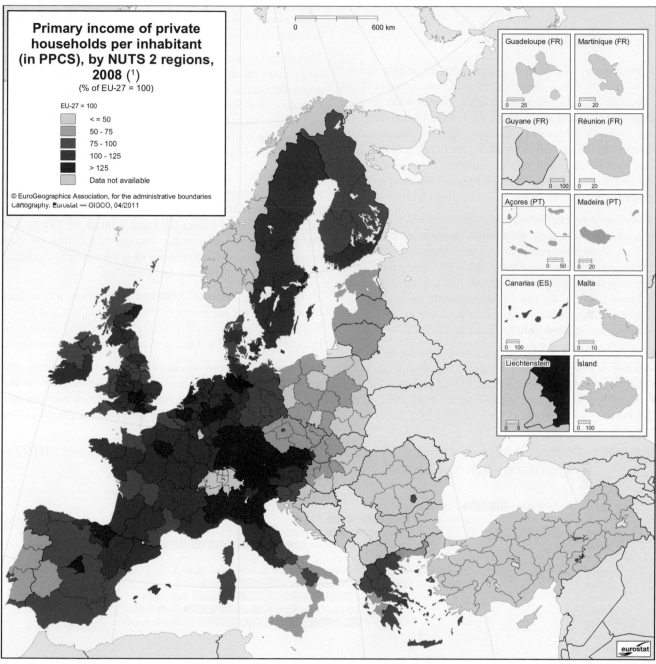

Primary income of private households per inhabitant (in PPCS), by NUTS 2 regions, 2008 ([1])
(% of EU-27 = 100)

EU-27 = 100

- <= 50
- 50 - 75
- 75 - 100
- 100 - 125
- > 125
- Data not available

© EuroGeographics Association, for the administrative boundaries
Cartography: Eurostat — GISCO, 04/2011

Guadeloupe (FR)   Martinique (FR)
Guyane (FR)   Réunion (FR)
Açores (PT)   Madeira (PT)
Canarias (ES)   Malta
Liechtenstein   Ísland

([1]) EU-27 and Bulgaria, Eurostat estimation.

Source: Eurostat (online data code: nama_r_ehh2inc).

narrowed considerably over the period 2000–08. This positive development can be attributed partly to the Romanian and Bulgarian economies catching up on the rest of the EU.

Disposable income

A comparison of primary income with disposable income shows the levelling influence of state intervention. More especially, this increases the relative income level in some regions of Italy and Spain, in the west of the United Kingdom and in parts of eastern Germany. Similar effects can be observed in the new Member States, particularly in Hungary, Romania, Bulgaria and Poland. However, the levelling-out of private income levels in the new Member States is generally less pronounced than in the EU-15 Member States.

Despite state redistribution and other transfers, most capital regions maintain their prominent position as having the highest disposable incomes in their respective countries. The regional values range from 3 800 PPCS per inhabitant in Severozapaden (Bulgaria) to 26 100 PPCS in the UK region of Inner London. Of the 10 regions with the highest per-inhabitant disposable income, four each are in the UK and in Germany, and one each in Spain and France.

The region with the highest disposable income in the new Member States is Bratislavský kraj (Slovakia) with 14 600 PPCS per inhabitant (99 % of the EU-27 average), followed by Vzhodna Slovenija (Slovenia) with 13 900 PPCS (94 %) and Praha (Czech Republic) with 13 200 PPCS (90 %).

A clear regional concentration is also evident when the ranking is extended to the top 30 regions: this group contains 13 German and six UK regions, along with three regions each in Austria and Italy, two in Spain and one each in Belgium, Greece and France.

The tail end of the distribution is very similar to the ranking for primary income. The bottom 30 include nine Polish and seven Romanian regions, six regions each in Bulgaria and Hungary, one Slovakian region and Estonia. State activity and other transfers significantly reduce the difference between the highest and lowest regional values in the 24 countries examined here, from a factor of around 9.8 to 6.8.

For disposable income there has been a significant trend towards a narrower spread in regional values over recent years: between 2000 and 2008 the difference between the highest and lowest values fell from a factor of 10.8 to 6.8. For primary and disposable income alike, this positive development is partly the result of the economic catching-up process in Romania and Bulgaria.

To summarise, between 2000 and 2008, there was a clear narrowing of the difference between the highest and lowest regional values for both primary income and disposable income (influenced by state interventions and other transfers).

The regional spread in disposable income within the individual countries is obviously much lower than for the EU as a whole, but varies considerably from one country to another. Figure 8.1 gives an overview of the spread of

Figure 8.1: Disposable income of private households per inhabitant (in PPCS), highest and lowest NUTS 2 region within each country, 2008 (^{1})

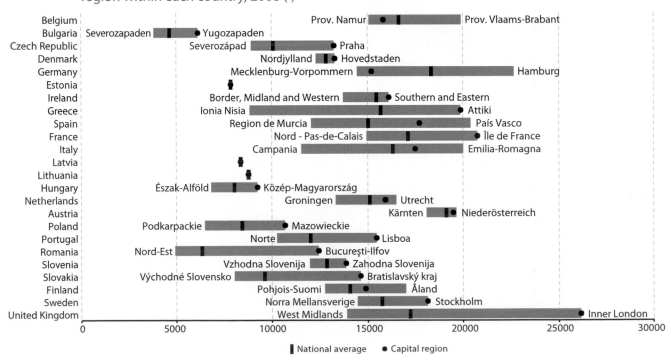

(^{1}) Bulgaria, Eurostat estimation; Départements d'outre-mer (FR9), Cyprus, Luxembourg and Malta, data not available.

Source: Eurostat (online data code: nama_r_ehh2inc).

disposable income per inhabitant between the regions with the highest and the lowest values for each country. We can see that, with a factor of almost 2.5, the regional disparity is greatest in Romania. This means that disposable income per inhabitant in Bucureşti - Ilfov is two and a half times as high as in the Nord-Est region. Greece, the UK and Slovakia also have high regional differences, with factors of between 1.8 and 2.2. In Italy, Spain, Poland, Bulgaria and Germany the highest values are, in each case, between 57 % and 73 % above the lowest.

The regional differences tend to be higher in the new Member States than in the EU-15. Of the new Member States, Slovenia — with 16 % — has the smallest spread between the highest and lowest values and thus comes close to Denmark (8 %) and Austria (9 %), which have the lowest regional income disparities in the entire EU. Ireland, the Netherlands and Sweden also have only moderate regional disparities, with the highest regional values between 17 % and 26 % above the lowest ones. Figure 8.1 also shows that the capital city regions of 14 of the 21 countries with more than one NUTS 2 region also have the highest income values. All seven new Member States with at least two NUTS 2 regions belong to this group.

The economic dominance of the capital regions is also evident when we compare their income values with the national averages. In three countries (Romania, Slovakia and the United Kingdom), the capital city regions exceed the national values by more than 50 %. Only in Belgium and Germany are the values for the capital lower than the national average.

To assess the economic situation in individual regions, it is important to know not just the levels of primary and disposable income but also their relationship to each other. Map 8.2 shows this quotient, which gives an idea of the effect of state activity and of other transfer payments. On average, disposable income in the EU-27 amounts to 86.7 % of primary income. The figure was 86.4 % in 2000, so over this eight-year period the scale of state intervention and other transfers has not changed.

The lowest values are to be found in the capital regions and other economic centres of the more affluent Member States, in particular Hovedstaden (Denmark) at 64.8 %, Utrecht (Netherlands) at 67.3 %, Stockholm (Sweden) at 72.7 % and Inner London (UK) at 72.8 %; the highest values are found in the rural Romanian regions Nord-Est at 120.3 %, Sud-Vest Oltenia at 114.3 % and Sud - Muntenia at 111.2 %

In general, the figures for the EU-15 Member States are lower than for the new Member States. On closer inspection, typical differences can be seen between the regions of the Member States. Disposable income in the capital cities and other prosperous regions of the EU-15 is generally less than 80 % of primary income. Correspondingly higher percentages can be observed in all the Member States in the less affluent areas, in particular on the southern and south-western peripheries of the EU, in the west of the United

Kingdom and in eastern Germany. The reason for this is that, in regions with relatively high income levels, a larger share of primary income is transferred to the state in the form of taxes. At the same time, state social benefits amount to less than in regions with relatively low income levels.

The regional redistribution of wealth is generally less significant in the new Member States than in the EU-15. For the capital regions the valucs are mostly between 75 % and 85 % and are almost without exception at the bottom end of the ranking within each country. This shows that incomes in these regions require much less support through social benefits than elsewhere. The difference between the capital region and the rest of the country is particularly large in Romania and Slovakia, at around 15 percentage points.

In the 24 EU Member States examined here, disposable income exceeds primary income in a total of 28 regions. These are seven Polish regions, five regions each in Portugal and Romania, four in Greece, three in Bulgaria, two in the UK, and one each in German and Italy. Map 8.2 clearly shows that these are particularly poor regions of the Member States in question. No clear differences were found in income support for private households between the new Member States and the EU-15 countries. When interpreting these results, however, we should bear in mind that it is not just monetary social benefits from the state which may cause disposable income to exceed primary income. Other transfer payments (e.g. transfers from people temporarily working in other regions) can play a role as well.

Dynamic development on the edges of the EU

The focus finally turns to an overview of longer-term trends in the regions compared with the EU-27 average. Map 8.3 uses an eight-year comparison to show how primary income per inhabitant (in PPCS) in the NUTS 2 regions changed between 2000 and 2008 compared to the average for the EU-27.

It shows, first of all, dynamic processes at work at the edges of the EU, particularly in Spain, the Czech Republic, Slovakia, Romania, the Baltic States, Finland and some parts of Greece and Ireland.

On the other hand, incomes have grown at a below-average rate in most of the EU's founding Member States. Belgium, Germany and Italy have been particularly hard hit; there, incomes fell back considerably, compared to the average, even in some regions which are not particularly prosperous.

The changes range from + 53 percentage points compared to the EU-27 average for Bucureşti - Ilfov (Romania) to – 20 percentage points for Brussels.

Despite overall clear evidence that the new Member States are catching up, the positive trend is not equally strong everywhere. In some regions of Hungary and

Map 8.2: Disposable income of private households as % of primary income, by NUTS 2 regions, 2008 (¹)

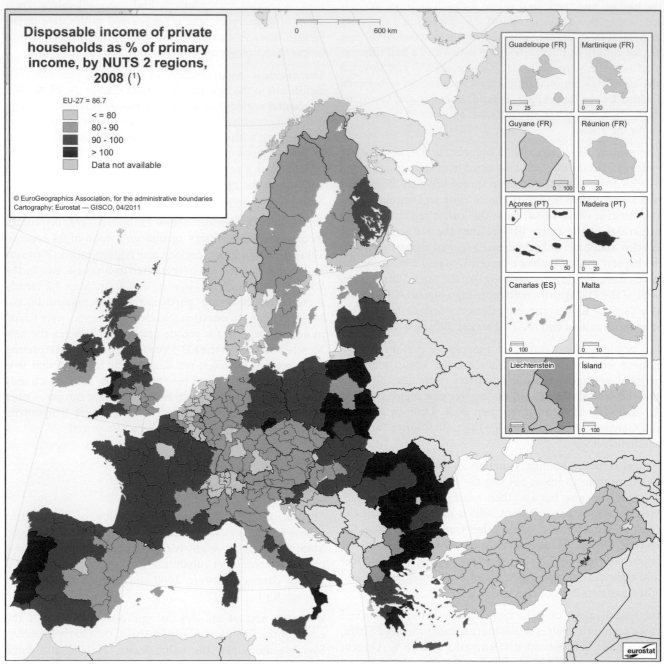

Disposable income of private households as % of primary income, by NUTS 2 regions, 2008 (¹)

EU-27 = 86.7

- < = 80
- 80 - 90
- 90 - 100
- > 100
- Data not available

© EuroGeographics Association, for the administrative boundaries
Cartography: Eurostat — GISCO, 04/2011

Guadeloupe (FR) Martinique (FR) 0 25 / 0 20

Guyane (FR) Réunion (FR) 0 100 / 0 20

Açores (PT) Madeira (PT) 0 50 / 0 20

Canarias (ES) Malta 0 100 / 0 10

Liechtenstein Ísland 0 5 / 0 100

0   600 km

eurostat

(¹) EU-27 and Bulgaria, Eurostat estimation.

Source: Eurostat (online data code: nama_r_ehh2inc).

Map 8.3: Development of primary income of private households per inhabitant, by NUTS 2 regions, 2008 as compared with 2000 (¹)
(in percentage points of the average EU-27 in PPCS)

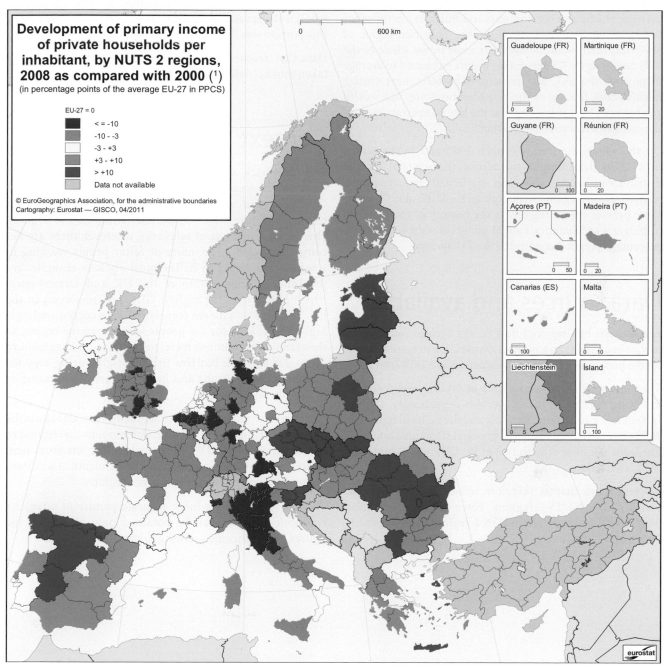

Development of primary income of private households per inhabitant, by NUTS 2 regions, 2008 as compared with 2000 (¹)
(in percentage points of the average EU-27 in PPCS)

EU-27 = 0

- < = -10
- -10 - -3
- -3 - +3
- +3 - +10
- > +10
- Data not available

© EuroGeographics Association, for the administrative boundaries
Cartography: Eurostat — GISCO, 04/2011

(¹) EU-27 and Bulgaria, Eurostat estimation; Greece, 2008 as compared with 2004.

Source: Eurostat (online data code: nama_r_ehh2inc).

Poland, disposable incomes only rose by a few percentage points compared to the EU average. Közép-Magyarország (Hungary) was the only region in a new Member State which fell back (by 3 percentage points) compared to the EU average. The figures for Romania and Bulgaria, on the other hand, are very encouraging. Even the Bulgarian region of Severozapaden (with the lowest income in the whole of the EU) caught up by 7.5 percentage points compared to average income in the EU. The structural problem nevertheless remains that, in most of the new Member States, the wealth gap between the capital city and the less prosperous areas of the countries has widened further.

On the whole, the trend between 2000 and 2008 resulted in a slight flattening at the top of the regional income distribution band, caused in particular by substantial relative falls in regions with high levels of income. Over the same period, the 10 regions at the bottom of the scale, all in Bulgaria or Romania, caught up by between 4.4 and 12.0 percentage points compared to the EU average.

Data sources and availability

Eurostat has had regional data on the income categories of private households for a number of years. The data are collected for the purposes of the regional accounts at NUTS level 2.

There are still no data available at NUTS level 2 for the following regions: France's overseas departments, Cyprus, Luxembourg and Malta. For Bulgaria the regional figures for 2008 were estimated using the regional structure from 2007. The same nominal growth rate as for GDP was assumed for the national data.

The text in this chapter, therefore, relates to only 24 Member States, or 264 NUTS 2 regions. Three of these 24 Member States consist of only one NUTS 2 region, namely Estonia, Latvia and Lithuania.

Owing to the limited availability of data, the EU-27 values for the regional household accounts had to be estimated. For this purpose, it was assumed that the share of the missing Member States in household income for the EU-27 as a whole was the same as for GDP. For the reference year 2008, this portion was 0.5 %.

Data that reached Eurostat after 25 March 2011 are not taken into account in this chapter.

Context

One drawback of regional GDP per inhabitant as an indicator of wealth is that a 'place-of-work' figure (the GDP produced in the region) is divided by a 'place-of-residence' figure (the population living in the region). This inconsistency is of relevance wherever there are net commuter flows — i.e. more or fewer people working in a region than living in it. The most obvious examples are the Inner London region of the UK and Luxembourg, which have by far the highest GDP per inhabitant in the EU. Yet this by no means translates into a correspondingly high income level for the people who live in the region, as thousands of commuters travel to London and Luxembourg every day to work but live in the neighbouring regions. Hamburg, Wien, Praha and Bratislava are other examples of this phenomenon.

Apart from commuter flows, other factors can also cause the regional distribution of actual income not to correspond to the distribution of GDP. These include income from rent, interest or dividends received by the residents of a certain region, but paid by residents of other regions.

This being the case, a more accurate picture of a region's economic situation can be obtained only by adding the figures for net income accruing to private households.

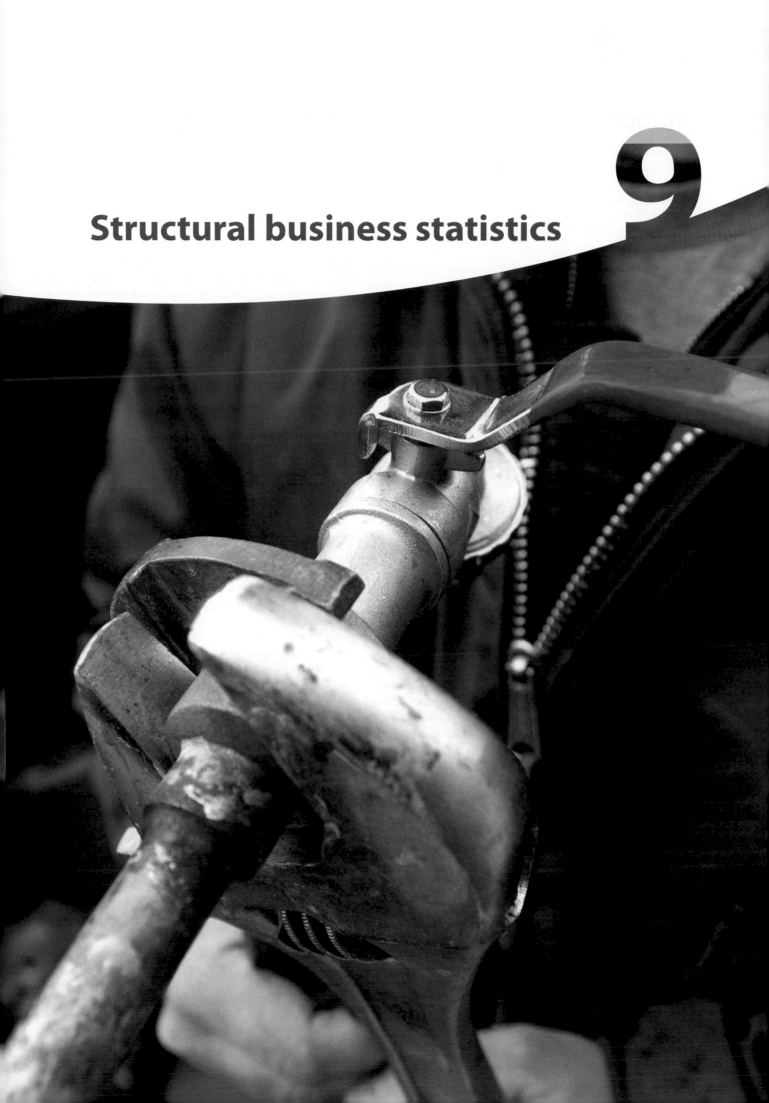

Structural business statistics

Introduction

There are significant disparities between European regions in terms of the importance of different activities within the business economy. While some activities are distributed relatively evenly across most regions, many others exhibit a considerable variation in the level of regional specialisation, often with a few regions having a particularly high degree of specialisation.

The share of a particular activity within the business economy gives an idea of which regions are the most or least specialised in that activity, regardless of whether the region or the activity is large or small. The reasons for regional specialisation are varied and include the availability of natural resources (for example, for mining and quarrying and forest-based manufacturing), the availability of skilled employees, costs, infrastructure, legislation, climatic and topographic conditions (particularly regarding tourism-related activities) and proximity to markets.

Main statistical findings

Regional specialisation

The shares of the non-financial business economy workforce working in the industrial sector and in the non-financial services sector in 2008 are shown in Maps 9.1 and 9.2. Relatively high shares of industrial employment were found in regions of Bulgaria, the Czech Republic, Germany, Hungary, Poland, Romania and Slovakia, with the Slovakian region of Západné Slovensko recording the highest share at 60.2 %.

Non-financial services employment accounted for over 80 % of the non-financial business economy workforce in at least nine regions, mainly in or bordering major urban areas such as Berlin, Hamburg and Köln in Germany, København in Denmark, Noord-Holland in the Netherlands, and Inner London and the surrounding south-east of England. The highest share was 92.5 % in Inner London.

Table 9.1 shows which region was the most specialised in 2007 on a more detailed activity level (all NACE divisions within each NACE section) and, as a comparison, the median and average share of the non-financial business economy workforce among all regions in the EU-27 and Norway.

Manufacturing activities which involve the primary processing stages of agricultural, fishing or forestry products tend to be concentrated in areas close to the source of the raw material. The regions most specialised in food manufacturing (NACE 10) were all located in rural areas in or close to agricultural production centres: Podlaskie (the most specialised of all the regions), Lubelskie and

Warmińsko-Mazurskie in the eastern part of Poland, Dél-Alföld in Hungary, Região Autónoma dos Açores in Portugal and Lincolnshire in the UK. Heavily forested Nordic and Baltic regions were the most specialised regions in the manufacture of wood and wood products (NACE 16) and in the related manufacturing of paper and paper products (NACE 17). Itä-Suomi (Finland) was the most specialised region in wood and wood products and Norra Mellansverige (Sweden) in pulp and paper.

Regions traditionally associated with tourism, i.e. in Portugal, Spain and Italy, were the most specialised in accommodation (NACE 55) and food service activities (NACE 56). Accommodation services accounted for more than 20 % of the workforce in Algarve in the south of Portugal, the Spanish Illes Balears and Provincia Autonoma Bolzano/Bozen in the north-east of Italy on the border with Austria. Algarve was also the most specialised in food service activities.

Construction activities (NACE 41–43) accounted for the highest shares of the workforce in Região Autónoma dos Açores in Portugal and in a few Spanish regions. Transport services are also influenced by location, with water transport (NACE 50) naturally being important for coastal regions and islands, while air transport (NACE 51) is also important for regions with or close to major cities, but also for island regions (especially those with a developed tourism industry). The small island region of Åland (Finland) is a centre for the ferry services between Sweden and Finland and other Baltic Sea traffic. Åland was very highly specialised in water transport, which accounted for over 35 % of persons employed in 2008, more than six times more than the next most specialised region, Vestlandet, and more than 10 times more than the third, Nord-Norge (both in Norway). Outer London was the region most specialised in air transport, followed by Noord-Holland (Dutch region of Amsterdam), Köln in Germany and the Portuguese islands in Região Autónoma dos Açores.

Specialisation in real estate activities (NACE 68), professional scientific and technical activities (NACE 69–75) and administrative and support service activities (NACE 77–82) may be based on access to a critical mass of clients (enterprises or households) or to a knowledge base (external researchers and qualified staff). Latvia was most specialised in real estate (NACE 68) in 2008, ahead of Rheinhessen-Pfalz and Koblenz (both in Germany) and Közép-Magyarország (Hungary). Inner London (UK) was most specialised in professional scientific and technical activities (NACE 69–75), while Flevoland (Netherlands) was most specialised in administrative and support service activities (NACE 77–82).

Figure 9.1 indicates that the widest spread (from lowest to highest) in the share of an activity in each region's non-financial business economy workforce concerned manufacturing activities. In contrast, the employment spread for activities like construction and distributive

Map 9.1: Employment in the industrial economy, by NUTS 2 regions, 2008 (^{1})
(%, share in total non- financial business economy employment)

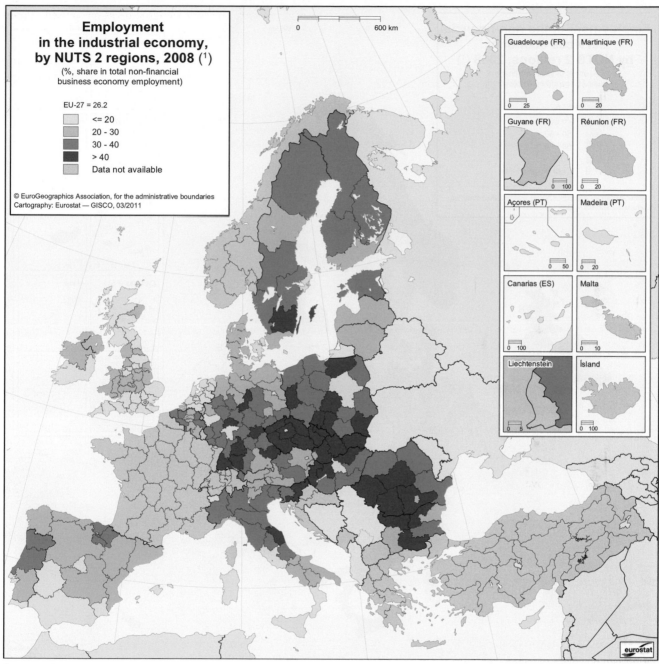

Employment
in the industrial economy,
by NUTS 2 regions, 2008 (^{1})

(%, share in total non-financial
business economy employment)

EU-27 = 26.2

	<= 20
	20 - 30
	30 - 40
	> 40
	Data not available

© EuroGeographics Association, for the administrative boundaries
Cartography: Eurostat — GISCO, 03/2011

Guadeloupe (FR) Martinique (FR)
Guyane (FR) Réunion (FR)
Açores (PT) Madeira (PT)
Canarias (ES) Malta
Liechtenstein Ísland

(^{1}) Norway, excluding sections B–E; EU-27, excluding Greece, France, Latvia (section F), Luxembourg and Malta.

Source: Eurostat (online data code: sbs_r_nuts06_r2).

Map 9.2: Employment in the non-financial services economy, by NUTS 2 regions, 2008 ([¹])
(%, share in total non- financial business economy employment)

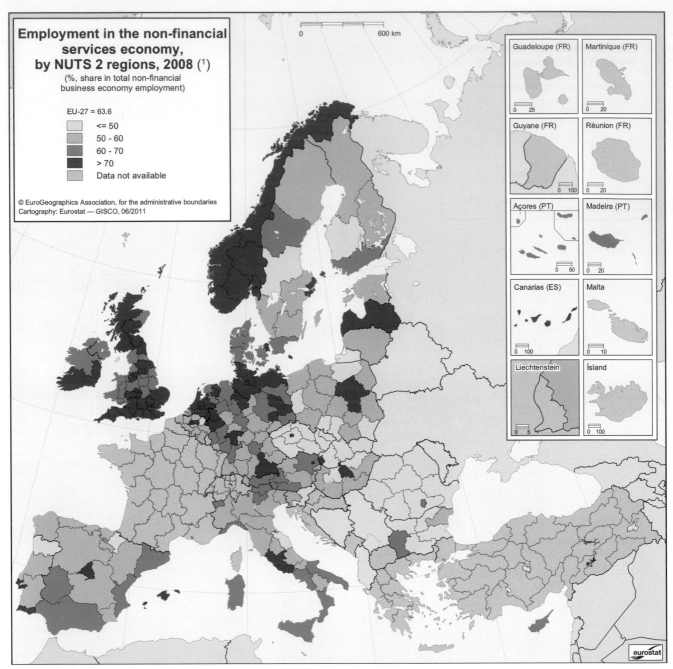

Employment in the non-financial services economy, by NUTS 2 regions, 2008 ([¹])

(%, share in total non-financial business economy employment)

EU-27 = 63.6

	<= 50
	50 - 60
	60 - 70
	> 70
	Data not available

© EuroGeographics Association, for the administrative boundaries
Cartography: Eurostat — GISCO, 06/2011

0   600 km

Guadeloupe (FR)   Martinique (FR)   0 25   0 20

Guyane (FR)   Réunion (FR)   0 100   0 20

Açores (PT)   Madeira (PT)   0 50   0 20

Canarias (ES)   Malta   0 100   0 10

Liechtenstein   Ísland   0 5   0 100

([¹]) Norway, excluding sections B–E; EU-27, excluding Greece, France, Latvia (section F), Luxembourg and Malta.

Source: Eurostat (online data code: sbs_r_nuts06_r2).

Table 9.1: Most specialised region by activity (NACE sections and divisions), EU-27 and Norway, 2007 ([1])
(%, share of total non-financial business economy employment of the region and the median and average share of all regions)

Activity (NACE)	All regions		Most specialised region	
	Median share (%)	Average share (%)	Name (NUTS 2 region)	Share of the region (%)
Mining and quarrying (B 05-09)	0.3	0.6	North Eastern Scotland (UKM5)	11.1
Mining of coal and lignite (05)	0.0	0.2	Śląskie (PL22)	9.3
Extraction of crude petroleum and natural gas (06)	0.0	0.1	North Eastern Scotland (UKM5)	3.4
Mining of metal ores (07)	0.0	0.0	Övre Norrland (SE33)	c
Other mining and quarrying (08)	0.2	0.2	Świętokrzyskie (PL33)	1.2
Mining support service activities (09)	0.0	0.1	North Eastern Scotland (UKM5)	7.5
Manufacturing (C 10-33)	24.1	25.0	Západné Slovensko (SK02)	54.7
Food (10)	2.9	3.1	Podlaskie (PL34)	8.4
Beverages (11)	0.3	0.4	La Rioja (ES23)	3.2
Tobacco products (12)	0.0	0.1	Trier (DEB2)	1.7
Textiles (13)	0.3	0.5	Prov. West-Vlaanderen (BE25)	5.3
Wearing apparel (14)	0.3	1.0	Severozapaden (BG31)	11.3
Leather and leather products (15)	0.1	0.3	Marche (ITE3)	6.6
Wood and wood products (16)	0.8	1.1	Itä-Suomi (FI13)	5.0
Paper and paper products (17)	0.4	0.6	Norra Mellansverige (SE31)	4.3
Printing and reproduction of recorded media (18)	0.6	0.6	West Yorkshire (UKE4)	1.5
Coke and refined petroleum products (19)	0.0	0.1	Opolskie (PL52)	c
Chemicals and chemical products (20)	0.6	0.9	Rheinhessen-Pfalz (DEB3)	8.3
Pharmaceutical products and preparations (21)	0.2	0.4	Prov. Brabant Wallon (BE31)	c
Rubber and plastic products (22)	1.2	1.4	Oberfranken (DE24)	5.8
Other non-metallic mineral products (23)	1.1	1.3	Prov. Namur (BE35)	4.8
Basic metals (24)	0.5	1.0	Norra Mellansverige (SE31)	9.6
Fabricated metal products (25)	2.8	3.0	Gießen (DE72)	8.3
Computer, electronic and optical products (26)	0.7	0.9	Pohjois-Suomi (FI1A)	5.5
Electrical equipment (27)	0.8	1.2	Oberpfalz (DE23)	7.4
Other machinery and equipment (28)	1.8	2.4	Tübingen (DE14)	12.6
Motor vehicles, trailers and semi-trailers (29)	0.9	1.8	Braunschweig (DE91)	c
Other transport equipment (30)	0.3	0.5	Lancashire (UKD4)	c
Furniture (31)	0.6	1.0	Warmińsko-mazurskie (PL62)	7.2
Other manufacturing (32)	0.5	0.6	Border, Midland and Western (IE01)	4.2
Repair and installation of machinery (33)	0.8	0.9	Moravskoslezsko (CZ08)	3.2
Electricity, gas, steam and air conditioning supply (D 35)	0.8	0.9	Sud-Vest Oltenia (RO41)	3.8
Water supply, sewerage, waste management (E 36-39)	0.9	1.0	Východné Slovensko (SK04)	2.9
Water supply (36)	0.2	0.3	Východné Slovensko (SK04)	c
Sewerage (37)	0.1	0.1	Trier (DEB2)	c
Waste management (38)	0.5	0.6	Prov. Luxembourg (B) (BE34)	c
Remediation (39)	0.0	0.0	Valle d'Aosta/Vallée d'Aoste (ITC2)	0.3
Construction (F 41-43)	10.8	10.9	Região Autónoma dos Açores (PT20)	22.7
Buildings (41)	3.2	3.8	Região Autónoma dos Açores (PT20)	13.4
Civil engineering (42)	1.3	1.3	Região Autónoma da Madeira (PT30)	4.8
Specialised construction activities (43)	5.3	5.2	Hedmark og Oppland (NO02)	12.7
Distributive trades (G 45-47)	24.6	24.4	Ciudad Autónoma de Melilla (ES64)	39.4
Motor trades and repair (45)	2.9	2.9	Brandenburg - Südwest (DE42)	5.6
Wholesale trade (46)	7.1	7.1	Oslo og Akershus (NO01)	13.7

Table 9.1: Most specialised region by activity (NACE sections and divisions), EU-27 and Norway, 2007 (^{1})
(%, share of total non-financial business economy employment of the region and the median and average share of all regions) *(cont.)*

Activity (NACE)	All regions		Most specialised region	
	Median share (%)	Average share (%)	Name (NUTS 2 region)	Share of the region (%)
Retail trade (47)	14.2	14.8	Ciudad Autónoma de Melilla (ES64)	26.2
Transport and storage (H 49-53)	7.5	8.3	Åland (FI20)	46.4
Land transport and pipelines (49)	4.2	4.5	Sjælland (DK02)	14.3
Water transport (50)	0.0	0.4	Åland (FI20)	37.4
Air transport (51)	0.0	0.2	Outer London (UKI2)	3.5
Supporting transport activities (52)	1.6	1.8	Bremen (DE50)	10.8
Postal and courier activities (53)	1.2	1.3	Köln (DEA2)	13.3
Accomodation and food service activities (I 55-56)	7.4	7.8	Algarve (PT15)	23.1
Accomodation (55)	1.6	2.2	Provincia Autonoma Bolzano/Bozen (ITD1)	13.5
Food and beverage service activities (56)	5.5	5.6	Algarve (PT15)	13.7
Information and communication (J 58-63)	2.7	3.6	Région de Bruxelles-Capitale/Brussels Hoofdstedelijk Gewest (BE10)	15.0
Publishing activities (58)	0.5	0.6	Oslo og Akershus (NO01)	3.5
Multimedia publishing (59)	0.1	0.2	Inner London (UKI1)	2.5
Programming and broadcasting (60)	0.1	0.2	Rheinhessen-Pfalz (DEB3)	1.1
Telecommunications (61)	0.5	0.7	Köln (DEA2)	7.6
Computer activities (62)	1.2	1.6	Utrecht (NL31)	8.1
Information service activities (63)	0.2	0.3	Bremen (DE50)	2.1
Real estate activities (L 68)	1.8	1.8	Latvija (LV00)	6.2
Professional, scientific and technical activities (M 69-75)	6.9	7.5	Inner London (UKI1)	24.3
Legal and accounting activities (69)	2.2	2.2	Inner London (UKI1)	8.3
Activities of head offices (70)	0.9	1.3	Inner London (UKI1)	6.4
Architectural and engineering activities (71)	2.0	2.1	North Eastern Scotland (UKM5)	11.9
Scientific research and development (72)	0.2	0.3	Trøndelag (NO06)	2.4
Advertising and market research (73)	0.5	0.7	Inner London (UKI1)	3.3
Other professional, scientific and technical activities (74)	0.6	0.7	Inner London (UKI1)	2.2
Veterinary activities (75)	0.1	0.2	Cornwall and Isles of Scilly (UKK3)	0.7
Administrative and support service activities (N 77-82)	8.5	8.7	Flevoland (NL23)	18.9
Rental and leasing activities (77)	0.4	0.5	North Eastern Scotland (UKM5)	1.9
Employment activities (78)	2.2	3.0	Groningen (NL11)	14.2
Travel agency and related activities (79)	0.3	0.4	Illes Balears (ES53)	1.5
Security and investigation (80)	0.8	0.9	Bucureşti - Ilfov (RO32)	5.0
Service to buildings and landscape activities (81)	2.5	2.7	Berlin (DE30)	8.2
Other administrative and business activities (82)	1.2	1.3	Köln (DEA2)	4.6
Repair of computers and personal and household goods (S 95)	0.3	0.3	Prov. Vlaams-Brabant (BE24)	0.7

(^{1}) EU-27, excluding Greece, Spain (divisions F41-F43), France, Latvia (section F), Luxembourg, Malta and Cyprus (division M72); Norway, excluding sections B-E.
c: confidential data.

Source: Eurostat (online data code: sbs_r_nuts06_r2).

Figure 9.1: Degree of regional specialisation by activity, EU-27 and Norway, by NUTS 2 regions, 2008 (¹)
(%, share of non-financial business economy employment)

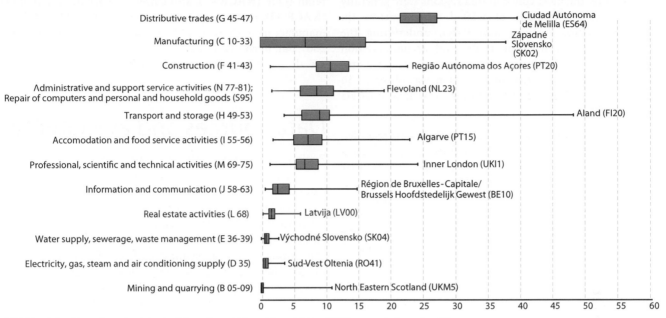

(¹) EU-27, excluding Greece, France, Latvia (section F), Luxembourg, Malta and Cyprus (division M72); Norway, excluding sections B-E.
Source: Eurostat (online data code: sbs_r_nuts06_r2).

trades, which tend to serve more local clients and are large, basic activities present in each region, was much narrower.

Manufacturing accounted for only 2.4 % of persons employed in Ciudad Autónoma de Melilla (Spain) and under 10 % in a further 11 regions, including the capital regions of the Netherlands, Spain and the United Kingdom. The distribution of the remaining regions was relatively symmetrical, from 10 % to almost half of the workforce in two Czech regions: Střední Morava with 47.7 % and Severovýchod with 48.3 %. Západné Slovensko (Slovakia) was the only region where the share of employment in manufacturing exceeded half the non-financial business economy workforce (54.7 %). In contrast, the spread of employment was much narrower in distributive trades (NACE section G), which was the activity displaying the highest median employment, present in all regions and serving more local clients. Shares ranged from 12.3 % in Région de Bruxelles-Capitale/Brussels Hoofdstedelijk Gewest (Belgium) and less then 15 % in Åland (Finland) and in another four regions in Belgium, to more than a third in Ciudad Autónoma de Ceuta and Ciudad Autónoma de Melilla (Spain).

On the other hand, transport and storage (NACE section H) and mining and quarrying (NACE section B) are two activities with a few strong outlier regions that are highly specialised. In fact, there were only two regions where the share of employment in transport, storage and communication exceeded 20 %. The highest specialisation of

the Finnish island region of Åland, where almost half of the workforce (46.4 %) was employed in this sector, is due almost exclusively to the importance of water transport. Åland was far ahead of Köln in Germany (20.4 %). Natural endowments play an important role in mining and quarrying. Many regions record little or no such activity, with only very few regions being highly specialised on account of deposits of metallic ores, coal, oil or gas. Mining and quarrying accounted for less than 0.1 % of persons employed in a quarter of all regions, and between 0.1 % and 0.5 % in half of the regions. However, it did account for over 4 % in five regions and as much as a 10th of the total non-financial business economy workforce in North Eastern Scotland (United Kingdom) and Śląskie (Poland).

Business concentration

While an analysis of specialisation shows the relative importance of different activities in the regions, regardless of the size of the region or the activity, an analysis of concentration looks at the dominance of certain regions within an activity, or activities within a region. In most activities, there are many examples of regions that are ranked highly in terms of both specialisation and concentration.

Map 9.3 gives an indication of how concentrated or diversified the regional business economy was in 2008, measured as the share of the five largest activities (NACE divisions) in the total non-financial business economy workforce. The level of concentration tends to be higher in regions where trade and services dominate the business economy, as industrial activities are more fragmented. By this measure, the most concentrated regions were generally in countries traditionally associated with tourism (in particular Spain, Portugal and Italy), underlining the importance of construction, trade, and accommodation and food service activities in tourism-oriented regions. In addition, high business concentration was observed in Danish, Irish, Polish and British regions as well as in Latvia and Lithuania.

In contrast, the lowest business concentrations were recorded mainly in regions with a relatively small services sector and a large manufacturing sector in eastern Europe (in particular in Slovakia, the Czech Republic and Hungary), although low shares were also recorded in Sweden and Finland (except for the island region of Åland). The five largest activities accounted for less than a third of total employment in five regions in the Czech Republic, two in Belgium and one in Spain.

Figure 9.2 shows the extent to which employment in certain activities was concentrated in a limited number of regions in 2008.

Four of the five mining and quarrying activities topped the rankings in terms of the share of total employment in the EU-27 and Norway, and of the 10 regions with the largest workforces. The most concentrated was the mining of metal ores (NACE 07), with persons employed in only a fifth of all the regions in 2008.

Air transport (NACE 51) and leather and leather products manufacturing (NACE 15) were also highly concentrated in the 10 largest regions, which together accounted for 43 % and 49 % of total employment respectively. In the case of air transport, this dominance is due to the concentration in large metropolitan regions where the large airports are situated: chief among them are the regions of Paris, Outer London, Köln, Amsterdam and Madrid. Leather and leather products manufacturing, on the other hand, is a small activity in Europe, heavily concentrated in Italy and Romania: three of the 10 regions with the largest workforces were situated in Italy, three in Romania and one each in Portugal, Spain, Slovakia and Bulgaria. The region with the largest workforce was Toscana in Italy, with 41 000 persons employed, but it ranked only third, accounting for almost 4 % of the total leather manufacturing workforce in the EU-27 and Norway. Concentration of this activity was slightly higher in Nord-Vest (Romania) and reached the highest level in Marche (6.6 %) in Italy.

In contrast to the more specialised types of mining and quarrying, 'other mining and quarrying' (NACE 08) was among the activities in which the 10 largest regions were least dominant, accounting for only 12 % of total sectoral employment. This is due to the widespread availability and local sourcing of many construction materials, such

as sand and stone, which dominate this type of quarrying in most regions. Of all the activities (NACE divisions), retail trade (NACE 47), specialised construction activities (NACE 43), motor trades and repair (NACE 45) and food manufacturing (NACE 10) had the lowest concentration in 2007, but, in contrast to 'other mining and quarrying', these are all major activities in terms of employment in the EU.

Data sources and availability

Regional structural business statistics (SBS) are collected under a regulation of the European Parliament and of the Council, using the definitions and breakdowns specified in the Commission implementing regulations. Data for the reference year 2008, presented in this chapter, were collected under Regulation (EC) No 295/2008 of 11 March 2008 concerning structural business statistics. The data cover the EU Member States and Norway. These and other SBS data sets are available on Eurostat's website (www.ec.europa.eu/eurostat) on the tag 'Statistics', under the theme 'Industry, trade and services/Structural business statistics'. Selected publications, data and background information are available in the section of the Eurostat website dedicated to European business: http://epp.eurostat.ec.europa.eu/portal/page/portal/european_business/introduction

Most data series are continuously updated and revised where necessary. This chapter reflects the data situation in March 2011.

Structural business statistics are presented by sectors of activity, for the first time according to the NACE Rev. 2 classification, with a breakdown to two-digit level (NACE divisions). The data presented here are restricted to the non-financial business economy. This includes sections B (Mining and quarrying), C (Manufacturing), D (Electricity, gas, steam and air conditioning supply), E (Water supply, sewerage and waste management), F (Construction), G (Distributive trades), H (Transport and storage), I (Accommodation and food service activities), J (Information and communication), L (Real estate activities), M (Professional, scientific and technical activities) and N (Administrative and support service activities) and division S95 (Repair of computers and personal and household goods). It excludes agricultural, forestry and fishing activities and public administration and other non-market services (such as education and health, which are currently not covered by the SBS), as well as financial services (NACE section K).

The observation unit for regional SBS data is the local unit, which is an enterprise or part of an enterprise situated in a geographically identified place. Local units are classified into sectors (by NACE) according to their main activity. At national level, the statistical unit is the enterprise. An enterprise can consist of several local units. It is possible for

Figure 9.2: Most concentrated activities (NACE divisions), EU-27 and Norway, by NUTS 2 regions, 2008 ([1])
(%, share of regions in total sectoral employment)

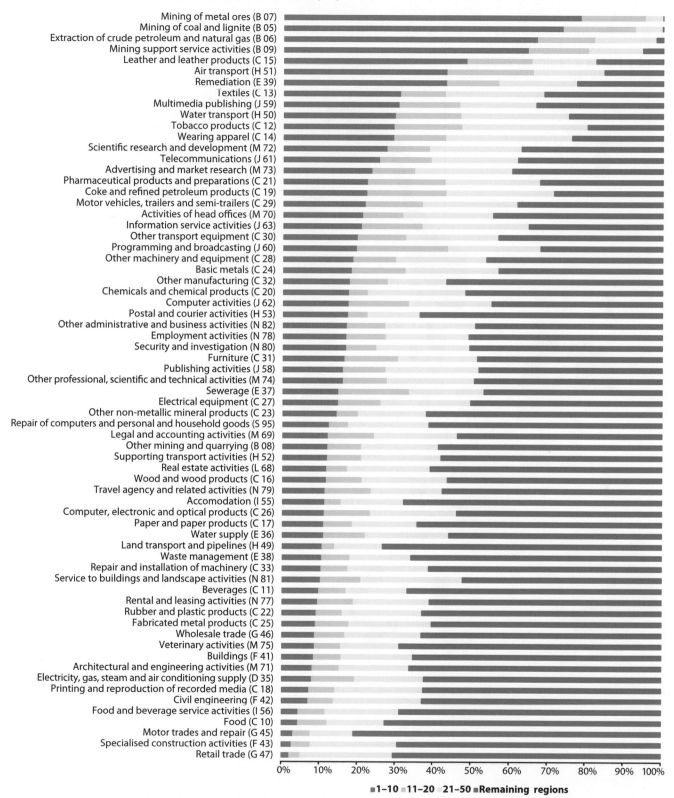

([1]) EU-27, excluding Greece, Spain (divisions F41-F43), France, Latvia (section F), Luxembourg, Malta and Cyprus (division M72); Norway, excluding sections B-E.

Source: Eurostat (online data code: sbs_r_nuts06_r2).

Map 9.3: Regional business concentration, by NUTS 2 regions, 2008 (^{1})
(%, share of five largest activities (NACE divisions) in total non- financial business economy employment)

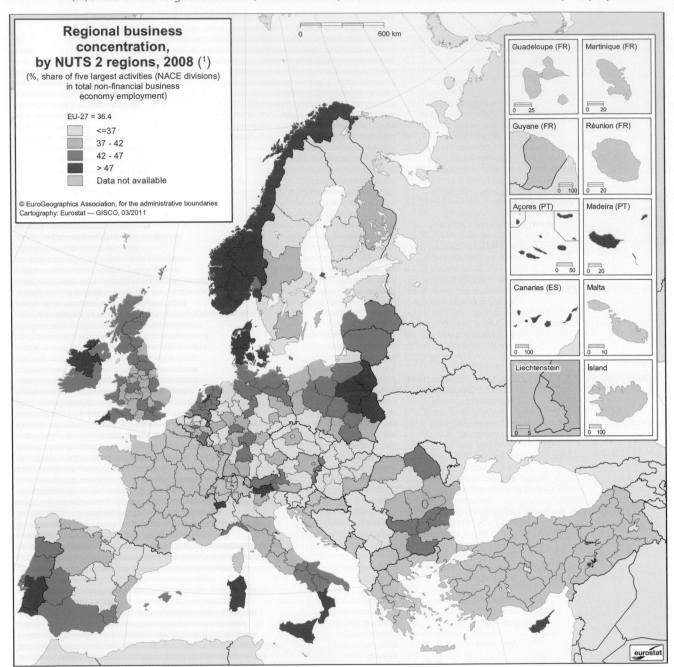

Regional business concentration, by NUTS 2 regions, 2008 (^{1})

(%, share of five largest activities (NACE divisions) in total non-financial business economy employment)

EU-27 = 36.4

- <=37
- 37 - 42
- 42 - 47
- > 47
- Data not available

© EuroGeographics Association, for the administrative boundaries
Cartography: Eurostat — GISCO, 03/2011

0   600 km

Guadeloupe (FR)   Martinique (FR)
0   25   0   20

Guyane (FR)   Réunion (FR)
0   100   0   20

Açores (PT)   Madeira (PT)
0   50   0   20

Canarias (ES)   Malta
0   100   0   10

Liechtenstein   Ísland
0   5   0   100

(^{1}) Norway, excluding sections B–E; EU-27, excluding Greece, France, Latvia (section F), Luxembourg and Malta.

Source: Eurostat (online data code: sbs_r_nuts06_r2).

the principal activity of a local unit to differ from that of the enterprise to which it belongs. Hence, national and regional structural business statistics are not entirely comparable. It should be noted that in some countries the activity code is assigned on the basis of the principal activity of the enterprise.

Structural business statistics define the **number of persons employed** as the total number of persons who work (paid or unpaid) in the observation unit, as well as persons who work outside the unit but who belong to it and are paid by it. It includes working proprietors, unpaid family workers, part-time workers and seasonal workers.

Context

Regional structural business statistics offer users who want to know more about the structure and development of the regional business economy a detailed, harmonised data source, describing for each activity the number of workplaces, number of persons employed, wage costs and investments made. This chapter shows how some of these data can be used to analyse different regional business characteristics: the focus, diversity and specialisation of regional business economies and the nature and characteristics of regional business services. The analysis in this chapter generally confirms the positive expectations for the business services sector, strengthening the belief that this will remain one of the key drivers of competitiveness and job creation within the EU economy in the coming years.

Globalisation, international market liberalisation and technological gains are likely to lead to further integration among Europe's regions (and beyond), bringing buyers and sellers of these services closer together.

Information society

Introduction

The introduction of the Internet and the Word Wide Web has led the development of what we call 'the information society'. The related developments have created new dimensions of economic, social or political participation for individuals or groups of individuals. Online activities have become ubiquitous, meaning that the actual geographic location where they are performed does not matter any more, as long as there is a connection to the Internet.

The term 'digital divide' has been coined to distinguish between those who have access to the Internet and are able to make use of new services offered on the World Wide Web and those who are excluded from these services. This chapter emphasises the geographic aspects of the digital divide.

Main statistical findings

Access to information and communication technologies

Access to information and communication technologies (ICT) is at the heart of the digital divide, and geographic location is just one aspect of that divide. Regional statistical data on access to the Internet within households and the availability of broadband for going online exist at European level. Fast Internet access is one specific action area of the Digital Agenda for Europe. New and innovative developments of electronic services rely on fast wired and wireless Internet access. It is therefore essential to foster and monitor the development of fast Internet access as part of the benchmarking framework. By 2013, all citizens within the EU should have access to broadband. By 2020, the minimum bandwidth of the broadband Internet connections should be 30 Mbps, with 50 % of the households having a speed of at least 100 Mbps. In contrast to supply-side statistics, Eurostat figures show the actual uptake of ICT by the population. In 2010, seven out of 10 (70 %) households on average in Europe with members aged between 16 and 74 years had access to the Internet at home and six out of 10 (61 % of households) accessed the Internet via broadband. These numbers have grown rapidly in recent years, with an average annual growth of 5 percentage points for Internet access and 6 percentage points for broadband access between 2008 and 2010. While access to the Internet makes it possible to participate in the information society, broadband connections enable Internet users to fully exploit the potential of the Internet. Many of the advanced Internet services, such as social networking sites, uploading and downloading of media content (video and audio files) or the use of online maps and satellite images, automatically require a broadband connection. Websites are becoming richer in content, and this constantly increases the demand for traffic volumes, even for less advanced services such as e-mail communication.

The maps in this chapter all show the average annual development in percentage points between 2008 and 2010 for the following indicators: Internet connections, broadband access, regular Internet use and online shopping. When interpreting these figures one has to bear in mind that it is easier to achieve high growth rates at a lower overall level. When approaching saturation, growth rates normally decrease or a greater effort has to be made to maintain the previous growth rates. In order to consider this state of affairs, the figures in this chapter show the average annual development in percentage points and at the same time the levels attained in 2010 for the four selected indicators.

The national differences in Internet connections and broadband access of households in 2010 are considerable. They range from 33 % in Bulgaria to 91 % in the Netherlands for Internet connections and from 23 % in Romania to 83 % in Norway and Sweden for broadband access. The European Union averages are 70 % for Internet connections and 61 % for broadband access, which means that some countries are lagging well behind the EU average. The figures show the situation in 2010 by country. In addition, Figures 10.1 and 10.2 — together with the corresponding maps — illustrate the average annual change in Internet and broadband connections. The EU average for the development of Internet connections between 2008 and 2010 is 4.9 percentage points and 6.1 percentage points for broadband access. The best performing countries as regards new Internet connections are the former Yugoslav Republic of Macedonia, Turkey, Poland, Greece and the Czech Republic, with an average annual increase of more than 7.3 percentage points, while the least performing countries are Sweden, Austria, Denmark and Norway, with an average annual increase of less than 3 percentage points.

A similar picture can be drawn for broadband access of households. Here, the best performers are Croatia, Germany, Poland, Greece and Italy, with an average annual increase of 9 percentage points or more. In Bulgaria and Denmark the average annual increase was 3 percentage points or less. When interpreting these results one has to bear in mind that it is easier to achieve high growth rates at a lower level, whereas growth rates tend to decrease when reaching higher levels. In order to maintain high growth, efforts and investments have to be intensified. This rule is borne out when one observes the take-up and development of Internet and broadband connections. Linear regressions between take-up and annual average growth are significant and yield a decrease in the growth of Internet connections at higher levels of connected households. It could be expected that countries like the Netherlands, Denmark, Austria or Sweden would exhibit low growth, as they have already reached high levels of Internet access.

Figure 10.1: Broadband connections in households, 2008–10 (^{1})
(share of households with broadband connection in 2010 and average annual change,
in percentage points)

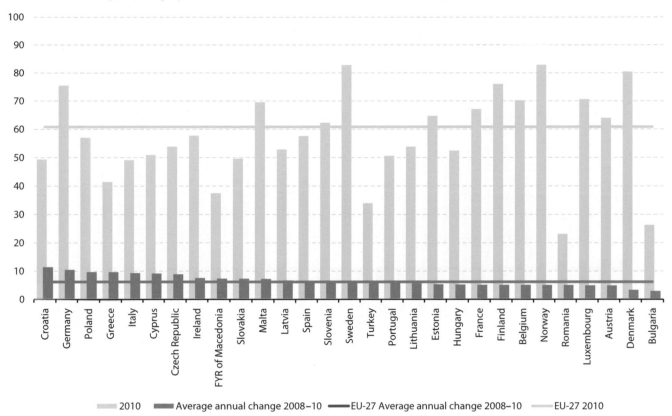

(^{1}) Netherlands, United Kingdom and Iceland, data not available.

Source: Eurostat (online data code: isoc_si_broad).

Taking these observations into account, countries could be classified according to levels of Internet and broadband access in below and above EU average levels which have already been reached. A similar grouping could be applied to the average annual development of Internet and broadband connections. France and Luxembourg perform above the EU average as regards the levels and the development of Internet connections, whereas Estonia, Lithuania, Slovenia, Slovakia, Bulgaria and Latvia are below average when it comes to the level and growth of Internet connections. The situation concerning broadband access is more mixed, i.e. the differences between the countries are more pronounced. Germany, Malta and Slovenia show an annual growth and take-up above the EU average between 2008 and 2010, while Turkey, Portugal, Lithuania, Hungary, Romania and Bulgaria are below the EU average.

The statistics on Internet connections and broadband access are closely related, as broadband is a type of Internet connection and efforts are being made at both European and national levels to foster broadband access to the Internet. However, not all countries and regions are equally successful in deploying fast Internet connections that enable users to make full use of the potential of the

Internet. Maps 10.1 and 10.2 show the increase in the take-up of Internet and broadband connections by households in the European regions between 2008 and 2010. Again, the abovementioned restrictions on the levels already reached and the effects on growth rates have to be taken into account when interpreting these figures. The regional differences in Internet access (see Figure 10.2) are quite large, with an average annual growth of 4.9 percentage points at EU level. The regions where the highest increases are recorded are Est (France), Nisia Aigaiou, Kriti (Greece), Střední Morava, Severozápad and Jihovýchod (Czech Republic) and Region Centralny (Poland), with an average of more than 9 percentage points. Regions with an increase of below 1 % point are Groningen, Friesland and Gelderland (Netherlands), Wien (Austria), Scotland (UK), Severoiztochen (Bulgaria), Trøndelag (Norway), Molise (Italy) and Mecklenburg-Vorpommern (Germany). Most of these regions are well above the EU average, except for Severoiztochen, Molise and Mecklenburg-Vorpommern. The latter region fell below the EU average in 2010 due to the stagnation in growth from 2008 to 2010. All regions in Greece, Hungary, Poland and Croatia are above the EU average for annual growth between 2008 and 2010.

Figure 10.2: Internet access in households, 2008–10 (¹)
(share of households with Internet access in 2010 and average annual change, in percentage points)

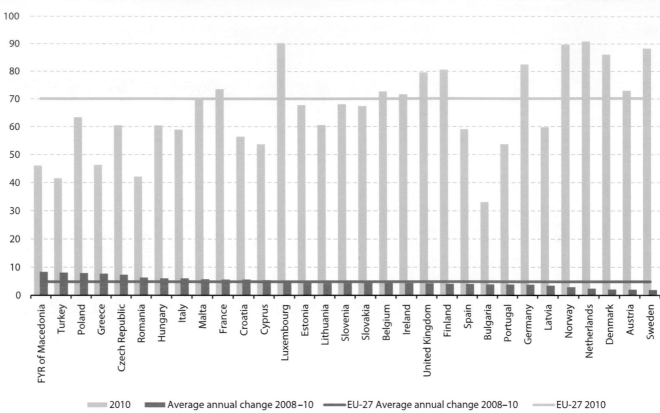

Legend:
■ 2010　■ Average annual change 2008–10　── EU-27 Average annual change 2008–10　── EU-27 2010

(¹) Iceland, data not available.

Source: Eurostat (online data code: isoc_ci_in_h).

The situation for broadband access is to some extent comparable to the development of Internet connections. The regions with the highest increase in broadband access are located in the United Kingdom (North East, North West), the Netherlands (Drenthe), the Czech Republic (Severozápad), Italy (Sardegna), Croatia Središnja i Istočna (Panonska) Hrvatska) and Germany (Brandenburg, Hessen, Sachsen, Sachsen-Anhalt, Schleswig-Holstein, Thüringen) with an average annual growth of at least 12 percentage points.

As with the development of the Internet connection, the regions with the lowest growth (below 1 % point) are located in the Netherlands, Bulgaria, Norway and the United Kingdom. With the exception of Severoiztochen (Bulgaria), the regions are well above the EU average in broadband take-up. All regions in Germany, Greece, Croatia, Ireland, Italy and Poland are above the EU average as regards the average annual growth of broadband access in percentage points.

E-commerce by individuals

Online shops and markets are creating additional opportunities to increase sales and reduce costs for businesses and they provide many advantages for consumers, such as 24-hour availability or easy price and product comparison. The Digital Agenda for Europe puts emphasis on online shopping, with a focus on achieving a digital single European market. Policy measures aim to lower national barriers for the online markets by opening access to content, such as buying and downloading of digital media content, simplifying cross-border transactions and payments and building trust in cross-border e-commerce. By 2015, 50 % of the population will be likely to buy online and 20 % will be likely to buy from vendors in other EU countries. So far, it is only the smaller countries or those sharing a common language with a larger neighbouring country, such as Luxembourg, Austria, Malta or Cyprus, that achieve high percentages of cross-border e-commerce.

In 2010, 40 % of the total population of the European Union purchased online within the 12 months before the survey. The annual average increase between 2008 and 2010 was 4 percentage points, which means that the 50 % goal of the Digital Agenda is likely to be reached by 2013, assuming that the current development continues in the future. It will be more difficult to achieve the second goal of 20 % cross-border online purchases, as the average at EU level was 9 % in 2010 with an average annual increase of only 1.5 percentage points.

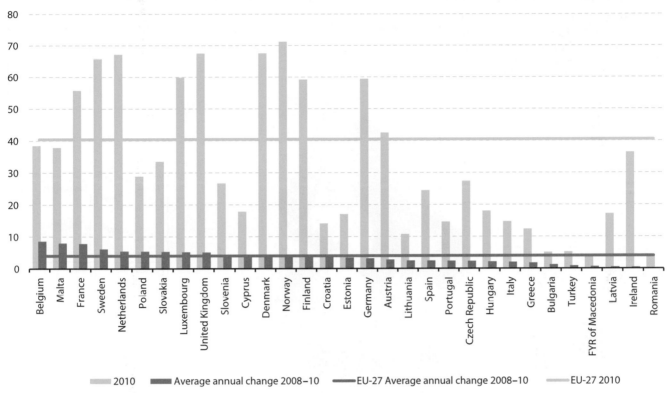
Figure 10.3: Online purchases by private persons, 2008–10 (¹)
(share of persons who ordered goods or services over the Internet for private use in 2010 and average annual change, in percentage points)

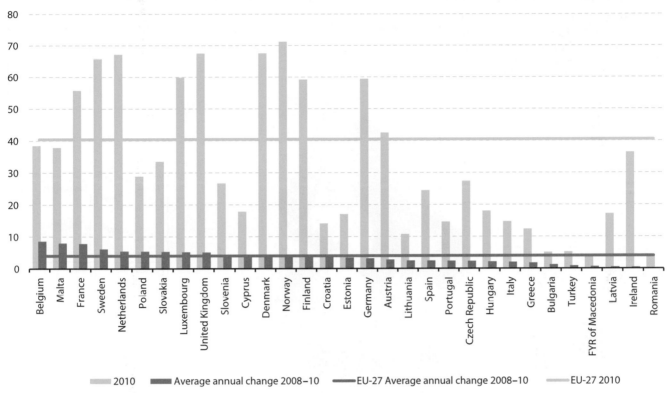

Legend: 2010 ■ Average annual change 2008–10 ■ EU-27 Average annual change 2008–10 ■ EU-27 2010

(¹) Iceland, data not available.

Source: Eurostat (online data code: isoc_ec_ibuy).

The countries with the highest growth in the percentage of the population shopping online between 2008 and 2010 are Belgium, Malta and France, with an increase of more than 7.5 percentage points annually. The countries with the lowest increases are Romania, Ireland, Latvia, the former Yugoslav Republic of Macedonia and Turkey, with less than 1 percentage point annually. France, Sweden, the Netherlands, Luxembourg, the United Kingdom and Denmark are the countries which are above the EU average in the share of population buying online: at the same time they are growing faster than the EU average. Looking at the ranking of countries according to the share of population buying online, Luxembourg, Malta, Belgium, Poland, Slovenia, Hungary, Estonia, Cyprus, Croatia, Turkey and Bulgaria all improved their position between 2008 and 2010.

The regions with the highest growth in the share of online buyers are all located in France (all regions except for Méditerranée), the Netherlands (Flevoland), Belgium (Prov. Antwerpen, Prov. Namur), the United Kingdom (Northern Ireland) and Sweden (Sydsverige). These regions are all above the EU average as regards the share of population buying online in 2010. By far the majority of regions in France, Belgium, the Netherlands, Poland and Slovakia are above the

EU average with regard to annual growth. The regions with an increase of less than 1 % are located in Sweden, Romania, the Netherlands, Ireland, the Czech Republic, Italy, Spain, Germany, Hungary, Latvia and Greece. In Romania, online shopping plays a marginal role in both the share of online shoppers and the annual increase in all except one of the regions.

Regular use of the Internet

Regular Internet use by individuals is defined as using the Internet at least once a week within a reference period of three months prior to the survey. The data show that people who use the Internet tend to use it regularly. In 2008, 91 % of Internet users within the European Union accessed it at least once a week. Between 2008 and 2010 this percentage increased to 94 %. The figures for the share of the population who use the Internet regularly are closely related to the figures for Internet connections. In addition, the percentage of regular Internet users who live in a household with broadband access is on average higher than the share of regular Internet users living in a household with narrowband access only. Consequently, countries or regions

Map 10.1: Development of broadband connections in households, by NUTS 2 regions, 2008–10 (¹)
(Average annual change of the share of households with broadband connections, in percentage points)

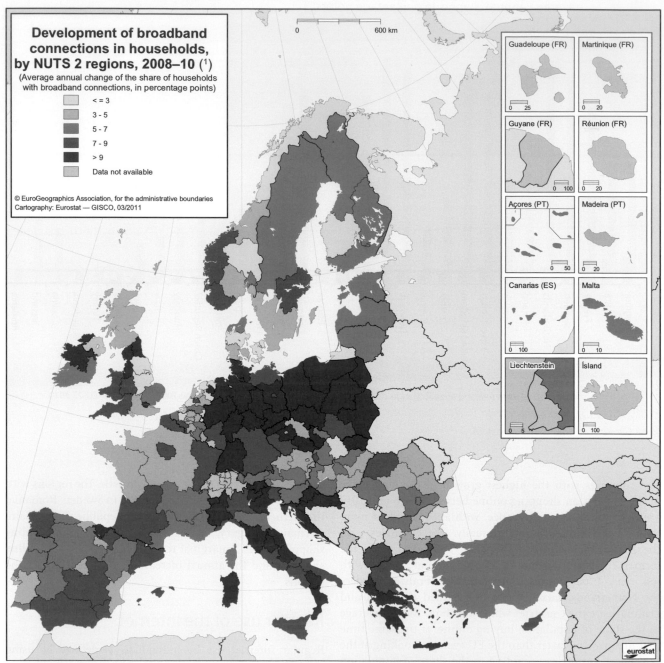

Development of broadband connections in households, by NUTS 2 regions, 2008–10 (¹)
(Average annual change of the share of households with broadband connections, in percentage points)

- < = 3
- 3 - 5
- 5 - 7
- 7 - 9
- > 9
- Data not available

© EuroGeographics Association, for the administrative boundaries
Cartography: Eurostat — GISCO, 03/2011

0   600 km

Guadeloupe (FR)   Martinique (FR)   0 25   0 20

Guyane (FR)   Réunion (FR)   0 100   0 20

Açores (PT)   Madeira (PT)   0 50   0 20

Canarias (ES)   Malta   0 100   0 10

Liechtenstein   Ísland   0 5   0 100

(¹) Netherlands and United Kingdom, 2008–09; Slovenia and Turkey, national level; Germany, Greece, France, Poland, Sweden and United Kingdom, by NUTS 1 regions; Finland, Åland combined with Länsi-Suomi .

Source: Eurostat (online data code: isoc_r_broad_h).

Map 10.2: Development of Internet access in households, by NUTS 2 regions, 2008–10 (¹)
(Average annual change of the share of households with Internet access, in percentage points)

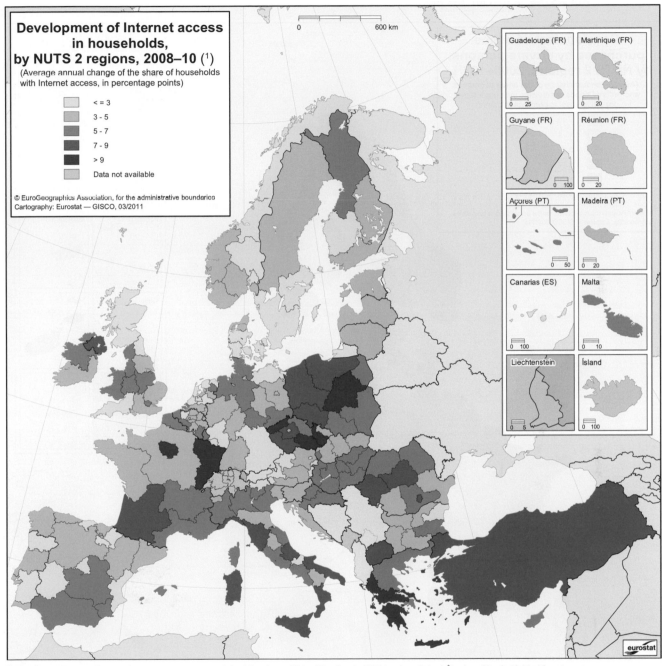

Development of Internet access in households, by NUTS 2 regions, 2008–10 (¹)
(Average annual change of the share of households with Internet access, in percentage points)

- <= 3
- 3 - 5
- 5 - 7
- 7 - 9
- > 9
- Data not available

© EuroGeographics Association, for the administrative boundaries
Cartography: Eurostat — GISCO, 03/2011

Guadeloupe (FR)
Martinique (FR)
Guyane (FR)
Réunion (FR)
Açores (PT)
Madeira (PT)
Canarias (ES)
Malta
Liechtenstein
Ísland

(¹) Slovenia and Turkey, national level; Germany, Greece, France, Poland, Sweden and United Kingdom, by NUTS 1 regions; Finland, Åland combined with Länsi-Suomi.

Source: Eurostat (online data code: isoc_r_iacc_h).

Map 10.3: Development of online purchases by private persons, by NUTS 2 regions, 2008–10 (¹)
(Average annual change of the share of persons who ordered goods or services, over the Internet, for private use, in percentage points)

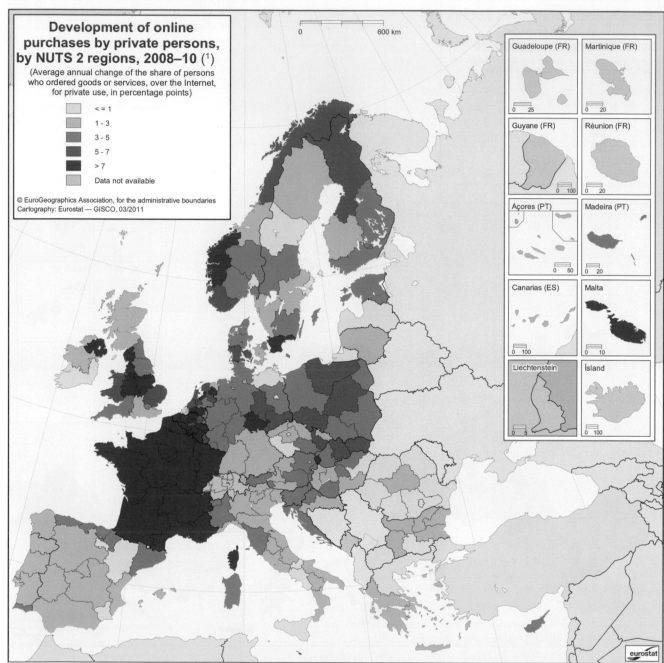

Development of online purchases by private persons, by NUTS 2 regions, 2008–10 (¹)

(Average annual change of the share of persons who ordered goods or services, over the Internet, for private use, in percentage points)

- < = 1
- 1 - 3
- 3 - 5
- 5 - 7
- > 7
- Data not available

© EuroGeographics Association, for the administrative boundaries
Cartography: Eurostat — GISCO, 03/2011

Guadeloupe (FR)
Martinique (FR)
Guyane (FR)
Réunion (FR)
Açores (PT)
Madeira (PT)
Canarias (ES)
Malta
Liechtenstein
Ísland

(¹) France and Sweden, 2009–10; Slovenia and Turkey, national level; Germany, Greece, France, Poland and United Kingdom, by NUTS 1 regions; Finland, Åland combined with Länsi-Suomi.

Source: Eurostat (online data code: isoc_r_iacc_h).

10

Figure 10.4: Regular use of the Internet, 2008–10 (¹)
(share of persons who accessed the Internet on average at least once a week in 2010
and average annual change, in percentage points)

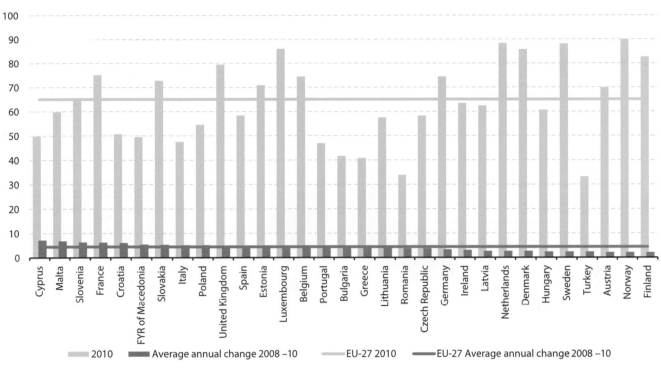

2010 ■ Average annual change 2008 –10   EU-27 2010   EU-27 Average annual change 2008 –10

(¹) Iceland, data not available.

Source: Eurostat (online data code: isoc_ci_ifp_fu).

with a higher share of broadband access at comparable levels of Internet household connections are expected to have a larger share of regular Internet users.

The aim of the Digital Agenda for Europe is to increase the regular use of the Internet from 60 % in 2009 to 75 % of the total population by 2015. The average annual increase in the share of regular Internet users among the total population in the European Union is 4.5 percentage points. Overall, the European average of the share of regular Internet users among the total population rose from 56 % in 2008 to 65 % in 2010. Assuming that the growth maintained this pattern, this target would already be reached by 2013. As in the case of the share of households with Internet connections, there is a negative correlation — albeit a weaker one — between the share of regular Internet users that has already been reached and its annual increase. The countries with a large share of regular Internet users and a high annual growth (both above EU average) are Slovenia, France, Slovakia, the United Kingdom, Estonia and Luxembourg. On the other hand, Portugal, Bulgaria, Greece, Romania, the Czech Republic and Turkey are the countries that are well below the EU average in terms of the share of regular Internet users and annual average growth. At regional level, the regions with a growth of less than 1 percentage point are Groningen (Netherlands), Trøndelag (Norway), Wien (Austria), Sør-Østlandet (Norway), Scotland (UK), Länsi-

Suomi (Finland) and Közép-Dunántúl (Hungary). All of these regions have a level above or close to the average (Közép-Dunántúl) in terms of the level of regular Internet usage that has already been reached. Regions which are more than 9 percentage points below the EU average with regard to the share of regular Internet users in 2010 and showing a annual increase of 3 percentage points or less are located in Romania (Nord-Vest, Sud-Est, Sud - Muntenia, Sud-Vest Oltenia), Bulgaria (Yuzhen tsentralen), Czech Republic (Severovýchod, Moravskoslezsko), Greece (Attiki), Hungary (Dél-Dunántúl, Észak-Alföld), Spain (Canarias) and Italy (Provincia Autonoma Bolzano/Bozen). The regions with the highest growth between 2008 and 2010 are located in Germany (Sachsen-Anhalt, Thüringen), Slovakia (Východné Slovensko), Belgium (West-Vlanderen), the United Kingdom (North West, Northern Ireland) and France (Île de France, Bassin Parisien) with an average annual growth of at least 8 percentage points. All regions in France, Poland and Croatia show an annual increase over the EU average of 4.5 percentage points.

Conclusions

Statistics on the use of information and communication technologies in households and by individuals are collected annually at regional level. The available statistics reveal

Map 10.4: Development of regular use of Internet, by NUTS 2 regions, 2008–10 (¹)
(Average annual change of share of persons who accessed the Internet, on average, at least once a week, in percentage points)

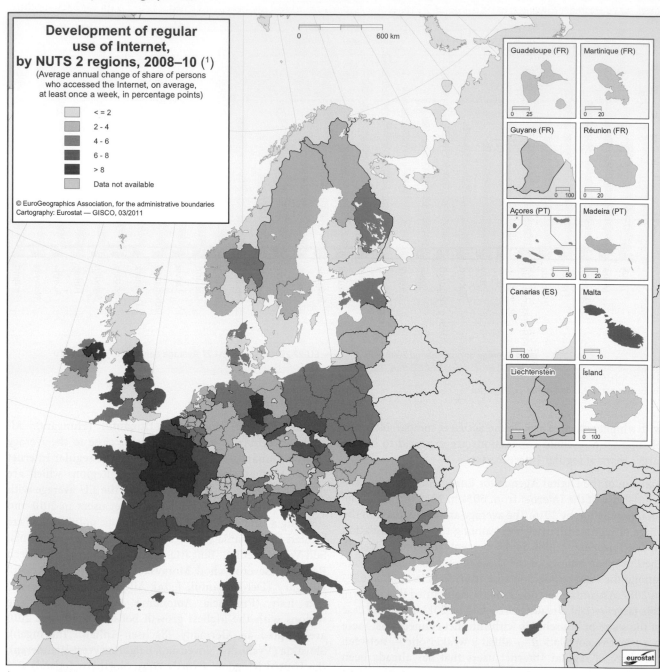

Development of regular use of Internet, by NUTS 2 regions, 2008–10 (¹)
(Average annual change of share of persons who accessed the Internet, on average, at least once a week, in percentage points)

- < = 2
- 2 - 4
- 4 - 6
- 6 - 8
- > 8
- Data not available

© EuroGeographics Association, for the administrative boundaries
Cartography: Eurostat — GISCO, 03/2011

(¹) Slovenia and Turkey, national level; Germany, Greece, France, Poland, Sweden and United Kingdom, by NUTS 1 regions.

Source: Eurostat (online data code: isoc_r_iuse_i).

considerable differences between 2008 and 2010 in the development of access and use among the regions of the European Union. Within the last few years, all Member States have increased access to and use of ICTs. However, there is a risk that the introduction of the Internet and related services is already compounding the existing differences in society, as was demonstrated for some regions which are lagging behind the average development at EU-27 level. In order to overcome this issue, the European Union has shaped explicit policy targets to achieve an inclusive information society. The policies are benchmarked according to the Benchmarking Digital Europe framework ([1]).

The maps in this chapter reveal specific spatial patterns that vary according to the chosen indicators. The countries where the majority of regions are experiencing a big increase in Internet access are Greece, Poland and the Czech Republic. This picture changes when observing the broadband access of households by region. As with Internet connections, the majority of regions in Greece, Poland and the Czech Republic show a high increase. Additionally, regions in Germany, Slovenia, Croatia and Italy experienced high growth compared to the EU average. In terms of the development of regular Internet use, there is a greater regional variation, with a bigger increase in Cyprus, Malta, Slovenia and France. The regions with the highest growth as regards the share of population shopping online between 2008 and 2010 are located in France, Belgium, Luxembourg and the Netherlands. Regions in the south and the south-east of the European Union are lagging behind in terms of the development of online shopping within the population.

In order to achieve the policy goals of inclusive participation in the information society, it will be necessary to maintain existing efforts to provide affordable access to the Internet via broadband and to educate people in the necessary skills to enable them to access and exploit the riches of the Internet.

Data sources and availability

European statistical data on the use of information and communication technologies have been available since 2003. Harmonised data have been published since 2006 based on Regulation (EC) No 808/2004 of the European Parliament and of the Council of 21 April 2004 concerning Community statistics on the information society. The regulation describes two modules or areas of statistical data production: namely statistics on the use of ICT in enterprises and statistics on ICT use in households and by individuals. Annual Commission regulations define the set of indicators for which data are collected by the EU Member States. Regional data on a limited list of indicators have been available at the

level of NUTS 1 since 2006 as a voluntary contribution by the Member States and since 2008 on a mandatory basis. Some Member States provide regional data at NUTS 2 level on a voluntary basis. The collection of data for each module is divided into a core part, i.e. access to ICT, and general use of ICT. Questions on access to ICT are addressed to the household, while questions on the use of ICT are answered by individuals within the household. Following the principles of the i2010 benchmarking framework, the model questionnaire includes a topic of special focus each year, i.e. e-government (2006), e-skills (2007), advanced services (2008), e-commerce (2009) and security (2010).

The scope of the survey comprises individuals aged between 16 and 74 years and households with at least one member within this age range. The reference period is the first three months of the calendar year.

The presentation of statistics on ICT use is restricted to a number of core indicators for which regional data are available. These regional indicators are 'access to the Internet at home by household', 'access to the Internet via broadband by household', 'regular Internet users', 'persons who have never used the Internet' and 'e-commerce by individuals'.

The term 'access' does not refer to 'connectivity', i.e. whether connections can be provided in the households' area or street, but to whether anyone in the household was able to use the Internet at home.

The term 'broadband connection' refers to the speed of data transfer for uploading and downloading data. Broadband requires a data transfer speed of at least 144 kbit/s. The technologies most widely used for broadband access to the Internet are a digital subscriber line (DSL) or cable modem.

Internet users are persons who have used the Internet within the last three months. Regular Internet users have used the Internet at least once a week within the three-month reference period.

For the purpose of the households module, e-commerce via the Internet is defined as placing orders for goods or services via the Internet. Purchases of financial investments, e.g. shares, confirmed reservations for accommodation and travel, participation in lotteries and betting and obtaining payable information services from the Internet or purchases via online auctions are included in the definition. Orders placed by manually typed e-mails are not accepted. Delivery or payment by electronic means is not a requirement for an e-commerce transaction.

Context

During the course of the last decades, information and communication technologies have penetrated all areas of economic and social life. They have accounted for a

([1]) http://ec.europa.eu/information_society/eeurope/i2010/docs/benchmarking/benchmarking_digital_europe_2011-2015.pdf

significant increase in the productivity of the economy and the growth of GDP, and are transforming our societies in a profound and unprecedented way. The introduction of the Internet and the World Wide Web has led to the development of what we call 'the information society'. With access to the Internet, it is very easy to obtain information on almost any topic. Search engines provide rapid and easy access to websites and information sources. Many activities, such as communicating and selling or buying goods and services, can be performed online. These developments have created new dimensions of economic, social or political participation for individuals or groups of individuals. As these activities are not bound by any specific geographic location, they have the potential to bridge large distances. In principle, the actual geographic location where these activities are performed does not matter any more, as long as there is a connection to the Internet. Nowadays, it is possible to maintain contact with family members or friends via social networking sites, share holiday pictures on the web or have a video call with a friend via the Internet. Electronic shopping sites offer the possibility of buying or selling items via the Internet. ICTs support working from home or from other places outside the enterprise, delivering greater flexibility in work organisation from which both the enterprise and the employee can benefit. The ubiquitous presence of ICTs has the potential to create completely new ways of participating in the economy and society.

As a basic condition, the participation of citizens and businesses in the information society depends on access to ICTs, i.e. the presence of electronic devices, such as computers, and fast connections to the Internet. The term 'digital divide' has been coined to distinguish between those who have access to the Internet and are able to make use of new services offered on the World Wide Web and those who are excluded from these services. The term explicitly includes access to ICTs as well as the related skills needed to participate in the information society. The digital divide can be classified according to criteria that describe the difference in participation according to gender, age, education, income, social group or geographic location. This chapter emphasises the geographic aspects of the digital divide.

Policies within the European Union at national and European levels have acknowledged the importance of bridging the digital divide to give citizens equal access to ICTs and to enable them to participate in the information society. The Digital Agenda for Europe [1], which is a successor to the i2010 strategy for growth and employment, outlines a number of actions in the area of very fast Internet access and sustainable digital society. Unlike the i2010 strategy, which focused on providing access to ICTs, the Digital Agenda emphasises the quality of services. One of the targets of the Digital Agenda is that all households should have broadband subscriptions at a minimum speed of 30 Mbps by 2020. The key benchmarking indicators are defined in the European Commission's 'Framework for benchmarking digital Europe 2011–15' [2], which is monitoring the development of the European information society and the degree of achievement of the policy objectives set out in the Digital Agenda for Europe, which is a flagship initiative under the Europe 2020 strategy for smart, sustainable and inclusive growth [3], to further develop an economy based on knowledge and innovation.

[1] http://eur-lex.europa.eu/LexUriServ/LexUriServ.do?uri=COM:2010:0245:FIN:EN:PDF
[2] http://ec.europa.eu/information_society/eeurope/i2010/docs/benchmarking/benchmarking_digital_europe_2011-2015.pdf
[3] http://eur-lex.europa.eu/LexUriServ/LexUriServ.do?uri=COM:2010:2020:FIN:EN:PDF

Tourism

11

Introduction

This chapter presents the regional pattern of tourism in the European Union in 2009. It mainly tracks tourism occupancy in tourist accommodation establishments. The tourism statistics used in this chapter refer to 'hotels and similar establishments' and 'tourist campsites' (for more details, see data sources and availability).

The number of overnight stays, which reflects both the length of stay and the number of visitors, is the key indicator for accommodation statistics, so this chapter concentrates mostly on this variable. It also presents figures on the capacity of collective tourist accommodation in European regions.

Main statistical findings

Tourism in the EU-27: trends and facts

Tourism in the European Union increased by 7.2 % overall from 2000 to 2009, giving an average annual change rate of 0.8 %. However, as shown in Figure 11.1, the tourist accommodation sector was affected by the financial crisis: from a peak at 1.94 billion in 2007, the number of overnight stays dropped successively in 2008 and 2009 to 1.88 billion nights, below the level of 2006.

According to the Eurostat *Statistics in focus* on 2010 first results, the tourist accommodation sector started to recover in 2010, with the number of nights spent at hotels and similar establishments increasing by 2.8 % compared with 2009 ([1]).

Before going further into regional details, it is worth making a key observation: three Member States accounted for nearly half of all nights spent in hotels and campsites in the European Union in 2009: Italy, France and Spain. As shown in Figure 11.2, adding Germany and the United Kingdom increases this to three quarters.

Top 20 tourist regions in the EU-27

Out of the 20 top tourist regions in the EU-27 in 2009 (in terms of nights spent at hotels and campsites), 17 regions were from Spain, Italy and France.

Figure 11.3 shows the 20 regions in the European Union with the highest number of overnight stays, broken down by hotels and campsites. These regions accounted for 36.5 % of all overnight stays in all 271 regions of the EU-27 for which data are available.

[1] For more details, see 'Slow recovery of the tourist accommodation sector in 2010', Statistics in focus No 6/2011.

With 63.6 million overnight stays, the Île-de-France region, which includes the French capital Paris, was well in the lead, followed by three Spanish regions: Cataluña (54.1 million), Illes Balears (45.9 million) and Canarias (45.3 million). The region of Veneto in Italy took fifth place (44.8 million). Almost one in seven tourism nights spent in hotels or campsites across the EU was spent in one of these top five regions.

Inner London (seventh place), Tirol in Austria (11th place) and Oberbayern in Germany (18th place), which includes the Bavarian metropolitan area of München, were the only regions in the top 20 that were not in one of the three leading tourism countries.

In 18 of the 20 regions, more nights were spent in hotels and similar establishments than on campsites. In two French regions, Languedoc-Roussillon and Aquitaine, however, the opposite was true, as they attracted more tourists to campsites than to other types of accommodation.

Number of overnight stays

Tourism in Europe is concentrated in the coastal regions. The Alpine regions also saw strong demand.

Map 11.1 gives an overview of the number of overnight stays by both residents and non-residents in the regions of Europe in 2009. In addition to the six countries represented in the top 20 EU regions (Italy, Spain, France, Austria, Germany and the United Kingdom), eight more countries had NUTS 2 regions reporting more than 8 million overnight stays: the Czech Republic (Praha), Greece (Kriti and Notio Aigaio), Cyprus, the Netherlands (Noord-Holland), Portugal (Algarve and Lisboa), Sweden (Västsverige and Stockholm), Switzerland (Région lémanique) and Croatia (Jadranska Hrvatska).

Trends in tourism over the period 2004–09

The main beneficiaries of the upswing in tourism over the period 2004–09 were regions from Poland, Lithuania, Bulgaria, Greece and the United Kingdom.

Map 11.2 shows the average annual change rate of nights spent at hotels and campsites in the period 2004–09. Tourism grew in most of the regions of the European Union over this period. Forty-four regions recorded an average annual change rate of over 5 %.

However, 72 regions recorded a negative average annual change rate. Most of these regions were in France, Italy, the Czech Republic, Germany, the Netherlands, Romania and the United Kingdom.

Figure 11.1: Evolution of nights spent in hotels and campsites in EU-27, 2000–09 ([1])
(million nights)

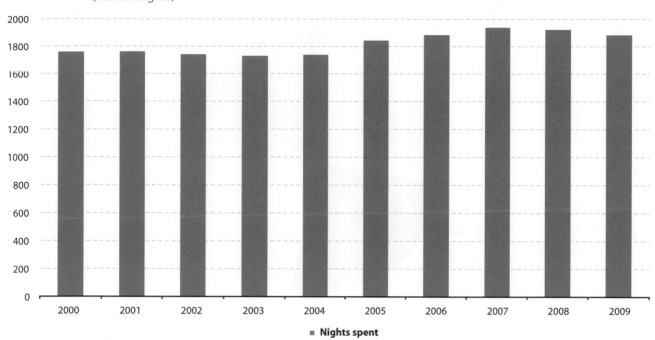

■ Nights spent

([1]) Estonia, only hotels for 2000 and 2001; Ireland, only hotels for 2001; 2008 and 2009 estimated; Cyprus, only hotels for 2000 and 2002; Malta, only hotels, 2000, 2001 and 2002 estimated.

Source: Eurostat (online data code: tour_occ_nin2).

Overnight stays in campsites

In the regions of western Europe (mainly coastal regions) and Scandinavian countries, campsites are more frequently used as accommodation than in central and eastern Europe.

In 2009, overnight stays spent on campsites accounted for less than 20 % of the total number of overnight stays in all 271 regions of the EU-27 for which data were available (the remaining 80 % were hotels). Map 11.3 shows significant disparities in the ratio of camping in regions across Europe. The regions with campsites accounting for more than 40 % were concentrated in nine countries: the United Kingdom, Netherlands, France, Sweden, Denmark, Norway, Belgium, Portugal and Croatia. No regions in Bulgaria, Estonia, Lithuania, Latvia or Romania had over 5 % share of nights spent on campsites. A large majority of regions in Poland and Austria had a less than 5 % share of overnight stays spent in campsites.

Top 20 tourist regions in the EU-27 visited by foreign tourists

In 2009, the top six tourist regions in the EU-27 visited by foreign (inbound) tourists (Illes Baleares, Canarias, Île-de-France, Cataluña, Inner London and Veneto) recorded as many nights of tourism as the next 14 put together.

Figure 11.4 shows the top 20 EU regions recording the highest number of total overnight stays in hotels and on campsites by

foreign tourists. These top 20 regions accounted for more than half of all overnight stays by non-residents across the EU-27.

Nine Member States were on the list of the top 20 tourist regions visited by foreign tourists: Spain, France, the United Kingdom, Italy, Austria, Greece, Cyprus, Portugal and the Czech Republic.

Share of inbound tourism

The share of inbound tourism, i.e. visits from abroad, differed very widely from region to region from around 2 % to over 97 %. Foreign overnight visitors accounted for more than 90 % of overnight stays in five EU regions in 2009: Malta, Luxembourg, the Czech region of Praha, the Greek region of Kriti and the Austrian region of Tirol. This was also true in Liechtenstein and the Croatian region of Jadranska Hrvatska.

Map 11.4 shows overnight stays by foreign visitors as a percentage of total overnight stays. Southern Europe's island regions recorded particularly high figures of foreign visitors as a percentage of total overnight stays, especially Malta, Cyprus, the Greek island regions, the Spanish Illes Balears and Canarias and the Portuguese Região Autónoma da Madeira. All of these regions recorded a share of non-resident nights above 80 %.

Inbound tourism also occupied a key position in the capital regions of some countries. This was true in Luxembourg, the Czech region of Praha, Bruxelles-Capitale/Brussels

Figure 11.2: Nights spent in hotels and campsites, share per Member State in EU-27 total, 2009
(%)

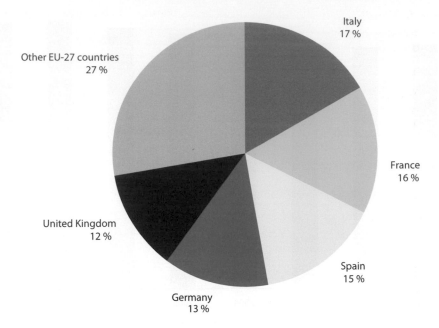

Source: Eurostat (online data code: tour_occ_nin2).

Figure 11.3: Top 20 EU-27 tourist regions, number of nights spent in hotels and campsites, by NUTS 2 regions, 2009
(million nights)

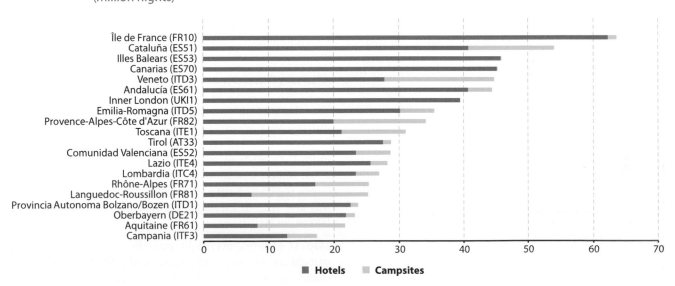

Source: Eurostat (online data code: tour_occ_nin2).

Map 11.1: Nights spent in hotels and campsites, by NUTS 2 regions, 2009 (¹)

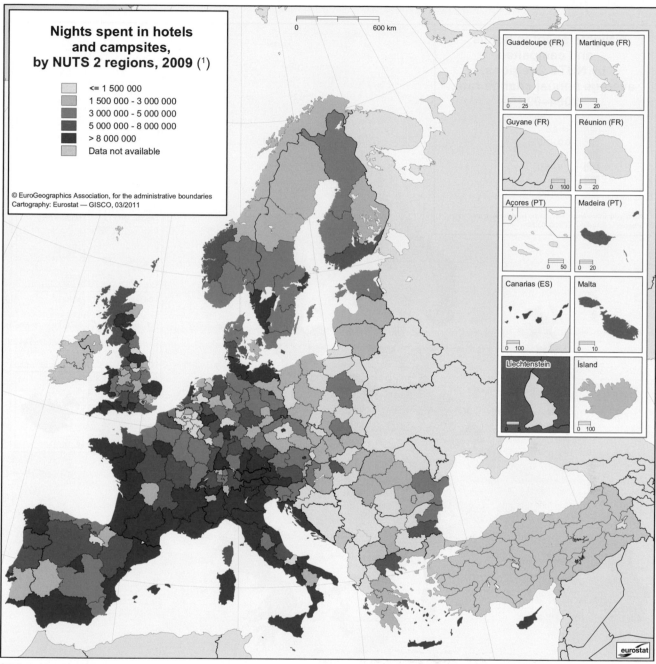

Nights spent in hotels and campsites, by NUTS 2 regions, 2009 (¹)

- <= 1 500 000
- 1 500 000 - 3 000 000
- 3 000 000 - 5 000 000
- 5 000 000 - 8 000 000
- > 8 000 000
- Data not available

© EuroGeographics Association, for the administrative boundaries
Cartography: Eurostat — GISCO, 03/2011

Guadeloupe (FR)   Martinique (FR)   Guyane (FR)   Réunion (FR)   Açores (PT)   Madeira (PT)   Canarias (ES)   Malta   Liechtenstein   Ísland

(¹) Malta and Switzerland, hotels only.

Source: Eurostat (online data code: tour_occ_nin2).

Map 11.2: Nights spent in hotels and campsites, by NUTS 2 regions, average annual change rate, 2004–09 (¹) (%)

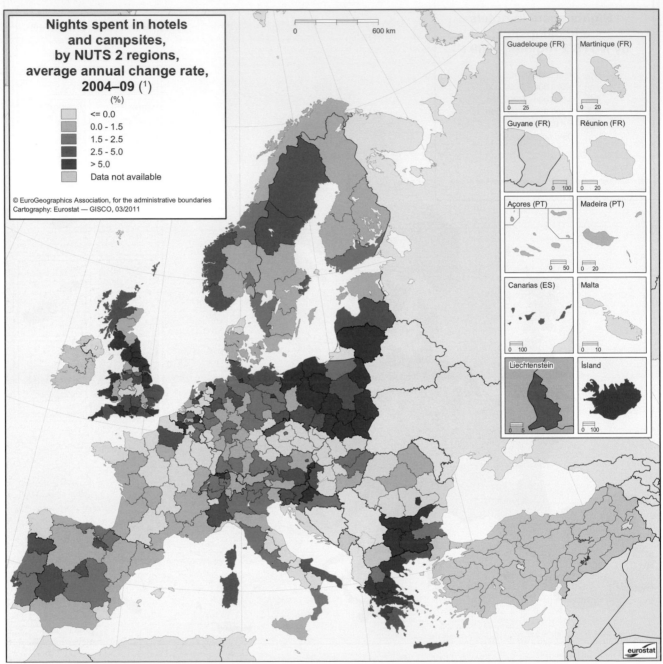

(¹) Malta and Switzerland, hotels only. Départements d'outre-mer (France) and Switzerland, average annual change rate 2005–09.

Source: Eurostat (online data code: tour_occ_nin2).

Map 11.3: Share of nights spent in campsites in total number of nights spent, by NUTS 2 regions, 2009 (¹)
(%)

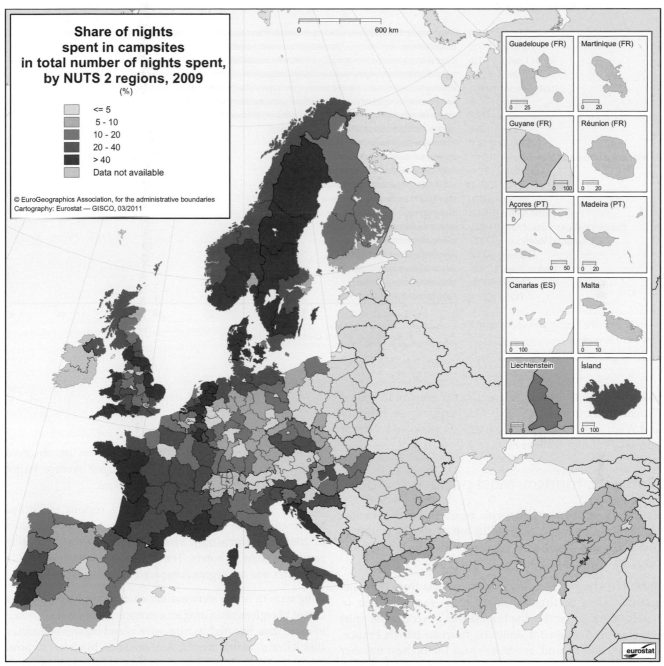

Share of nights spent in campsites in total number of nights spent, by NUTS 2 regions, 2009 (%)

- <= 5
- 5 - 10
- 10 - 20
- 20 - 40
- > 40
- Data not available

© EuroGeographics Association, for the administrative boundaries
Cartography: Eurostat — GISCO, 03/2011

Guadeloupe (FR)   Martinique (FR)
Guyane (FR)   Réunion (FR)
Açores (PT)   Madeira (PT)
Canarias (ES)   Malta
Liechtenstein   Ísland

Source: Eurostat (online data code: tour_occ_nin2).

Figure 11.4: Top 20 EU-27 tourist regions, number of nights spent by non-residents in hotels and campsites, by NUTS 2 regions, 2009
(million nights)

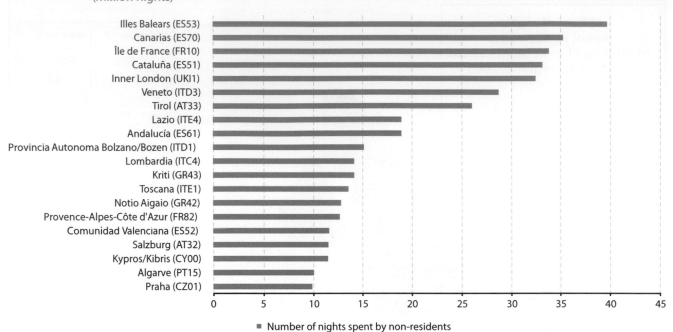

■ Number of nights spent by non-residents

Source: Eurostat (online data code: tour_occ_nin2).

Hoofdstedelijk Gewest in Belgium, Inner London in United Kingdom, the region of Közép-Magyarország in Hungary and Wien in Austria. All of these regions recorded a share of non-resident nights above 80 %.

Domestic tourism: most popular regions

Resident tourists most often visit regions near the seaside. In 2009, this was the case for 15 out of the 24 countries (including five land-locked countries) for which a regional breakdown was available.

Table 11.1 shows the region where residents from the same country spent the highest number of overnight stays in hotels or on campsites. The seaside was generally the most popular destination for domestic tourism but in France, Germany and Poland, residents spent the highest number of nights in the capital region. In Austria, Switzerland, Slovakia and the Czech Republic, mountain regions were the most popular.

In most regions, the share of the most popular region in 2009 remained more or less unchanged compared to 2004. However, the regions of Prov. West-Vlaanderen in Belgium and Jadranska Hrvatskalost in Croatia lost ground compared to 2004 while the regions of Kentriki Makedonia in Greece, Nyugat-Dunántúl in Hungary and Noord-Holland in the Netherlands gained ground.

Average length of stay: hotel versus campsites

The longest average visitor trips in campsites are observed mainly in coastal regions while the longest average visitor stays in hotels are mainly in island regions.

Maps 11.5 and 11.6 show the NUTS 2 regions in Europe by average length of trip of visitors in hotels and campsites in 2009. Unsurprisingly, visitors tended to stay longer in campsites than in hotels. The EU average length of stay in campsites was 4.0 nights compared to 2.5 nights in hotels.

Long stays in hotels were mainly observed in island regions. Out of 12 regions recording an average length of stays in hotels of more than five nights, nine were island regions (Canarias, Illes Balears, Malta, Região Autónoma da Madeira, Kypros/Kibris and four Greek island regions). Long stays in hotels were also recorded in mountain regions (mainly Austria) and in central and eastern European countries (Bulgaria, Poland, Hungary, Slovenia, Slovakia and Romania).

Long stays in campsites were mainly observed in coastal regions: this was quite clear in Italy and France and to a lesser extent in Spain (mainly the Mediterranean coast). In Italy, out of 21 regions, only two recorded an average length of stays shorter than five nights: Sicilia and Valle d'Aosta/Vallée d'Aoste. In France, all the regions of the

Map 11.4: Share of non-resident nights spent in hotels and campsites, by NUTS 2 regions, 2009 (¹)
(%)

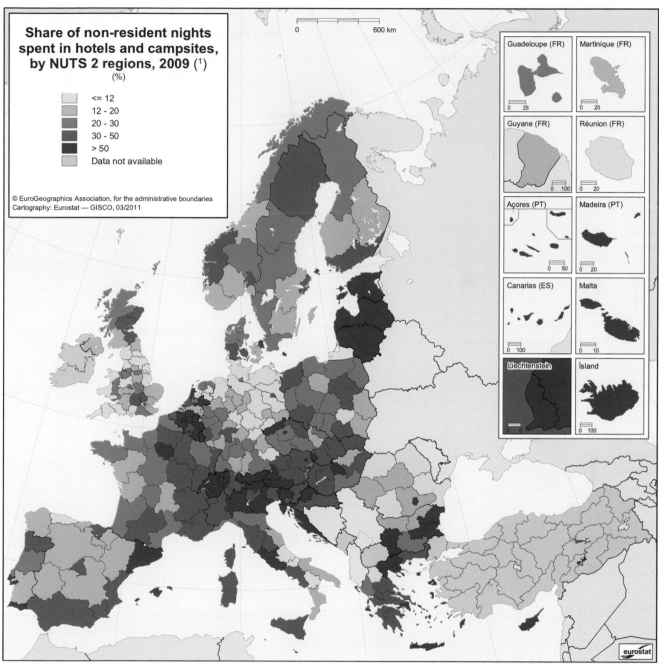

Share of non-resident nights spent in hotels and campsites, by NUTS 2 regions, 2009 (¹)
(%)

- <= 12
- 12 - 20
- 20 - 30
- 30 - 50
- > 50
- Data not available

© EuroGeographics Association, for the administrative boundaries
Cartography: Eurostat — GISCO, 03/2011

Guadeloupe (FR)
Martinique (FR)
Guyane (FR)
Réunion (FR)
Açores (PT)
Madeira (PT)
Canarias (ES)
Malta
Liechtenstein
Ísland

(¹) Malta and Switzerland, hotels only.

Source: Eurostat (online data code: tour_occ_nin2).

Table 11.1: Most popular tourist region per country (domestic tourism), number of nights spent by residents in hotels and campsites, by NUTS 2 regions, 2009 (^{1})

	Resident nights in the country (million nights)	Most popular tourist region		
		Region	Regional share (%)	Regional share, 2004 (%)
Belgium	6.76	Prov. West-Vlaanderen (BE25)	34	41
Bulgaria	4.69	Yugoiztochen (BG34)	23	22
Czech Republic	11.36	Severovýchod (CZ05)	24	23
Denmark	14.73	Syddanmark (DK03)	31	30
Germany	194.10	Oberbayern (DE21)	9	9
Estonia	1.09		–	–
Ireland	9.96	Southern and Eastern (IE02)	68	67
Greece	19.35	Kentriki Makedonia (GR12)	19	15
Spain	126.46	Andalucía (ES61)	20	20
France	195.98	Île de France (FR10)	15	14
Italy	178.47	Emilia-Romagna (ITD5)	15	15
Cyprus	1.33		–	–
Latvia	0.66		–	–
Lithuania	0.80		–	–
Luxembourg	0.11		–	–
Hungary	7.72	Nyugat-Dunántúl (HU22)	25	21
Malta (^{1})	0.35		–	–
Netherlands	33.68	Noord-Holland (NL32)	17	13
Austria	23.32	Steiermark (AT22)	20	20
Poland	17.53	Mazowieckie (PL12)	14	15
Portugal	18.34	Algarve (PT15)	25	26
Romania	14.11	Sud-Est (RO22)	28	30
Slovenia	2.85	Vzhodna Slovenija (SI01)	59	60
Slovakia	3.63	Stredné Slovensko (SK03)	38	36
Finland	12.73	Etelä-Suomi (FI18)	37	36
Sweden	31.29	Västsverige (SE23)	24	23
United Kingdom	166.14	Dorset and Somerset (UKK2)	6	4
Iceland	0.73		–	–
Liechtenstein	0.004		–	–
Norway	19.61	Sør-Østlandet (NO03)	20	22
Switzerland (^{1}) (^{2})	15.45	Ostschweiz (CH05)	27	28
Montenegro	:		–	–
Croatia	2.92	Jadranska Hrvatska (HR03)	77	82
FYR of Macedonia	0.39		–	–
Turkey	:		:	:

(^{1}) Switzerland and Malta, hotels only.

(2) Switzerland, regional share, 2005.

Source: Eurostat (online data code: tour_occ_nin2).

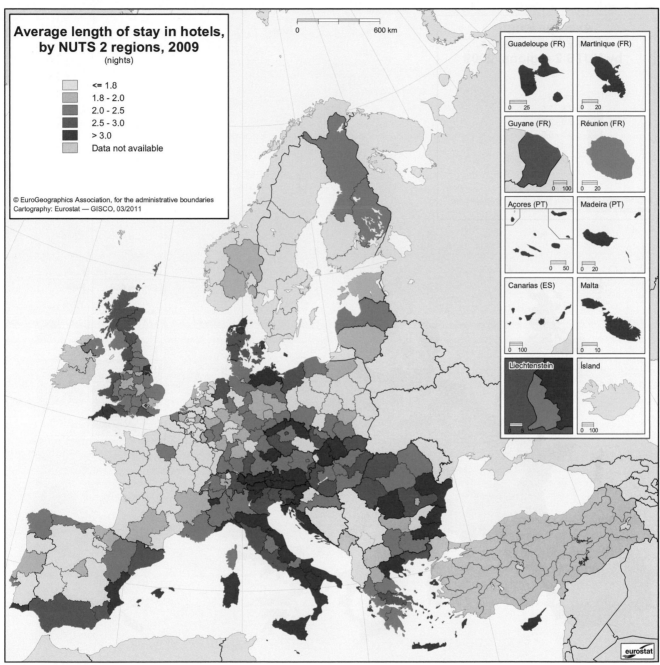

Map 11.5: Average length of stay in hotels, by NUTS 2 regions, 2009
(nights)

Average length of stay in hotels, by NUTS 2 regions, 2009
(nights)

- <= 1.8
- 1.8 - 2.0
- 2.0 - 2.5
- 2.5 - 3.0
- \> 3.0
- Data not available

© EuroGeographics Association, for the administrative boundaries
Cartography: Eurostat — GISCO, 03/2011

0   600 km

Guadeloupe (FR)   Martinique (FR)
0   25   0   20

Guyane (FR)   Réunion (FR)
0   100   0   20

Açores (PT)   Madeira (PT)
0   50   0   20

Canarias (ES)   Malta
0   100   0   10

Liechtenstein   Ísland
0   5   0   100

Source: Eurostat (online data code: tour_occ_nin2; tour_occ_arn2).

Map 11.6: Average length of stay in campsites, by NUTS 2 regions, 2009
(nights)

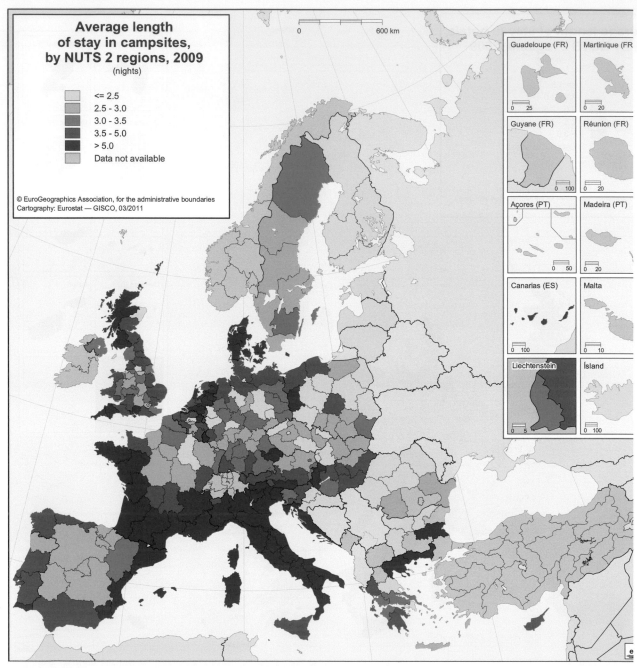

**Average length
of stay in campsites,
by NUTS 2 regions, 2009**
(nights)

- <= 2.5
- 2.5 - 3.0
- 3.0 - 3.5
- 3.5 - 5.0
- > 5.0
- Data not available

© EuroGeographics Association, for the administrative boundaries
Cartography: Eurostat — GISCO, 03/2011

Guadeloupe (FR) Martinique (FR

Guyane (FR) Réunion (FR)

Açores (PT) Madeira (PT)

Canarias (ES) Malta

Liechtenstein Ísland

Source: Eurostat (online data code: tour_occ_nin2 and tour_occ_arn2).

Figure 11.5: EU-27 top 20 regions by accommodation capacity, number of bed places in hotels and campsites, by NUTS 3 regions, 2009
(1 000 bed places)

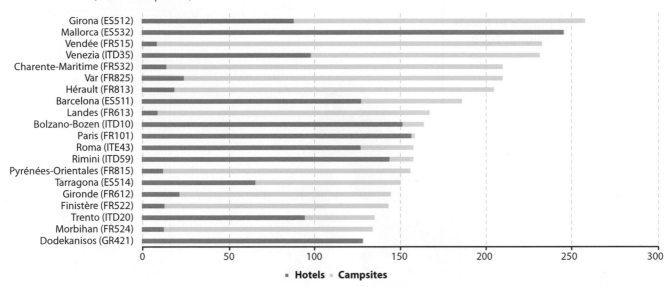

Source: Eurostat (online data code: tour_cap_nuts3).

Mediterranean and Atlantic coast recorded an average length of trips longer than five nights. Long stays in campsite were also recorded in Denmark, the Benelux countries, Austria, Hungary and the United Kingdom.

The number of overnight stays in a region is the product of the number of visitors and their average length of stay. The importance of each of the two factors depends on the nature of the region. For example, urban regions frequently have very large numbers of visitors, but they tend to stay for only a few days. A large proportion of visitors to these regions are often there for professional reasons. But even tourists staying for private reasons tend to opt for short stays. By contrast, stays are generally substantially longer in the typical holiday regions visited chiefly for recreational purposes. Average lengths of stay can also indicate the extent to which tourism is important to a region.

Top 20 regions by accommodation capacity

Ten out of the top 20 regions (NUTS 3 level) ranked according to their accommodation capacity in hotels and campsites were in France in 2009. The other regions were all in Spain or Italy, with one exception in 20th place: the Greek region of Dodekanisos.

Figure 11.5 shows the 20 regions at NUTS 3 level in the European Union with the highest number of bed places, broken down by hotels and campsites. These regions account for 16.1 % of the total number of bed places in all 271 regions of the EU-27 for which data were available.

In these top 20 regions, campsites accounted for 56.3 % of all bed places. The share reached 83.4 % in France.

Accommodation capacity in hotels

Ten regions offer more than 100 000 bed places in hotels: four Spanish regions (Mallorca, Barcelona, Madrid, Málaga), three in Italy (Bolzano/Bozen, Rimini, Roma), one in France (Paris), one in Greece (Dodekanisos) and one in England (Inner London — West).

Map 11.7 gives an overview of the number of bed places in hotels by NUTS 3 regions in 2009. Regions with a high number of bed places in hotels (> 10 000 places) tallied with the regions recording a high number of overnight stays. They were mainly concentrated around the coastal and Alpine regions.

Map 11.8 shows the average number of bed places by NUTS 3 regions in 2009. Big establishments were mainly concentrated in regions of Denmark, other Scandinavian countries and the Mediterranean coast of Spain and also in island regions. As the data collection systems have not been harmonised, the results can be biased and must be analysed with caution. Some countries collect data from all establishments while others only collect data from establishments with a number of bed places above a specific threshold (e.g. 40 bed places for Denmark).

Conclusion

According to the UN World Tourism Organisation, Europe is the most frequently visited region in the world. In 2009,

Map 11.7: Number of bed places in hotels, by NUTS 3 regions, 2009

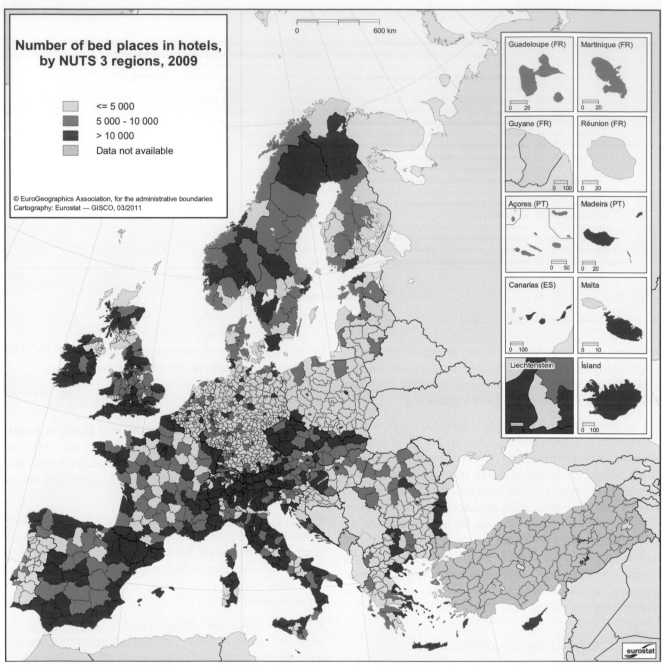

Number of bed places in hotels, by NUTS 3 regions, 2009

- <= 5 000
- 5 000 - 10 000
- > 10 000
- Data not available

© EuroGeographics Association, for the administrative boundaries
Cartography: Eurostat — GISCO, 03/2011

Guadeloupe (FR) Martinique (FR) Guyane (FR) Réunion (FR) Açores (PT) Madeira (PT) Canarias (ES) Malta Liechtenstein Ísland

Source: Eurostat (online data code: tour_cap_nuts3).

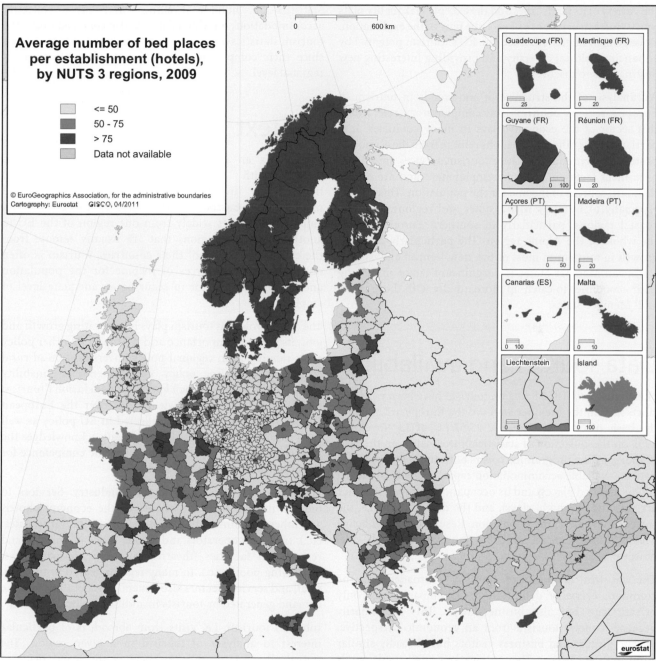

Map 11.8: Average number of bed places per establishment (hotels), by NUTS 3 regions, 2009

Average number of bed places per establishment (hotels), by NUTS 3 regions, 2009

- <= 50
- 50 - 75
- > 75
- Data not available

© EuroGeographics Association, for the administrative boundaries
Cartography: Eurostat   GISCO, 04/2011

0   600 km

Guadeloupe (FR)   0 25
Martinique (FR)   0 20
Guyane (FR)   0 100
Réunion (FR)   0 20
Açores (PT)   0 50
Madeira (PT)   0 20
Canarias (ES)   0 100
Malta   0 10
Liechtenstein   0 5
Ísland   0 100

Source: Eurostat (online data code: tour_cap_nuts3).

five of the top 10 countries for visitors in the world were European Union Member States. The wealth of its cultures, the variety of its landscapes and the exceptional quality of its tourist infrastructure are likely to be part of the explanation. Enlargement hugely enriched the EU's tourism potential by enhancing cultural diversity and providing interesting new destinations to discover.

An analysis of the structure of and trends in tourism in Europe's regions confirms the compensatory role which this sector of the economy plays in many countries. It is particularly significant in regions remote from the economic centres of their country. There tourism services are often a prominent factor in securing employment and are one of the main sources of income for the population. This applies especially to Europe's island states and regions, to many coastal regions, particularly in southern Europe, and to the whole of the Alpine region. The particularly dynamic growth in tourism in most of the 'new' central and eastern European Member States is a significant factor in helping their economies to catch up more rapidly with those of the 'old' Member States.

Data sources and availability

Harmonised statistical data on tourism have been collected since 1996 in the Member States of the European Union on the basis of Council Directive 95/57/EC of 23 November 1995 on the collection of statistical information in the field of tourism. The programme covers both the supply side, i.e. data on available accommodation capacity (establishments, rooms and bed places) and its occupancy (number of visitor arrivals and overnight stays), and the demand side, i.e. the travel behaviour of the population. Results by region below Member State level are available only for the supply side, however.

The statistical definition of 'tourism' is broader than the common, everyday definition. It encompasses not only private trips but also business trips. This is primarily because it views tourism from an economic perspective. Private visitors and business visitors have broadly similar consumption patterns. They both make significant demands on transport, accommodation and restaurant services. To providers of these services, it is of secondary interest whether their customers are private tourists or on business. Tourism promotion departments are keen to combine both aspects by emphasising the attractiveness of conference locations as tourist destinations in their own right and feature these services in marketing activities.

The tourism statistics presented in this chapter cover only 'hotels and similar establishments' and 'tourist campsites'. Statistics on 'holiday dwellings' and 'other collective accommodation', on which data are also collected under the tourism statistics directive, are not included in this analysis since their comparability is still limited, particularly at regional level.

Context

Tourism is an important and fast-evolving economic activity with social, cultural and environmental implications, involving large numbers of small and medium-sized businesses. Its contribution to growth and employment varies widely from one region of the EU to another. In rural regions that are usually remote from the economic centres of their countries, tourism is often one of the main sources of income for the population and a prominent factor in securing an adequate level of employment.

The crucial role that tourism plays in generating growth and jobs, its growing importance and its impact on other policy areas ranging from regional policy, diversification of rural economies, maritime policy, employment, sustainability and competitiveness to social policy and inclusion ('tourism for all') are widely acknowledged all over the European Union. Therefore, tourism is reflected in EU policy as well as in national policies. The Lisbon Treaty acknowledges the importance of tourism, outlining a specific competence for the European Union in this field.

Tourism is a typical cross-cutting industry. Services to tourists involve several branches of the economy: hotels and other accommodation, gastronomy (restaurants, cafés, etc.), transport operators and a wide range of cultural and recreational facilities (theatres, museums, leisure parks, swimming pools, etc.). In many regions geared to tourism, retail and services sectors also benefit considerably from the demand generated by tourists in addition to local demand.

Inbound tourism, i.e. visits from abroad, is of particular interest to analyses of tourism in a given region. The statistically important factor here is the usual place of residence of the visitors, not their nationality. Foreign visitors, particularly from far-away countries, usually spend more per day than visitors from the same country during their trips and thus generate greater demand for the local economy. Their expenditure also contributes to the balance of payments of the country visited. They therefore help to offset foreign trade deficits.

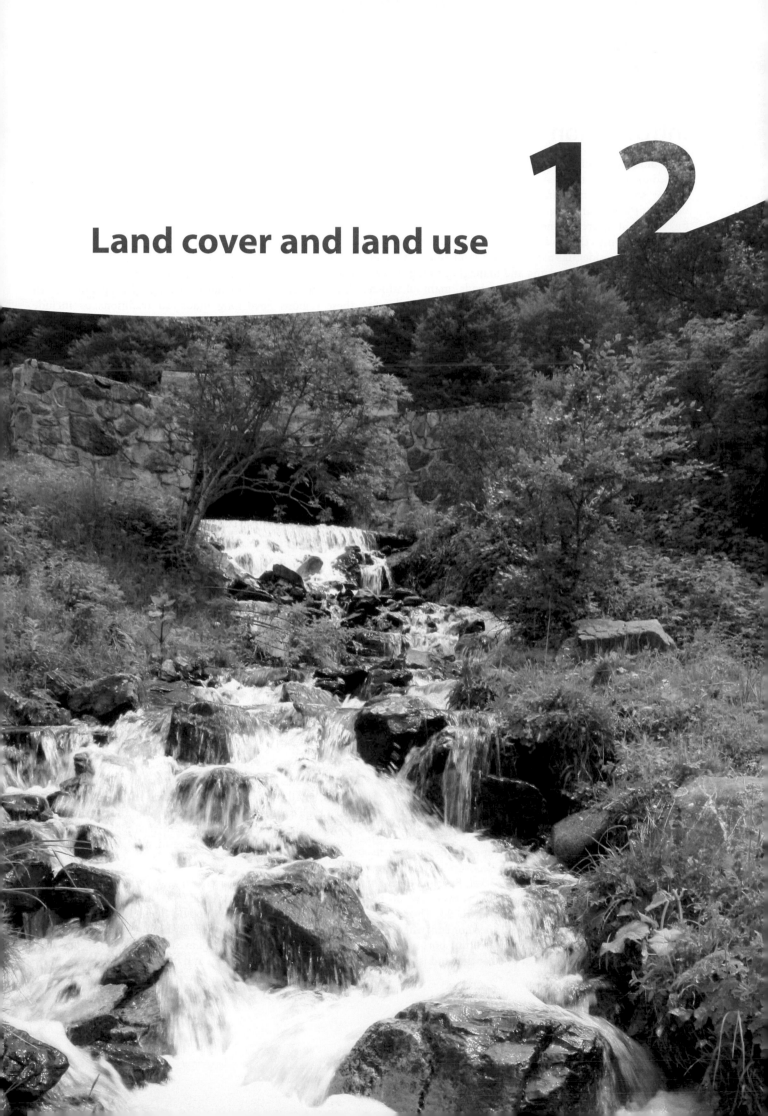

Land cover and land use **12**

Introduction

Most biological and human activities are land-based. Land is accounted for in two ways: as biogeographical land cover and as socioeconomic land use. Land cover indicates the visible surface of land (e.g. crops, grass, water, broad-leaved forest or built-up area). Land use indicates the socioeconomic purpose for which the land is used (e.g. agriculture, forestry, recreation or residential use). Data on land cover and land use are essential for observing and managing a range of key environmental and socioeconomic trends, many of which are linked to the sustainable use of resources and climate change.

In one of its land data collection systems, Eurostat collects land cover and land use data in the field through an area frame survey called LUCAS. It was launched in spring/autumn 2009 simultaneously in 23 EU countries. Bulgaria, Cyprus, Malta and Romania were not covered by the 2009 survey. Field surveyors visited the identified points and collected information on land cover, land use and selected agroenvironmental indicators for 234 700 points distributed among 23 Member States (the EU-23). Landscape diversity was recorded along a 250 m-long line eastwards from each point (the LUCAS transect). Each visit was documented by numerous photographs, which form an important part of the LUCAS dataset, especially in terms of landscape description.

Eurostat has drawn up land use and land cover statistics to NUTS level 2 on the basis of the data collected on these points. The LUCAS microdata for each single point are freely available on the Eurostat website.

This chapter presents regional data on land cover and land use from different perspectives. In addition to data on pure land cover and land use, there are maps that combine land cover and land use and depict landscape diversity analyses.

Main statistical findings

Artificial areas

Artificial areas include built-up areas and unbuilt surfaced areas such as transport networks and associated areas. Artificial areas dominate the landscape in cities and towns. At EU-23 level, 4.3 % of all land is covered by buildings and transport features. At regional level, Europe's diversity becomes evident. Map 12.1 gives an overview of the distribution of artificial areas in the EU-23. The highest share of artificial areas is found in Inner London, where 80 % of land is either built up or devoted to transport networks. Even in Outer London, almost 60 % of the land is artificial.

Many large city regions such as Greater Manchester, Praha, Bremen, Wien, Berlin and Hamburg have between 25 % and 45 % of their land covered by buildings and surfaced areas. These cities appear very compact because NUTS 2 regions are defined as a relatively small area around the city itself, unlike in many other metropolises such as Paris. The actual urban structure also appears to be quite dense.

Outside the large urban agglomerations, the most densely built-up regions are located in the Benelux countries, southern and central England, the Ruhr area in Germany, Attiki in Greece, Northern Italy and Île de France. All these regions have long industrial traditions or include a metropolis with a large number of inhabitants. This has paved the way for dense urbanisation, which is reflected in the high share of artificial areas. Another clearly visible trend is that coastal regions, even at NUTS level 2, are more densely built up and have more transport networks than areas inland, particularly in Spain and France.

The other extreme is northern Finland, Sweden and the Highlands and Islands in Scotland. In these parts of Europe, the share of artificial cover is below 1 % of all land. The Baltic States and large parts of ex-socialist countries in central and eastern Europe are also predominantly rural and sparsely populated.

More than 8.8 % of EU land used for residential, commercial and industrial purposes

An analysis of the socioeconomic use of land gives a more dynamic view. Map 12.2 shows the distribution of industrial, service and infrastructure-related areas and residential land in Europe, with the exclusion of recreational, leisure and sport-related areas.

The socioeconomic use of land reflects to a large extent the physical land cover, but there are some differences. For example, land use for residential, commercial and industrial purposes differs from land covered by built-up and other artificial areas because some areas covered by vegetation and/or water are used for residential purposes (gardens, parks, small ponds, etc.). For these reasons, the same regions have high shares of both artificial land and land used for residential, commercial and industrial purposes. At EU level, 8.8 % of land is used for residential, commercial and industrial purposes.

The most intensively used areas for these purposes are London (89.4 % in Inner London, 72.1 % in Outer London), Région de Bruxelles-Capitale/Brussels Hoofdstedelijk Gewest, Greater Manchester, Praha, Bremen, Wien, Berlin and Hamburg, all of which have over 40 % of the land used for residential, commercial and industrial purposes.

Map 12.1: Artificial areas as share of land cover, by NUTS 2 regions, 2009 (¹)
(in % of the total area of the region)

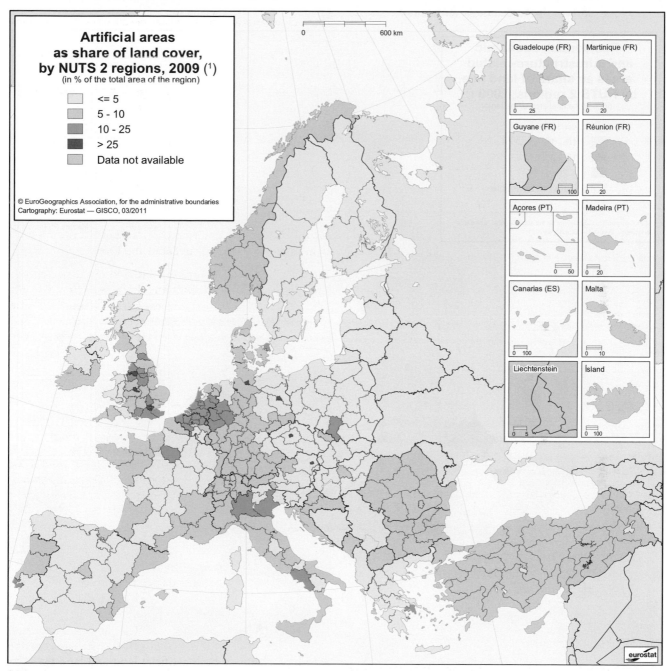

Artificial areas
as share of land cover,
by NUTS 2 regions, 2009 (¹)
(in % of the total area of the region)

- <= 5
- 5 - 10
- 10 - 25
- > 25
- Data not available

© EuroGeographics Association, for the administrative boundaries
Cartography: Eurostat — GISCO, 03/2011

Guadeloupe (FR)   Martinique (FR)
Guyane (FR)   Réunion (FR)
Açores (PT)   Madeira (PT)
Canarias (ES)   Malta
Liechtenstein   Ísland

(¹) Bulgaria, Cyprus, Malta and Romania were not included in the LUCAS 2009 survey.

Source: Eurostat (online data code: lan_lcv_art).

Map 12.2: Residential, economic and infrastructure-related areas as share of land use, by NUTS 2 regions, 2009 (¹)
(in % of the total area of the region)

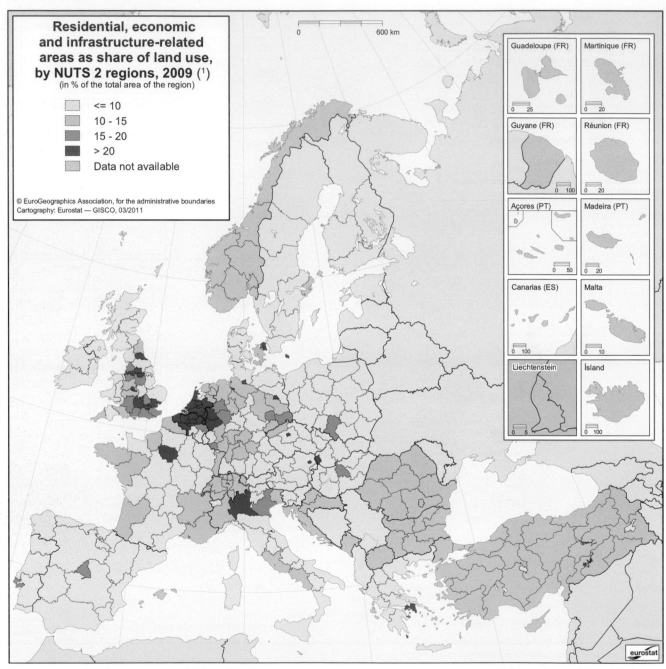

Residential, economic and infrastructure-related areas as share of land use, by NUTS 2 regions, 2009 (¹)
(in % of the total area of the region)

- <= 10
- 10 - 15
- 15 - 20
- > 20
- Data not available

© EuroGeographics Association, for the administrative boundaries
Cartography: Eurostat — GISCO, 03/2011

Guadeloupe (FR)   Martinique (FR)
Guyane (FR)   Réunion (FR)
Açores (PT)   Madeira (PT)
Canarias (ES)   Malta
Liechtenstein   Ísland

(¹) Bulgaria, Cyprus, Malta and Romania were not included in the LUCAS 2009 survey.

Source: Eurostat (online data code: lan_lu_ovw).

Cropland covers Europe evenly

Map 12.3 shows the share of land covered by cultivated areas (¹) in the EU-23 countries. Cropland represents more than an eighth of the total area in most parts of Europe (although with different concentrations), with the only exceptions being very remote areas (northern regions in Finland, Sweden, United Kingdom and Ireland), large cities and mountainous areas.

The largest share of cultivated areas (between 45 % and 68 % of the NUTS 2 regions) is in regions of eastern and central European countries, such as Hungary, the Czech Republic and Poland, where very large collective farming is still practised, in northern parts of France (Picardie, Nord - Pas-de-Calais, Haute- and Basse-Normandie and Poitou-Charentes), eastern England, some regions of Germany (Leipzig, Sachsen-Anhalt, Hannover), Puglia and Sicilia in Italy and Denmark. All these regions have fertile lands and a long tradition of agriculture, which explains the significant share of croplands.

Grasslands maintain Europe's livestock farming

Map 12.4 shows the grasslands used for agricultural purposes. They are mainly concentrated in regions with less fertile soils and where forests have been either cut during the past centuries to fuel economic growth or disappeared due to climate factors. This is the case in Ireland, most of the United Kingdom (except eastern parts) and the Netherlands. Grassland used for agricultural purposes directly reflects the intensity of livestock farming. In France, the cheese and meat-producing regions of Auvergne and Limousin are very heavily dominated by grassland.

Areas with a relatively low share of grassland in agricultural use are located in harsher climate conditions, some in northern and others in southern Europe. In Greece and in eastern and southern Spain (Andalucía, Comunidad Valenciana, Cataluña and Région de Murcia), the climate is too arid for natural grasslands. The land is dominated more by shrubs. Finland and Sweden have very few agricultural grasslands.

Forests and woodlands dominate the European landscape

Woodlands are the most common land cover type in Europe with a 39 % share, covering over 15 % of the land in most regions of Europe (Map 12.5). The few exceptions (less than a seventh woodland) include Ireland, most parts of England, coastal areas of the Netherlands and Belgium, Puglia and

(¹) Permanent grass is not included in this category, even when used for grazing, as it is classified as natural cover.

Sicilia in Italy, the island of Kriti in Greece, the north-west costal regions of France (Pays de la Loire, Basse-Normandie and Nord - Pas-de-Calais) and the Hamburg and Schleswig-Holstein regions in northern Germany.

In most regions in Finland, Sweden and Slovenia, more than 50 % of land is covered by woodland. The Baltic States are also dominated by forests. Large forest areas are a typical landscape feature in northern Europe and mountainous regions are usually covered by woodland. Typical examples are all regions in the Alps (France, Germany, Austria and Slovenia), the mountains in Greece, the Apennines (Italy), Pyrénées (Spain and France) and the Ardennes (Belgium). Central and south-western parts of Germany and most of Portugal are also rich in woodland.

European landscapes are diverse

Landscape is composed of the terrain, the land cover texture and visible features, such as trees and buildings. Giving a definition of landscape that describes its status and changes is a challenging task. Landscape is not only a mixture of the above elements but it also stems from perceptions and is scale dependent. The LUCAS data enable regional-level comparisons to be made of specific aspects of the landscape. One is the degree of variation of land cover types. This can be measured by the number of different land cover categories in the LUCAS 250 m transect and summarised using the Shannon Evenness Index (SEI).

As Map 12.6 shows, areas with high diversity are generally found in countries with mountainous or hilly areas. Slovenia, Portugal, Austria, Italy and Luxembourg score highly on land cover variance measured by the SEI. Relatively homogeneous countries, which have a strong dominance of one land cover type, typically have a low SEI value in landscape diversity. Examples are the United Kingdom and Ireland, which are dominated by grasslands, and Finland and Estonia, which are covered largely by woodlands. Countries close to the EU average value of SEI (Germany, Spain, France and Poland) have a balanced mixture with no clear dominant land cover type.

The SEI computed at NUTS level 2 shows that four out of five regions in Portugal rank amongst the top 25 %, as do three out of five Danish regions, six out of nine Austrian regions and eight out of the 11 Belgian regions. In Denmark and Belgium, land cover patches (particularly cropland) seem to be smaller than the European average and they often alternate with other types of land cover. This gives high landscape diversity in these regions. Italy and France are crossed from north to south by a strip of regions with a highly diverse landscape. In Italy, the line mainly follows the Apennine Mountains. In France, a combination of reasons seems to underpin landscape diversity in western regions. In the north (Bretagne), rather diverse land use leads to analogous diversity in the landscape. In the south (Midi-

Map 12.3: Cropland as share of land cover, by NUTS 2 regions, 2009 (¹)
(in % of the total area of the region)

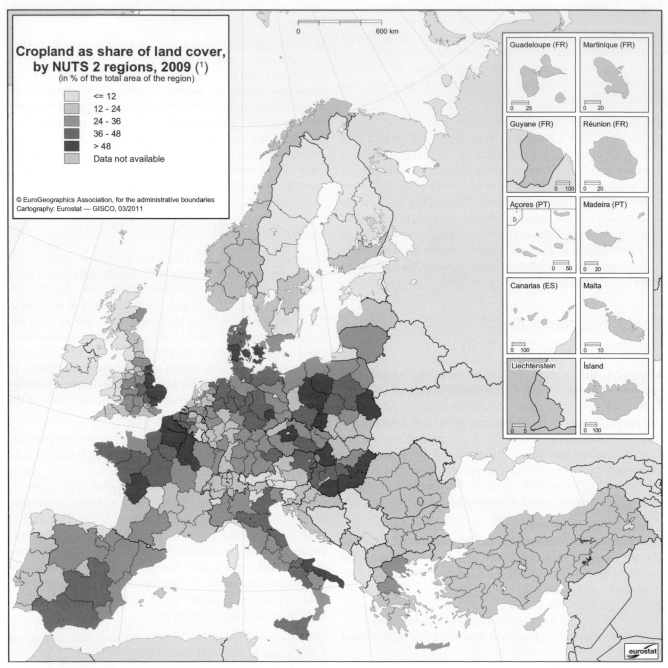

Cropland as share of land cover, by NUTS 2 regions, 2009 (¹)
(in % of the total area of the region)

- <= 12
- 12 - 24
- 24 - 36
- 36 - 48
- \> 48
- Data not available

© EuroGeographics Association, for the administrative boundaries
Cartography: Eurostat — GISCO, 03/2011

Guadeloupe (FR)　Martinique (FR)

Guyane (FR)　Réunion (FR)

Açores (PT)　Madeira (PT)

Canarias (ES)　Malta

Liechtenstein　Ísland

(¹) Bulgaria, Cyprus, Malta and Romania were not included in the LUCAS 2009 survey.

Source: Eurostat (online data code: lan_lcv_ovw).

Map 12.4 Grassland in agricultural use as share of land cover, by NUTS 2 regions, 2009 ([^1])
(in % of the total area of the region)

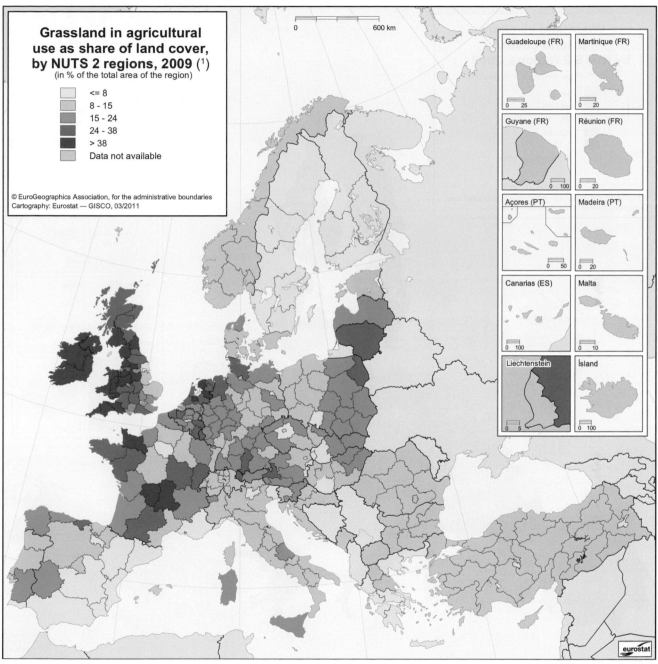

Grassland in agricultural
use as share of land cover,
by NUTS 2 regions, 2009 ([^1])
(in % of the total area of the region)

- <= 8
- 8 - 15
- 15 - 24
- 24 - 38
- > 38
- Data not available

© EuroGeographics Association, for the administrative boundaries
Cartography: Eurostat — GISCO, 03/2011

Guadeloupe (FR) Martinique (FR)
Guyane (FR) Réunion (FR)
Açores (PT) Madeira (PT)
Canarias (ES) Malta
Liechtenstein Ísland

([^1]) Bulgaria, Cyprus, Malta and Romania were not included in the LUCAS 2009 survey.

Source: Eurostat (online data code: lan_lcv_grs).

Map 12.5: Woodland as share of land cover, by NUTS 2 regions, 2009 (^{1})
(in % of the total area of the region)

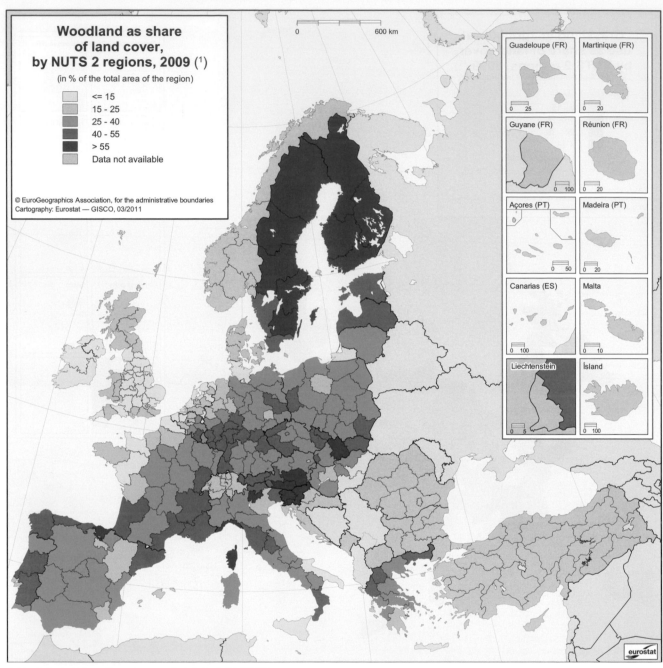

Woodland as share
of land cover,
by NUTS 2 regions, 2009 (^{1})

(in % of the total area of the region)

- <= 15
- 15 - 25
- 25 - 40
- 40 - 55
- > 55
- Data not available

© EuroGeographics Association, for the administrative boundaries
Cartography: Eurostat — GISCO, 03/2011

Guadeloupe (FR) Martinique (FR) Guyane (FR) Réunion (FR) Açores (PT) Madeira (PT) Canarias (ES) Malta Liechtenstein Ísland

(^{1}) Bulgaria, Cyprus, Malta and Romania were not included in the LUCAS 2009 survey.

Source: Eurostat (online data code: lan_lcv_woo).

12

Map 12.6: Landscape diversity expressed as Shannon Evenness Index, by NUTS 2 regions, 2009 (¹)

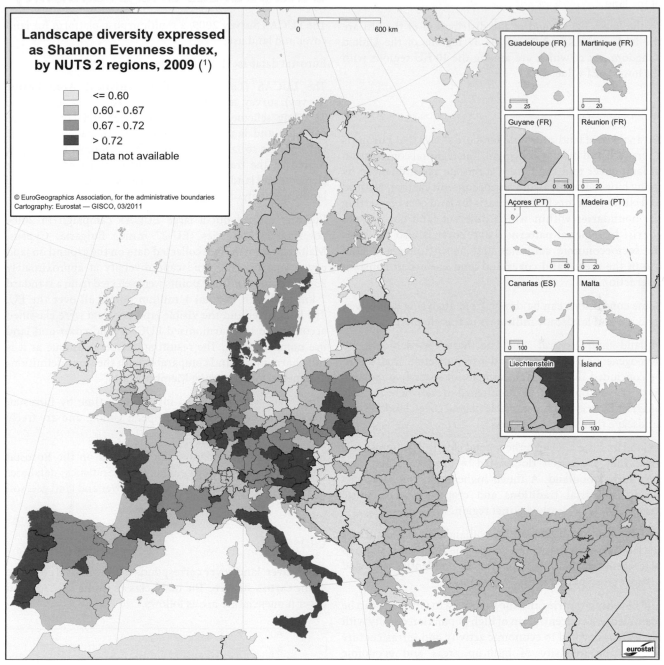

Landscape diversity expressed as Shannon Evenness Index, by NUTS 2 regions, 2009 (¹)

- <= 0.60
- 0.60 - 0.67
- 0.67 - 0.72
- > 0.72
- Data not available

© EuroGeographics Association, for the administrative boundaries
Cartography: Eurostat — GISCO, 03/2011

Guadeloupe (FR) Martinique (FR)

Guyane (FR) Réunion (FR)

Açores (PT) Madeira (PT)

Canarias (ES) Malta

Liechtenstein Ísland

(¹) Bulgaria, Cyprus, Malta and Romania were not included in the LUCAS 2009 survey.

Source: Eurostat (online data code: lan_lcs_sei).

Pyrénées), diversity is more directly linked to the orography of the land.

At the lower (25 %) end of the distribution of the SEI are the Irish regions and 24 of the 37 regions of the United Kingdom, six of which are among the 10 EU regions with the lowest SEI value.

Conclusions

An analysis of land cover and land use shows that Europe is a very rich and diverse continent. The regional composition of land cover and the land use mosaic are influenced by many biogeographical and socioeconomic factors. Natural and climatic factors form the basis for land cover by setting the boundaries within which different land cover types coexist in regional patterns. Land cover is also the basis for socioeconomic activities and hence influences land use in the area. Land cover and land use are in constant interaction.

Some conclusions can be drawn from analysing land cover, land use and landscape indicators in this chapter:

Finland and central and northern Sweden are so homogeneous according to all use indicators that it can be concluded that they are examples of sparsely populated northern European forest-dominated areas where the role of agriculture is much less visible in land cover, land use and landscape than in other regions.

Ireland and the UK form the second clearly distinguishable area. They are largely dominated by grasslands and have very little woodland. A much higher population density, strong industrial traditions and crop-based agriculture make England a clearly distinct region.

The distribution of cropland, woodland and grassland and the landscape diversity of the rest of the analysed area are so heterogeneous that it is more difficult to identify large and distinct cross-border areas.

The Benelux countries and the Ruhr area in Germany can be identified as a concentration of high population density with large areas devoted to economic activity and infrastructure due to the intensity of built-up areas and economic infrastructure and residential use.

Countries in central and eastern Europe have fewer artificial areas and areas devoted to economic infrastructure and services.

Data sources and availability

The LUCAS Survey 2009, a multipurpose platform for land cover and land use.

Eurostat database: LAN.

The **LUCAS (Land Use/Cover Statistical Area Frame Survey)** survey is a field survey based on an area-frame sampling scheme. Data on land cover and land use are collected and landscape photographs are taken to detect any changes to land cover/use or to European landscapes. Moreover, the transect, a 250 m walk along which linear elements and land cover changes are recorded, is used in the landscape analysis.

Eurostat carried out a large LUCAS campaign in 2009, covering 23 countries (EU-27 minus Bulgaria, Cyprus, Malta and Romania). It collected data on the ground on land cover, land use and landscape diversity at approximately 234 700 points ([1]). These points were selected from a standard 2 km grid with in total 1 million points all over the EU. The land cover and the visible land use data were classified according to the harmonised LUCAS land cover and land use nomenclatures. The resulting dataset is unique as it is fully harmonised and comparable with the same definitions and methodology among Member States.

These data were published for the first time by Eurostat, the statistical office of the European Union, and are freely available to users.

More detailed information can be found on the Eurostat website (http://ec.europa.eu/eurostat /Statistics database/ General and regional statistics/Land cover and land use, soil and landscape).

Glossary

Land cover: land cover corresponds to the physical coverage of the earth's surface. The main classes in the LUCAS land cover nomenclature are as follows.

A00	Artificial land
B00	Cropland
C00	Woodland
D00	Shrubland
E00	Grassland
F00	Bareland
G00	Water
H00	Wetland

Land use: refers to the socioeconomic purpose of the land. The main classes in the LUCAS land use nomenclature are as follows.

U110	Agriculture
U120	Forestry
U130	Fishing
U140	Mining and quarrying
U150	Hunting
U210	Energy production
U220	Industry and manufacturing
U310	Transport, communication networks, storage and protective works
U320	Water and waste treatment
U330	Construction
U340	Commerce, finance and business
U350	Community services
U360	Recreational, leisure and sport
U370	Residential
U400	Unused

Transect: the LUCAS 2009 transect is a 250 m straight line going east and stemming from one LUCAS point. Data collected along the transect include the occurrence of land cover types and of linear features recorded in the order in which they are encountered.

Shannon Evenness Index: provides information on area composition and richness. It covers the number of different land cover types (m) observed along the straight line and their relative abundances (P_i). It is calculated by dividing the Shannon Diversity Index by its maximum (h (m)). Therefore it varies between 0 and 1 and is relatively easy to interpret.

$$SEI = SDI / \max(SDI) = -\sum_{i}^{m} (P_i * \ln(P_i)) / \ln(m)$$

Context

Land is the basis for most biological and human activities on the earth. Agriculture, forestry, industries, transport, housing and other services all use land as a natural and/or an economic resource. Land is also an integral part of ecosystems and indispensable for biodiversity, carbon cycle, etc. Therefore harmonised and reliable data and information on land cover/use status and changes are crucial for various policy sectors and stakeholders.

The LUCAS survey is part of the Eurostat work programme. The next survey will take place in 2012.

Coastal regions

13

Introduction

The following chapter depicts the population of European Union coastal regions. It will emphasise the characteristics of these regions, taking into account the country to which they belong and the maritime basin they border. It will also take a special look at the female population of these unique EU regions.

Main statistical findings

EU coastal regions bordering the maritime basins

EU coastal regions (¹) belong to the 22 Member States that have a coastline. They are statistical regions defined at NUTS 3 level with a coastline or with more than half of their population living less than 50 km from the sea. These regions are distributed along oceans and seas bordering the EU coastline. As Map 13.1 shows, EU coastal regions border six main maritime basins: the Baltic Sea, the North Sea, the North East Atlantic Ocean, the Mediterranean Sea, the Black Sea and the outermost regions. However, the outermost coastal regions cannot be really considered as bordering a maritime basin. In these areas, the distance between the regions and their metropolis is the first criterion considered for this group.

Population of the EU coastal regions

In 2008, around 205 million people lived in the EU coastal regions, i.e. 41 % of the EU population or 44 % of the coastal Member States' population. As Table 13.1 shows, the share of the national population living in a coastal region mainly depends on the geographical characteristics of a country, such as the length of the coastline and its configuration. For island states, such as Cyprus, or peninsulas such as Denmark, the share is 100 % because all regions in these countries are deemed to be coastal. At the other end of the scale, 2009 figures show the share of inhabitants of coastal regions was only 5 % in Romania and 9 % in Germany.

The EU population living along maritime basins

The most populated EU coastline is the Mediterranean. As Figure 13.1 shows, in 2009, the coastal regions bordering the Mediterranean housed 36 % of the EU coastal regions' population, followed by the North East Atlantic Ocean coastal regions (30 %). This distribution is linked to the

attractiveness of the area but is mainly impacted by geographic criteria, such as coast length and the number of coastal regions in each basin. In total, 142 EU coastal regions belong to the seven Member States bordering the Mediterranean Sea and only five EU coastal regions in Romania and Bulgaria border the Black Sea.

Structure of the EU coastal regions' population by maritime basins

The structure of the EU coastal regions' population by age and gender shows quite different profiles according to the maritime basin. Figure 13.2 shows the different basins' age pyramids as compared with the age pyramid of the EU population as a whole.

Indeed, as clearly shown by the age pyramid of the EU outermost coastal regions, there was a greater share of people aged less than 40 years in these coastal regions than in the EU population as a whole. This is even more pronounced for people aged under 15 years. The structural difference is mainly due to the age structure of French overseas regions.

By contrast, the age pyramid of the EU coastal regions bordering the Baltic Sea shows an overrepresentation of people aged over 50 years as compared with the EU population as a whole.

The age pyramids also show a structural difference between the genders. In the EU coastal regions bordering the North Sea, there is an overrepresentation of the group including men aged over 40 years as compared with the EU population as a whole. Overrepresentation of this age group among women appears to be less pronounced.

The EU coastal regions population by maritime basins and urban–rural typology

The profile of the population living along the maritime basins also depends on the urban–rural type of the coastal regions bordering each basin. Indeed, the urban–rural type of the EU coastal regions has an impact on the kind of demographic pressure exerted on the coastal area and on socioeconomic issues. There has been a recent revision of urban–rural typology, taking into account the population density observed by grid cells of 1 km² and the population living in contiguous grid cell groups (²).

In 2009, as shown in Figure 13.3, 64 % of the population of EU coastal regions bordering the North Sea lived in predominantly urban regions. This is mainly due to the presence of large cities such as London, Hamburg and

(¹) See definition of EU coastal region in 'Data sources and availability'.

(²) See definition of the new urban–rural typology in 'Data sources and availability'.

Map 13.1: Coastal regions in the European Union, by sea basins and by NUTS 3 regions

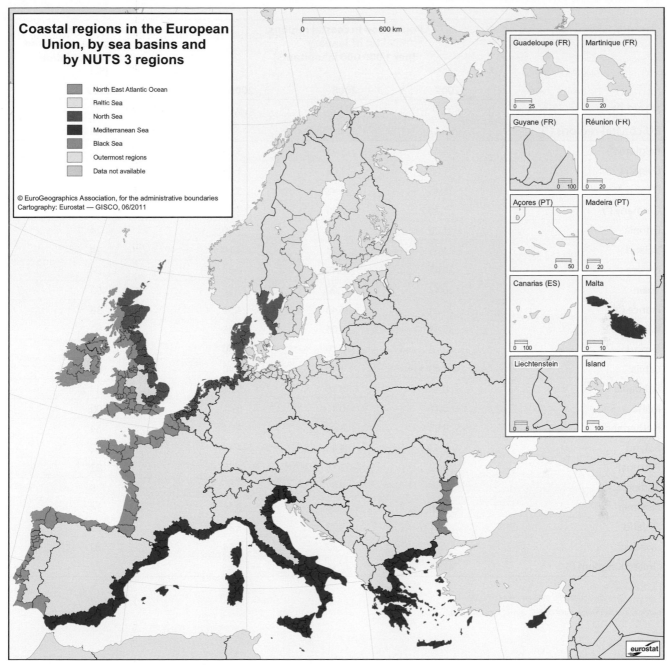

Coastal regions in the European Union, by sea basins and by NUTS 3 regions

- North East Atlantic Ocean
- Baltic Sea
- North Sea
- Mediterranean Sea
- Black Sea
- Outermost regions
- Data not available

© EuroGeographics Association, for the administrative boundaries
Cartography: Eurostat — GISCO, 06/2011

0   600 km

Guadeloupe (FR)   0 25

Martinique (FR)   0 20

Guyane (FR)   0 100

Réunion (FR)   0 20

Açores (PT)   0 50

Madeira (PT)   0 20

Canarias (ES)   0 100

Malta   0 10

Liechtenstein   0 5

Ísland   0 100

Source: Eurostat.

Table 13.1: Population in EU coastal regions by country

	Population in coastal regions, 1st of January (per 1 000 000 inhabitants)			Share of population in coastal regions compared to national population (%)
	2007	**2008**	**2009**	**2009**
EU-27 (¹)	495.3	497.7	499.7	41
EU coastal regions (¹)	203.2	204.7	:	44
Belgium (²)	3.43	3.45	3.48	32
Bulgaria	1.08	1.08	1.09	14
Denmark	5.45	5.48	5.51	100
Germany (²)	7.20	7.20	7.18	9
Estonia	1.00	1.00	1.00	74
Ireland	4.05	4.14	4.18	94
Greece	10.45	10.49	10.54	94
Spain	26.47	27.00	27.32	60
France (²)	24.24	24.40	24.52	38
Italy	35.83	36.06	36.25	60
Cyprus	0.78	0.79	0.80	100
Latvia	1.40	1.40	1.40	62
Lithuania	0.38	0.38	0.38	11
Malta	0.41	0.41	0.41	100
Netherlands	8.83	8.86	8.91	54
Poland	4.43	4.43	4.44	12
Portugal	8.72	8.75	8.77	83
Romania	0.97	0.97	0.97	5
Slovenia	0.28	0.28	0.28	14
Finland	3.31	3.33	3.35	63
Sweden	7.40	7.47	7.54	81
United Kingdom (¹)	47.07	47.36	:	77

(¹) 2008 instead of 2009.
(²) Belgium, Germany and France, estimated data for 2009.

Source: Eurostat (online data codes: demo_r_pjanaggr3).

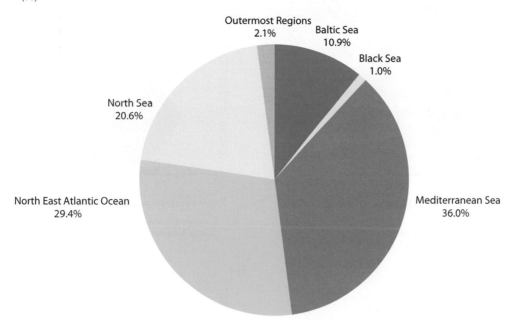

Figure 13.1: Distribution of population in EU coastal regions by maritime basin, 1 January 2009 (¹)
(%)

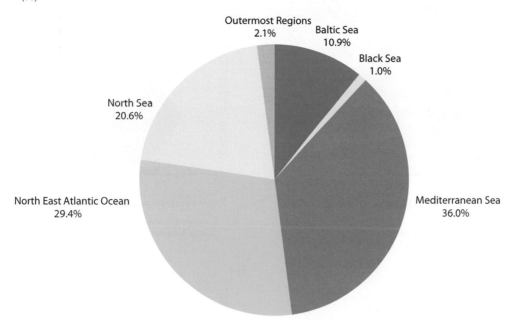

Outermost Regions
2.1%

Baltic Sea
10.9%

Black Sea
1.0%

North Sea
20.6%

North East Atlantic Ocean
29.4%

Mediterranean Sea
36.0%

(¹) United Kingdom, 2008 instead of 2009; Belgium, Germany and France, estimated data.

Source: Eurostat (online data code: demo_r_pjanaggr3).

Rotterdam and the high population density in the Belgian, Dutch and German coastal regions.

By contrast, only 25 % of the population of EU coastal regions bordering the Baltic Sea lived in predominantly urban regions. Although these regions are home to major cities areas such as Copenhagen, Riga, Stockholm and Helsinki, the regions bordering this basin are predominantly rural, especially along the Finnish, Swedish and Estonian coastlines.

The population of EU coastal regions bordering the Black Sea lived in predominantly rural regions (12 %) or intermediate regions (88 %). None of the regions bordering this basin are considered to be predominantly urban. This is mainly a country effect as Romania and Bulgaria house few predominantly urban regions.

Geographic criteria also influence the distribution of the population in these regions. The fact that the majority (72 %) of the population of EU coastal outermost regions lived in predominantly urban regions is linked to the fact that these regions are quite small islands, mainly volcanic, and consequently housing space is limited.

Change in EU coastal regions' population

In 2008, the population of the EU coastal regions increased by 0.6 % or 0.2 percentage points more than in the European Union as a whole. However, there were significant disparities between individual coastal regions and between coastal regions bordering each basin.

Population change or growth is the difference between the number of inhabitants in an area at the end and the beginning of a period. Relative population growth, evaluated here by the crude rate of population growth, has two components: natural population growth (balance between live births and deaths) and net migration. Map 13.2 showing the crude rate of population growth of the EU coastal regions in 2008 can be compared to Map 13.3 showing the crude rate of net migration of these regions in the same period.

In 2008, along the Mediterranean coastline, the crude rate of population growth was usually higher in the EU coastal regions of the western and central coast than in the east. This growth can be explained by net migration. The crude rates of population growth were higher in coastal regions such as the Spanish regions of Almería (27 ‰), the French region of Aude (11 ‰) or the Italian region of Viterbo (16 ‰) where net migration reached 20 ‰ in the region of Almería, 11 ‰ in the region of Aude and 18 ‰ in the region of Viterbo. By contrast, the crude rates of population growth were negative in the Greek region of Lakonia (– 6 ‰) partly explained by the crude rate of net migration (– 2 ‰) and in the Italian region of Napoli, where the crude rate of population growth (– 3 ‰) was deeply impacted by net migration (– 6 ‰). By contrast, in some regions, the trend in the crude rate of population growth went in the opposite direction to net migration, such as in the Greek region of Arkadia where the crude rate of population growth was – 5 ‰ despite a positive net migration (1 ‰).

Figure 13.2: Age pyramids for EU coastal regions by maritime basin and compared to EU-27, 2009

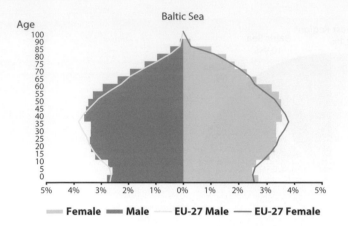

Baltic Sea

Female ▬ Male ▬ EU-27 Male —— EU-27 Female

Source: Eurostat rural development database.

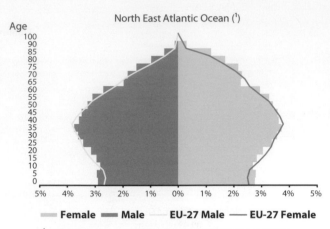

North East Atlantic Ocean (¹)

Female ▬ Male ▬ EU-27 Male —— EU-27 Female

(¹) United Kingdom, data not available; Ireland, 2006 instead of 2009.
Source : Eurostat rural development database.

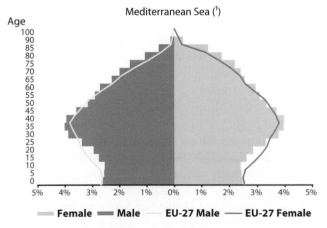

Black Sea (¹)

Female ▬ Male ▬ EU-27 Male —— EU-27 Female

(¹) Romania, data not available.
Source: Eurostat rural development database.

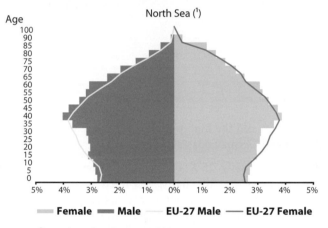

North Sea (¹)

Female ▬ Male ▬ EU-27 Male —— EU-27 Female

(¹) United Kingdom, data not available.
Source: Eurostat rural development database.

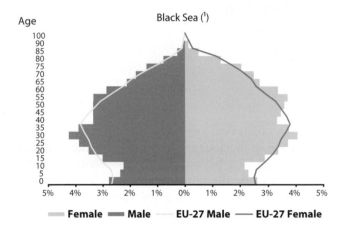

Mediterranean Sea (¹)

Female ▬ Male ▬ EU-27 Male —— EU-27 Female

(¹) Greece, data not available.
Source: Eurostat rural development database.

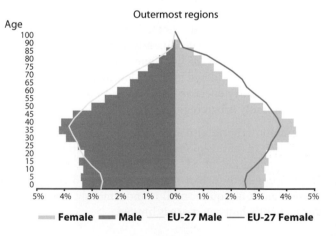

Outermost regions

Female ▬ Male ▬ EU-27 Male —— EU-27 Female

Source: Eurostat rural development database.

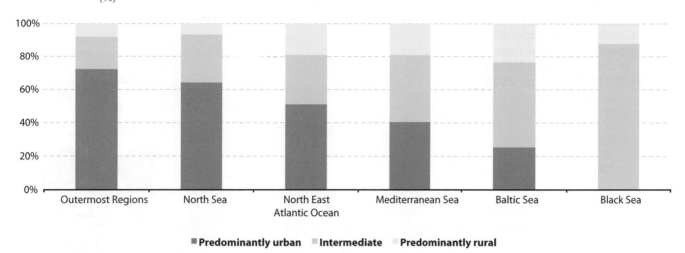
Figure 13.3: Distribution of population in EU coastal regions by maritime basin and urban-rural typology, 1 January 2009 (¹)
(%)

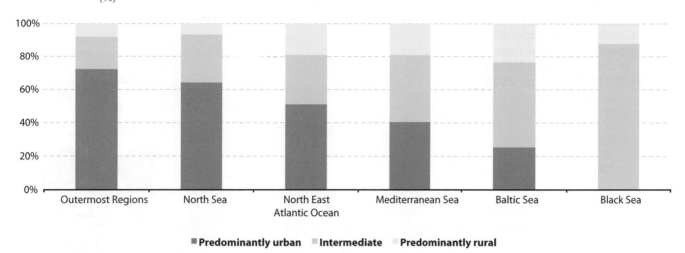

■ **Predominantly urban** ■ **Intermediate** ■ **Predominantly rural**

(¹) United Kingdom, 2008 instead of 2009; Belgium, Germany and France, estimated data.
Source: Eurostat (online data code: demo_r_pjanaggr3).

Along the Black Sea coastline, in 2008, population changes in the coastal regions bordering this basin were rather more even. However, the crude rates of population change varied in the same way as net migration, such as in the Bulgarian coastal region of Varna, where the population grew by (8‰) due to net migration (8‰), and in the Romanian coastal region of Tulcea, where population growth was negative (– 6‰), reflecting net migration (– 3‰).

In 2008, along the North East Atlantic Ocean coastline, the crude rates of population growth were higher in the Irish coastal regions, such as in the Mid-East region (20‰) partly explained by net migration (6‰). The crude rates of population growth were also high along the west French coastline, such as in the region of Landes (11‰), explained by net migration (10‰), and in some Portuguese regions such as the region of Algarve (9‰), explained by net migration (8‰). By contrast, the crude rate of population growth was negative in the Portuguese region of Alentejo Litoral (– 7‰), partly due to net migration (– 2‰). The Spanish region of Lugo bucked this trend with a negative crude rate of population growth (– 4‰) despite positive net migration (4‰).

Along the North Sea coastline, the highest crude rates of population growth were in the English, Belgian and Dutch regions, partly explained by net migration in Belgium and the Netherlands. By contrast, the negative crude rate of population growth in the German regions is also partly due to net migration. However, during this period, in the Dutch region of Delfzijl en omgeving, the crude rate of population growth was negative (– 15‰), explained by net migration (– 14‰), and growth in the German region of Hamburg was positive (9‰), also due to net migration (9‰).

In 2008, along the Baltic Sea coastline, the highest crude rates of population growth were mainly in the predominantly urban regions, such as the Finnish region of Uusimaa (12‰), partly explained by net migration (7‰), the Swedish region of Stockholms län (16‰), partly due to net migration (10‰), and the Latvian region of Pieriga (13‰), due to net migration (14‰).

In 2008, population changes in outermost coastal regions were mixed. In the Spanish coastal region of Gran Canaria, population growth was 13‰ mainly due to net migration (10‰). By contrast, in the French coastal region of Guadeloupe, population growth was 6‰ despite a net migration of – 3‰.

Share of women in the population of EU coastal regions

As Map 13.4 shows, in 2009, the share of women in the EU coastal regions population was fairly even. Along the Baltic Sea coastline, the share of women in the Swedish and Finnish coastal regions was below the EU average, but it was above average in the Latvian, Estonian and Lithuanian coastal regions.

In the same period, along the Mediterranean coastline, there was also a contrast between the Spanish and Greek coastal regions, which had a lower female population, and the French and north Italian coastal regions, which had a higher female population.

The North Atlantic Ocean Spanish coastal regions had a higher share of women than the Mediterranean coastline, and as compared with the EU average.

Map 13.2: Crude rate of population growth in coastal regions in the European Union, by NUTS 3 regions, 2008 (¹)
(per 1 000 inhabitants)

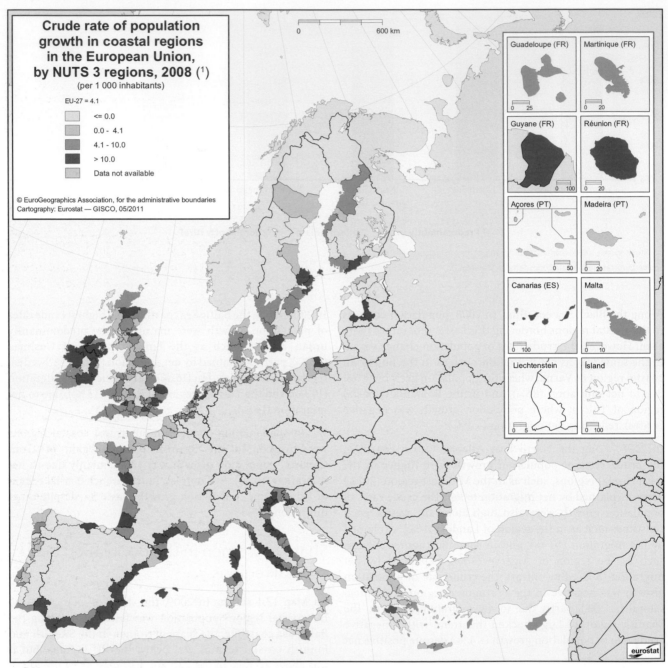

Crude rate of population growth in coastal regions in the European Union, by NUTS 3 regions, 2008 (¹)
(per 1 000 inhabitants)

EU-27 = 4.1

- <= 0.0
- 0.0 - 4.1
- 4.1 - 10.0
- > 10.0
- Data not available

© EuroGeographics Association, for the administrative boundaries
Cartography: Eurostat — GISCO, 05/2011

Guadeloupe (FR)   Martinique (FR)
Guyane (FR)   Réunion (FR)
Açores (PT)   Madeira (PT)
Canarias (ES)   Malta
Liechtenstein   Ísland

(¹) Belgium, Germany, Illes Balears and Canarias (Spain), France and United Kingdom, 2007.

Source: Eurostat (online data codes: demo_r_gind3).

Map 13.3: Net migration (crude rate, including corrections) in coastal regions in the European Union, by NUTS 3 regions, 2008 (¹)
(per 1 000 inhabitants)

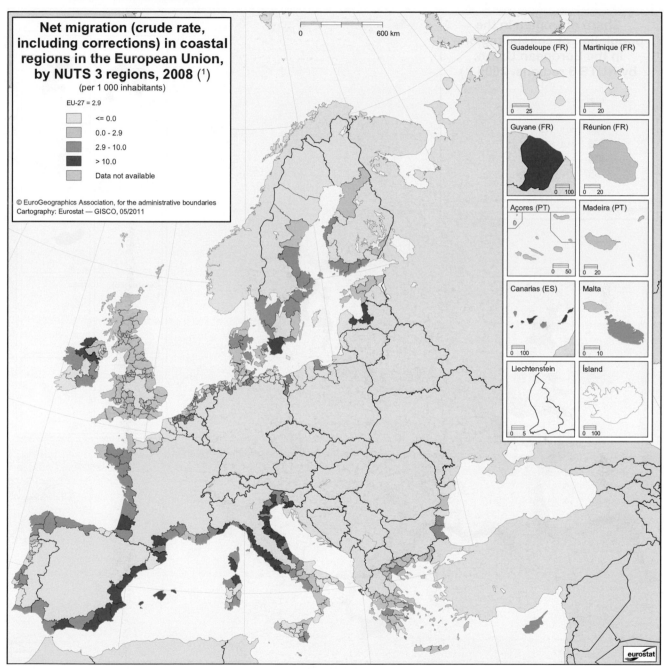

Net migration (crude rate, including corrections) in coastal regions in the European Union, by NUTS 3 regions, 2008 (¹)
(per 1 000 inhabitants)

EU-27 = 2.9

<= 0.0
0.0 - 2.9
2.9 - 10.0
> 10.0
Data not available

© EuroGeographics Association, for the administrative boundaries
Cartography: Eurostat — GISCO, 05/2011

(¹) Belgium, Germany, Illes Balears and Canarias (Spain) and France, 2007.

Source: Eurostat (online data codes: demo_r_gind3).

Map 13.4: Share of women in the population of coastal regions in the European Union, by NUTS 3 regions, 2009 (¹)
(%)

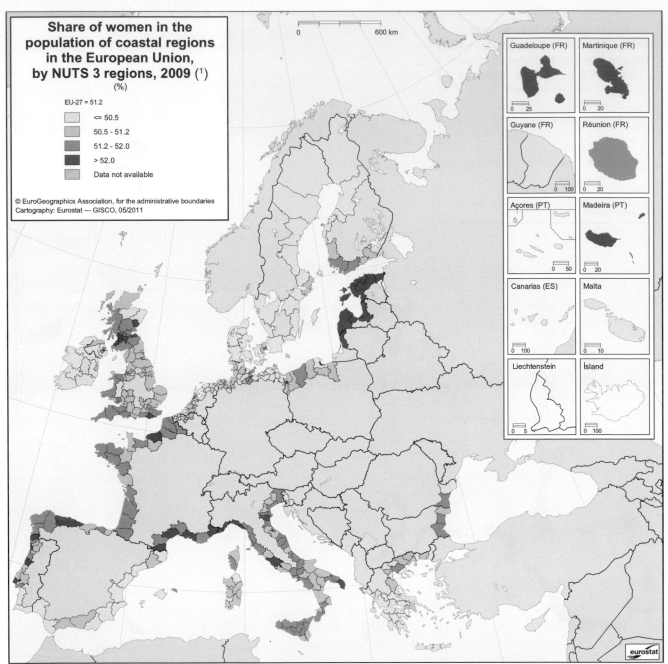

(¹) Population at 1 January; Belgium, Germany and France, estimated value; Illes Balears and Canarias (Spain) and United Kingdom, 2008.

Source: Eurostat (online data codes: demo_r_pjanaggr3).

Active population of the EU coastal regions

In 2009, the active population ([3]) of the EU coastal regions was around 97 million persons, i.e. 41 % of the whole EU active population. In general, the active population grew in the EU coastal regions faster than in the EU. However, the rise in active population differed greatly between countries. Between 2007 and 2009, as Table 13.2 shows, the active population in Germany remained fairly stable, rising from 3 652 000 persons to 3 669 000 persons, giving a 0.2 % average annual growth rate. During the same period, the active population of Malta increased by an annual average rate of 2.1 %.

Share of women in the active population of EU coastal regions

In 2009, the share of women in the active population of the EU coastal regions varied from 33.7 % in Malta to 50.5 % in Latvia. In general, as Map 13.5 shows, the share of women in the active population of the EU coastal regions along the Mediterranean and Black Sea basins was lower than the EU average, except for the Mediterranean French regions and the Spanish region of Barcelona. By contrast, the share was higher than the EU average in the EU coastal regions along the Baltic Sea. The share of women in the active population was more varied in the EU coastal regions along the other maritime basins.

Unemployment in EU coastal regions

In 2009, as shown in Map 13.6, the risk of unemployment ([4]) in the EU coastal regions was no higher than the national average. In 53 % of EU coastal regions, unemployment was lower than the national average. In general, proximity to the sea was not a discriminatory factor. Thus, in the southern and the Mediterranean coastal regions of Spain, the active population was more exposed to unemployment. This was also the case for the southern Italian coastal regions, eastern German coastal regions and French and Spanish outermost coastal regions. By contrast, the majority of the active population of the coastal regions along the North East Atlantic Ocean was less exposed to unemployment.

Female unemployment in EU coastal regions

In 2009, as shown in Map 13.7, the female active population was at greater risk of unemployment, in particular in the

([3]) See definition of active population in 'Data sources and availability'.
([4]) See definition of unemployment in 'Data sources and availability'.

coastal regions along the southern coastlines of France, Spain and Italy, several Greek regions and in the French and Spanish coastal outermost regions. Female unemployment rates can be compared to the share of women in the active population illustrated in Map 13.5. In the coastal regions along the southern Italian coastline and in several Greek coastal regions, the share of women in the active population was below the EU average and female unemployment was higher than the EU average. By contrast, in the Swedish and Finish coastal regions, the share of women in the active population was above the EU average and female unemployment was below the EU average.

Data sources and availability

EU coastal regions: a coastal region of the European Union is a statistical region defined at NUTS level 3 of the geographical nomenclature that has a coastline or more than half of its population living less than 50 km from the sea. The EU has 446 such regions, belonging to the 22 Member States which have a coastline. Of these 446 coastal regions, 372 have a coastline, while 73 meet the second criterion. Lastly, the German region of Hamburg has been added to the list, given the strong influence of the sea there.

The 22 Member States which have a coastline are: Belgium, Bulgaria, Denmark, Germany, Estonia, Ireland, Greece, Spain, France, Italy, Cyprus, Latvia, Lithuania, Malta, the Netherlands, Poland, Portugal, Romania, Slovenia, Finland, Sweden and the United Kingdom.

Urban–rural typology: the typology is based on a definition of urban and rural grid cells by 1 km². Urban grid cells fulfil two conditions: (1) a population density of at least 300 inhabitants per km² and (2) a minimum population of 5 000 inhabitants in contiguous cells above the density threshold. Other cells are considered as rural.

Based on the share of the rural population (i.e. living in rural grid cells), the NUTS 3 regions have been classified into the following three groups:

- **predominantly urban regions**: the rural population is less than 20 % of the total population;
- **intermediate regions:** the rural population is between 20 % and 50 % of the total population;
- **predominantly rural regions**: the rural population is 50 % or more of the total population.

Active population and unemployment: the active population comprises the population in employment plus the population of unemployed. The definitions and references relating to the active population and unemployment correspond to those used in the Labour Force Survey.

Table 13.2: Active population aged 15 years and over in EU coastal regions by country

	Active population in coastal regions (per 1 000 persons)			Share of women in the active population of coastal regions (%)
	2007	2008	2009	2009
EU-27	236 549.5	238 992.0	239 810.2	45.3
Belgium (¹)	1 571.2	:	:	44.8
Bulgaria (²)	495.7	503.3	:	44.8
Denmark	2 913.7	2 951.9	2 952.5	47.1
Germany	3 652.3	3 656.2	3 669.5	45.9
Estonia	526.2	530.6	527.3	49.7
Ireland	:	:	2 047.2	44.1
Greece	4 611.2	4 621.7	4 665.7	41.5
Spain	13 294.8	13 687.5	13 791.1	44.0
France (³)	10 321.0	10 418.8	10 571.1	47.4
Italy	13 990.3	14 172.1	14 005.1	39.1
Cyprus	393.4	397.4	402.6	44.9
Latvia	761.2	771.7	752.7	50.5
Lithuania	176.2	181.3	185.7	50.2
Malta	167.1	170.6	174.2	33.7
Netherlands	4 734.2	4 777.3	4 827.4	46.1
Poland	1 700.2	1 705.7	1 738.3	44.6
Portugal (¹)	4 585.2	:	:	47.0
Romania	416.7	418.6	416.9	38.5
Slovenia	142.4	144.1	142.3	44.8
Finland (²)	1 727.9	1 755.6	:	48.5
Sweden	3 940.9	3 998.8	4 017.6	47.5
United Kingdom (⁴)	20 272.7	22 930.0	24 144.5	46.1

(¹) Share of women calculated for 2007 instead of 2009.
(²) Share of women calculated for 2008 instead of 2009.
(³) France, share of women estimated value.
(⁴) United Kingdom, 2007 excluding Scotland and Northern Ireland; 2008 excluding Highlands and Islands and Northern Ireland.

Source: Eurostat (online data codes: lfst_r_lfp3pop).

Crude rate of population growth is the ratio of total population growth during the year to the average population of the area in question that year. The value is expressed per 1 000 inhabitants.

Crude rate of net migration is the ratio of net migration during the year to the average population in that year. The value is expressed per 1 000 inhabitants.

Context

On 10 October 2007, the Commission adopted the Blue Paper launching an integrated maritime policy for the European Union. The aims of this policy are to maximise the sustainable use of oceans and seas, enhance Europe's knowledge and innovation potential in maritime affairs, ensure development and sustainable growth in coastal regions, strengthen Europe's maritime leadership and raise the profile of maritime Europe. This policy stresses the importance of coastal regions due to their geographic location and aims to develop sea basin strategies.

Map 13.5: Share of women aged 15 years and over in the active population of coastal regions in the European Union, by NUTS 3 regions, 2009 (^{1})
(%)

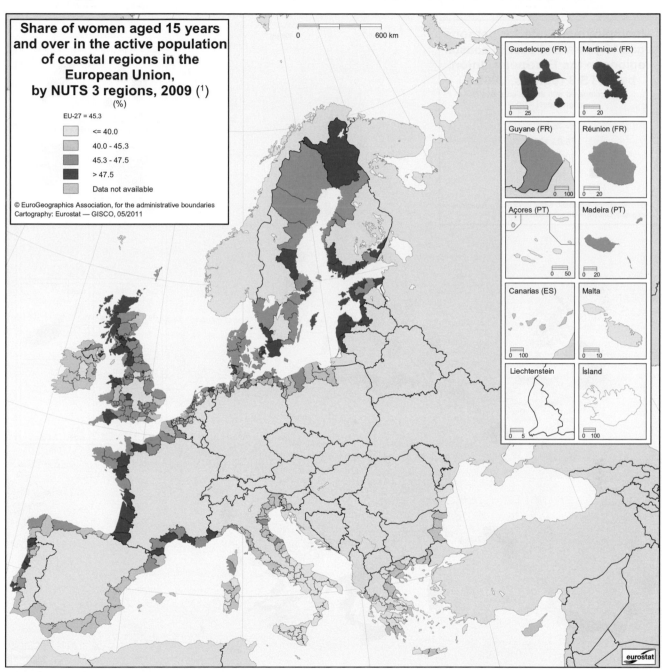

Share of women aged 15 years and over in the active population of coastal regions in the European Union, by NUTS 3 regions, 2009 (^{1})
(%)

EU-27 = 45.3

- <= 40.0
- 40.0 - 45.3
- 45.3 - 47.5
- > 47.5
- Data not available

© EuroGeographics Association, for the administrative boundaries
Cartography: Eurostat — GISCO, 05/2011

Guadeloupe (FR) Martinique (FR) Guyane (FR) Réunion (FR) Açores (PT) Madeira (PT) Canarias (ES) Malta Liechtenstein Ísland

(^{1}) Bulgaria, Malta and Finland, 2008; Belgium, France and Portugal, 2007.

Source: Eurostat (online data code: lfst_r_lfp3pop).

Map 13.6: Unemployment rate for persons aged 15 years and over in coastal regions in the European
Union, by NUTS 3 regions, 2009 (¹)
(as compared with the national level, national level = 100)

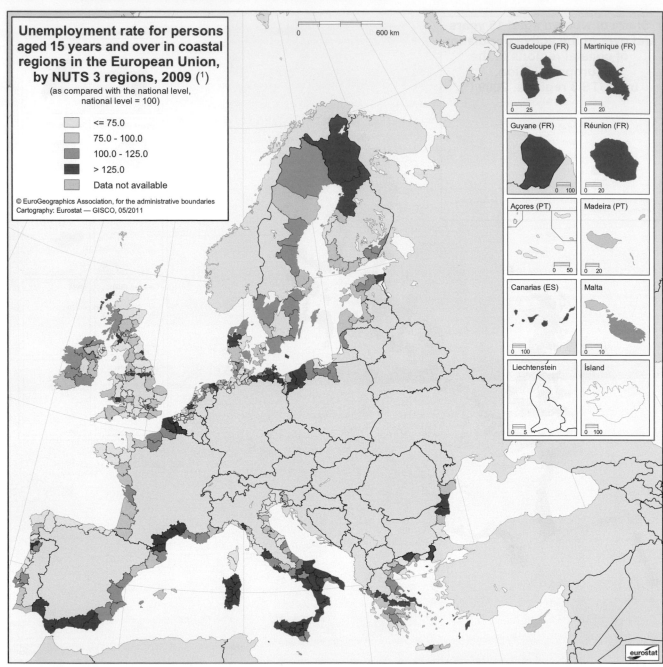

**Unemployment rate for persons
aged 15 years and over in coastal
regions in the European Union,
by NUTS 3 regions, 2009 (¹)**
(as compared with the national level,
national level = 100)

- <= 75.0
- 75.0 - 100.0
- 100.0 - 125.0
- > 125.0
- Data not available

© EuroGeographics Association, for the administrative boundaries
Cartography: Eurostat — GISCO, 05/2011

0   600 km

Guadeloupe (FR)   Martinique (FR)
0   25   0   20

Guyane (FR)   Réunion (FR)
0   100   0   20

Açores (PT)   Madeira (PT)
0   50   0   20

Canarias (ES)   Malta
0   100   0   10

Liechtenstein   Ísland
0   5   0   100

(¹) Bulgaria, Malta and Finland, 2008; France and Portugal, 2007; Belgium, 2006.

Source: Eurostat (online data code: lfst_r_lfu3rt).

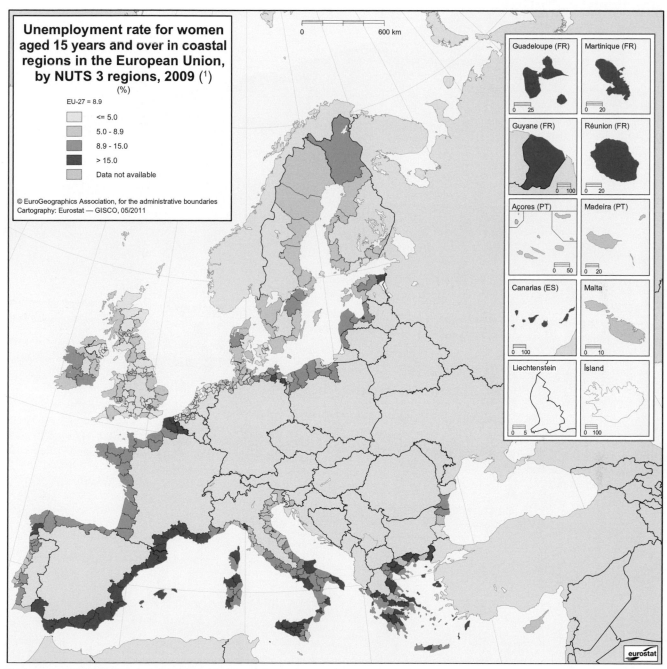

Map 13.7: Unemployment rate for women aged 15 years and over in coastal regions in the European Union, by NUTS 3 regions, 2009 (¹)
(%)

(¹) Bulgaria, Malta and Finland, 2008; France and Portugal, 2007; Belgium, 2006.

Source: Eurostat (online data code: lfst_r_lfu3rt).

Transport

Introduction

Transport policy is at the heart of efforts to reduce regional inequality and improve regional cohesion. The aim of regional transport statistics is to describe regions using a set of transport indicators and to quantify the flows of goods and passengers between, within and through regions. Regional transport statistics show patterns of variation across regions, where transport-related variables are often closely correlated with levels of economic activity.

This chapter is divided into four main sections. The first deals with passenger transport by road in the regions of Europe, studying the motorisation rate (passenger cars per inhabitant) in the regions and the role public transport vehicles (such as buses, trolleybuses and motor coaches) play. It highlights striking differences in the structure of passenger transport by road between regions in the western parts and in the central and eastern parts of the European Union. The second section examines the stock of freight vehicles in European regions and their weight in the total number of road vehicles, revealing regional patterns of transport infrastructure and differences between regions with respect to their economic characteristics and transport systems. The third and fourth sections review the top 20 European regions in terms of passenger and freight transport by air and sea and transport growth between 2003 and 2009.

The data are presented in four topical maps and four tables. The figures are taken from a larger set of regional transport statistics available in Eurostat's databases.

Main statistical findings

Stock of passenger cars, buses and coaches

There are clear differences in the number of passenger cars per inhabitant (known as the 'motorisation rate') within the regions of the European Union. The highest regional rate registered in the European Union was 10 times higher than the lowest.

The highest motorisation rate was in Valle d'Aosta in Italy, which was almost 40 % higher than the next highest region (Flevoland in the Netherlands). Eleven of the 20 regions with the highest motorisation rate in 2009 were in Italy.

Generally, the figures show an east–west divide in the European Union, with more passenger cars per inhabitant registered in western European regions than in the regions of central and eastern Europe. Exceptions were in Denmark, Ireland and Greece (except the Attiki region around Athens),

which had relatively low motorisation rates. In central and eastern Europe, regions with relatively high motorisation rates are found in the Czech Republic, Lithuania and parts of Poland.

Within the European Union, the seven regions with the lowest numbers of passenger cars per inhabitant were all in Romania, with the lowest in the Nord-Est region. These were followed by Peloponnisos in Greece, Vychodne Slovensko in Slovakia and Inner London in the United Kingdom.

The motorisation rates recorded in the European Union are often linked to economic issues. For instance, the top region, Valle d'Aosta, has especially low petrol prices. A number of regions close to larger cities also have a high number of passenger cars, suggesting a larger number of commuters. Examples of this are Flevoland in the Netherlands, Cheshire in the United Kingdom, Lazio in Italy and Attiki in Greece. Several island regions also have high motorisation rates, including Åland in Finland, Illes Balears in Spain, Sicilia in Italy and Corse in France.

The number of passenger cars per inhabitant is calculated on the basis of the stock of vehicles as of 31 December and population figures as of 1 January the following year.

Interestingly, the figures for public transport vehicles such as buses, trolleybuses and motor coaches are in contrast to those for passenger cars per inhabitant. The share of public transport vehicles in the total number of road vehicles for passenger transport also differs clearly between western Europe and central and eastern Europe. The regions in central and eastern Europe record the highest shares of public transport vehicles, which make up a much smaller share in most western European regions.

Out of the 10 European regions with the highest shares of public transport vehicles, five are Romanian, four Bulgarian and the other is Latvian. The highest share is found in Yugoiztochen, the region with the lowest population density in Bulgaria. This is followed by the Sud-Est region in Romania.

The regions in western Europe with the highest shares of public transport vehicles are all found in the United Kingdom. However, there are stark contrasts between these regions: on one hand they are the regions with a low population density, including the Highlands and Islands, West Wales and the Valleys and Cumbria, and on the other hand they are the densely populated urban regions of Inner London and Merseyside.

Generally, the United Kingdom stands out as having high numbers of passenger cars per inhabitant and at the same time a relatively high share of buses, trolleybuses and motor coaches in the total number of passenger road vehicles.

The share of public transport vehicles is calculated per 10 000 passenger road vehicles as of 31 December.

Stock of road freight vehicles

The picture is quite different when looking at road freight vehicles, where no systematic differences can be seen between west and east European regions.

The two regions with the highest number of registered freight vehicles are both located on the Mediterranean Sea: Andalucía and Cataluña in Spain. These two regions play a key role in freight transport in the western Mediterranean, with direct ferry connections not only to the Spanish islands, Ceuta and Melilla, but also from Andalucía to Morocco and Algeria and between Cataluña and Italy.

The region with the third highest number of freight vehicles is Lombardia, with its main city Milan, which is one of the key economic centres of Italy. The geographical position of this region also seems to play a key role in the regional need for freight vehicles: Lombardia, located at the heart of international freight corridors between Italy, France, Switzerland and Austria, registers a very high volume of trans-Alpine freight transport.

The other regions registering more than half a million freight vehicles are all economic centres dominated by the national capital or a major city: Île de France (Paris), Comunidad de Madrid, Istanbul, Mazowieckie (Warszawa), Rhône-Alpes (Lyon), Comunidad Valenciana (Valencia), Oberbayern (München) and Etelä-Suomi (Helsinki).

The share of freight vehicles out of all road vehicles in a region depends on a number of different factors. These include the regional transport system and its infrastructure for different modes of freight transport, such as the capacity of motorways, railway lines, ports and airports. They also include the economic characteristics of the region, i.e. whether the regional economy is driven by manufacturing or services, and whether the region is located on key European freight corridors.

Reflecting these fundamental differences, there are huge disparities in the regional structure of vehicle stocks. The highest regional share of freight vehicles is found in the Nordjylland region in Denmark (38.6 %). This is more than five times higher than in the region with the lowest share, Inner London in the United Kingdom (7.4 %).

The highest shares of freight vehicles are registered in regions in northern Europe: eight of the 10 regions with the highest shares of freight vehicles are located in Denmark or Finland, indicating a large role for road transport in the freight transport systems of these countries. All three regions with the highest shares are Danish: Nordjylland, Syddanmark, and Midtjylland. Next are four Finnish regions (Åland, Pohjois-Suomi, Itä-Suomi and Länsi-Suomi), two Greek regions (Peloponnisos and Sterea Ellada) and a further Danish region (Sjælland).

At the other end of the scale, five of the 10 EU regions with the lowest shares of freight vehicles in all road vehicles are located in the United Kingdom, with Inner London, Outer London and Merseyside (Liverpool) joining Attika in Greece (Athina) and Liguria in Italy in the top five.

Air transport

The rapid growth of air transport has been one of the most significant developments in the transport sector, both in Europe and all over the world. Intra-EU air transport of passengers (including domestic flights) more than doubled between 1995 and 2009. The events of 11 September 2001 stalled growth in 2002, but it rapidly bounced back. The liberalisation of the air transport market in the European Union greatly helped this development, most evident in the expansion of low-cost airlines. This led to the rapid growth of several smaller regional airports, which are less congested and charge lower landing fees than large airports in the capital regions. However, from 2008 to 2009 most airports experienced a sharp decline in passenger and freight transport, reflecting the fall in economic activity and international trade during the worldwide economic crisis.

Eurostat's databases track regional air transport statistics on passengers and freight. The figures show passenger and freight movements by NUTS 2 region, measured in thousand passengers and thousand tonnes. Passenger data are divided into passengers embarking, disembarking and in transit. Freight statistics are divided into tonnes of freight and mail loaded and unloaded.

Currently, data on air transport are collected under Regulation (EC) No 437/2003 of the European Parliament and of the Council on statistical returns in respect of the carriage of passengers, freight and mail by air. This regulation provides detailed monthly data on airports handling more than 150 000 passengers a year. The data collected at airport level are then aggregated at NUTS 2 regional level.

This section on air transport focuses on the total number of passengers and the total number of tonnes loaded and unloaded in NUTS 2 regions in Europe. Tables 14.1 and 14.2 show the top 20 regions with the highest number of air passengers, and the highest volume of air freight and mail in 2009.

The top-ranking regions in terms of the total number of air passengers are the regions that are home to capital cities in western Europe. The list is headed by Île-de-France, with a total of 82.8 million passengers for Paris-Charles de Gaulle and Paris-Orly airports, followed by Outer London (Heathrow) with 65.9 million passengers, Darmstadt with Frankfurt/Main airport (50.6 million), Comunidad de Madrid (47.9 million), Noord-Holland (Amsterdam/Schiphol: 43.5 million) and Lazio with Roma/Fiumicino and Roma/Ciampino airports (38.2 million).

Map 14.1: Motorisation rate, by NUTS 2 regions, as of 1 January 2009 (¹)
(number of passenger cars per inhabitant)

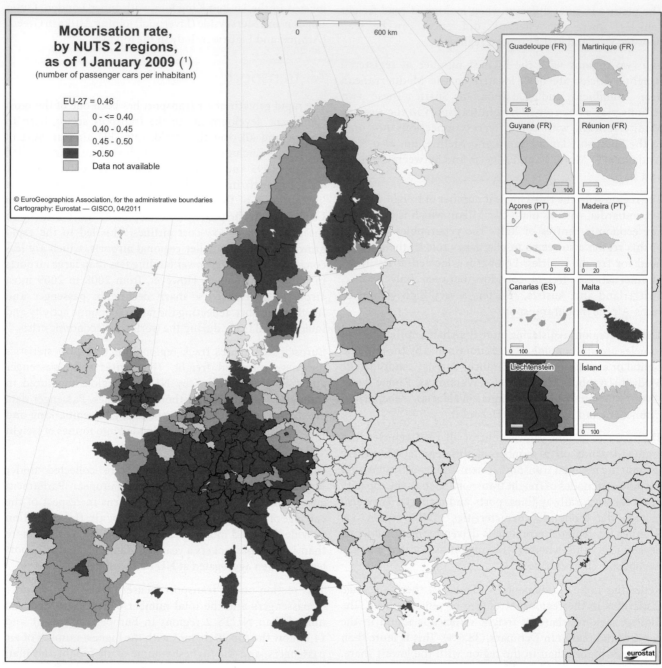

Motorisation rate,
by NUTS 2 regions,
as of 1 January 2009 (¹)

(number of passenger cars per inhabitant)

EU-27 = 0.46

- 0 - <= 0.40
- 0.40 - 0.45
- 0.45 - 0.50
- >0.50
- Data not available

© EuroGeographics Association, for the administrative boundaries
Cartography: Eurostat — GISCO, 04/2011

(¹) Belgium and United Kingdom, 2008 data for population.

Source: Eurostat (online data code: tran_r_vehst).

Map 14.2: Shares of public transport vehicles (motor coaches, buses and trolleybuses) in the total number of passenger road vehicles, by NUTS 2 regions, as of 31 December 2009 (^{1})
(per 10 000 passenger road vehicles)

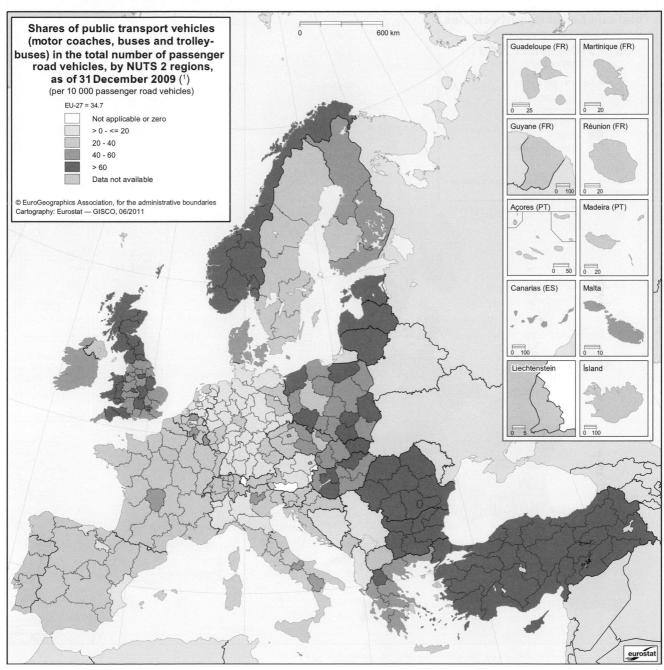

Shares of public transport vehicles (motor coaches, buses and trolley-buses) in the total number of passenger road vehicles, by NUTS 2 regions, as of 31 December 2009 (^{1})
(per 10 000 passenger road vehicles)

EU-27 = 34.7

- Not applicable or zero
- > 0 - <= 20
- 20 - 40
- 40 - 60
- > 60
- Data not available

© EuroGeographics Association, for the administrative boundaries
Cartography: Eurostat — GISCO, 06/2011

0   600 km

Guadeloupe (FR)   Martinique (FR)   0 25   0 20

Guyane (FR)   Réunion (FR)   0 100   0 20

Açores (PT)   Madeira (PT)   0 50   0 20

Canarias (ES)   Malta   0 100   0 10

Liechtenstein   Ísland   0 5   0 100

eurostat

(^{1}) Denmark, data at national level as of 31 December 2008; Ireland, data at national level excluding motorcycles over 50 cm³.

Source: Eurostat (online data code: tran_r_vehst).

Map 14.3: Total number of freight vehicles, by NUTS 2 regions, as of 31 December 2009 (¹)
(1 000 vehicles)

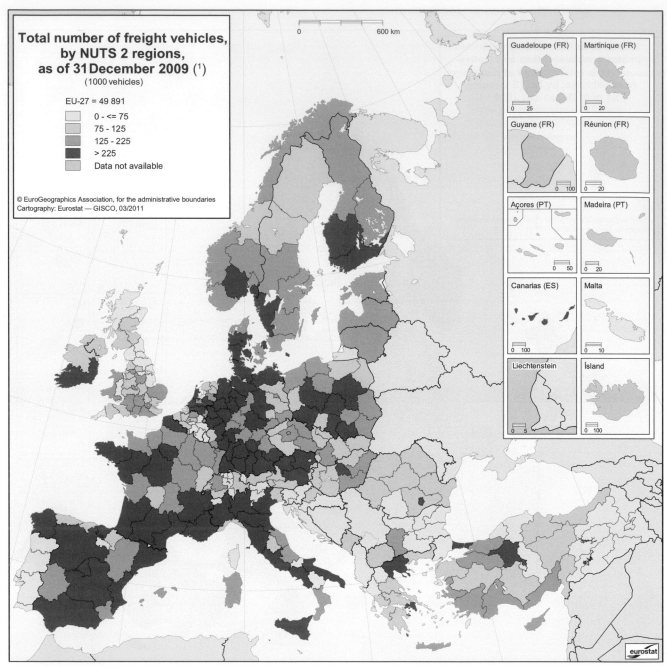

Total number of freight vehicles, by NUTS 2 regions, as of 31 December 2009 (¹)
(1000 vehicles)

EU-27 = 49 891

- 0 - <= 75
- 75 - 125
- 125 - 225
- > 225
- Data not available

© EuroGeographics Association, for the administrative boundaries
Cartography: Eurostat — GISCO, 03/2011

(¹) Denmark, data as of 31 December 2008; Portugal, data as of 31 December 2008, excluding trailers and semi-trailers; Switzerland, data excluding special purpose road vehicles.

Source: Eurostat (online data code: tran_r_vehst).

Map 14.4: Shares of freight vehicles in the total number of vehicles, by NUTS 2 regions,
as of 31 December 2009 (¹)
(%)

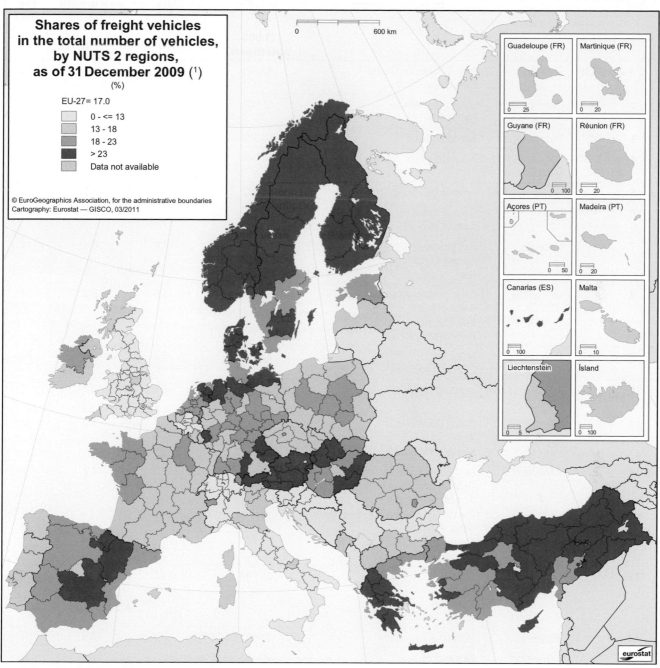

(¹) Denmark, data as of 31 December 2008; Switzerland, data excluding special purpose road vehicles.

Source: Eurostat (online data code: tran_r_vehst).

Table 14.1: Top 20 NUTS 2 regions with highest number of air passengers, 2009

Rank-ing	NUTS	Region	Airports contributing by NUTS 2 regions	Total passengers in 2009 (1 000 passengers)	Growth rate 2008/09 (%)	Average an-nual growth 2003–08 (%)	Rank-ing 2003
1	FR10	Île de France	Paris-Charles De Gaulle Paris-Orly	82 776	-4.5	4.2	1
2	UKI2	Outer London	London Heathrow Biggin Hill	65 904	-1.5	1.1	2
3	DE71	Darmstadt	Frankfurt/Main	50 573	-4.9	2.1	3
4	ES30	Comunidad de Madrid	Madrid/Barajas	47 944	-4.8	7.3	5
5	NL32	Noord-Holland	Amsterdam/Schiphol	43 532	-8.2	3.6	4
6	ITE4	Lazio	Roma/Fiumicino Roma/Ciampino	38 172	-3.5	7.8	9
7	ES51	Cataluña	Barcelona Girona/Costa Reus	34 234	-7.8	8.4	11
8	ITC4	Lombardia	Milano/Malpensa Bergamo/Orio Al Serio Milano/Linate Brescia/Montichiari	32 984	-5.6	3.6	7
9	DE21	Oberbayern	München Oberpfaffenhofen	32 560	-5.3	7.5	12
10	UKJ2	Surrey, East and West Sussex	London Gatwick	32 360	-5.3	2.7	6
11	ES53	Illes Balears	Palma De Mallorca Ibiza Menorca/Mahon	27 515	-6.2	3.0	10
12	ES70	Canarias (ES)	Las Palmas/Gran Canaria Tenerife Sur/Reina Sofia Arrecife/Lanzarote Puerto Del Rosario/Fuerteventura Tenerife Norte Santa Cruz De La Palma Hierro	26 223	-12.0	1.2	8
13	IE02	Southern and Eastern	Dublin Cork Shannon Kerry	25 540	-12.6	8.0	13
14	CH04	Zürich	Zürich	21 911	-0.7	5.5	17
15	DEA1	Düsseldorf	Düsseldorf Mönchengladbach Essen-Mülheim Niederrhein	20 115	2.5	6.7	22
16	UKH3	Essex	London Stansted Southend	19 953	-10.9	3.6	15
17	DK01	Hovedstaden	Kobenhavn/Kastrup Bornholm	19 609	-9.6	4.2	16
18	UKD3	Greater Manchester	Manchester	18 630	-11.5	1.5	14

Rank-ing	NUTS	Region	Airports contributing by NUTS 2 regions	Total passengers in 2009 (1 000 passengers)	Growth rate 2008/09 (%)	Average annual growth 2003–08 (%)	Rank-ing 2003
19	ES61	Andalucia	Malaga Sevilla Jerez Granada Almeria	18 592	-10.4	5.6	19
20	NO01	Oslo og Akershus	Oslo/Gardermoen Kjeller	18 183	-1.9	8.0	24

Source: Eurostat (online data codes: tran_r_avpa_nm).

The big airports in and around western Europe's capitals also serve as central hubs for intercontinental air traffic. This is especially true for Heathrow (London), Charles de Gaulle (Paris), Frankfurt/Main and Schiphol (Amsterdam) airports.

Although this is not visible from Table 14.1, a significant number of smaller regional airports are among the fastest growing, due to the success of low-cost carriers using them as their main hubs.

Düsseldorf was the only one of the top 20 airports for passenger transport to record an increase in passenger numbers between 2008 and 2009. Zürich, Outer London (Heathrow) and Oslo og Akershus (Gardermoen) had the lowest losses in passenger numbers, with less than 2 %. The other top 20 regions for air passenger transport faced losses of more than 3.5 %, with the highest losses in the Canarias (– 12 %) and Southern and Eastern Ireland (Dublin, Cork and Shannon, – 12.6 %). By contrast, all of the top 20 regions recorded positive average annual growth over the previous five-year period.

For air freight and mail, Darmstadt (Frankfurt/Main) leads the top 20 European regions with 1.88 million tonnes, followed by Outer London (Heathrow: 1.35 million tonnes), Noord-Holland (Amsterdam/Schiphol: 1.32 million tonnes) and Île-de-France (Paris: 1.27 million tonnes). Volumes at other European airports are significantly lower, indicating that the biggest European airports serve as the main European hubs for air freight and mail. Relatively high volumes can also be observed in Luxembourg (0.63 million tonnes), Köln (Köln-Bonn: 0.55 million tonnes), Leipzig/Halle (0.51 million tonnes) and Lombardia (Milano/Bergamo/Brescia: 0.50 million tonnes).

While the total volume of air freight is limited compared with the much higher volumes of freight transported by road, rail, inland waterways and especially sea, air freight is important and growing steadily for articles with high added value, perishable goods (especially food) and express parcels.

Air freight volumes fell even further than the volume of air passengers from 2008 to 2009, with 10 of the top 20 regions for air freight and mail transport recording losses of 10 % or more. The only regions in the top 20 to record an increase over this period were Leipzig/Halle (+ 18.4 %) and Province de Liège (+ 5.2 %). Much of the increase in Leipzig/Halle can be explained by a major international express mail company moving its European hub from Brussels to Leipzig/Halle in the middle of 2008. Correspondingly, the air freight volume for Vlaams-Brabant (Bruxelles) fell by 40.7 % in this period. Hovedstaden (København/Kastrup) also experienced a dramatic fall, with 38.5 % less air freight handled in 2009 than in 2008.

Maritime transport

The number of passengers embarking or disembarking in EU ports fell slightly (– 2.2 %) in 2009, after remaining stable over the previous five-year period. However, the volume of freight handled in EU ports dropped by 12.5 % in 2009, after growing by more than 13 % over the previous five-year period. Despite this fall, maritime transport plays an important role in transporting goods in extra-EU trade. The geographical spread of the main European seaports illustrates the flexibility of maritime transport, allowing large volumes to be loaded and unloaded close to the main recipients and producers. Landlocked Member States (Czech Republic, Luxembourg, Hungary, Austria and Slovakia) are not active in this sector.

Eurostat's databases contain regional maritime transport statistics on passengers and freight. They show passenger and freight movements by NUTS 2 region, measured in thousand passengers and tonnes. Passenger data are divided into passengers embarking and disembarking. Freight statistics are divided into tonnes of freight loaded and unloaded. Two series are available on maritime passenger transport, based on different methods. One series started in 1997 and ended in 2003 and was replaced by a new time series with different definitions in 2004 (now excluding passengers on cruises).

Table 14.2: Top 20 NUTS 2 regions with highest volume of air freight and mail, 2009
(1 000 tonnes of total freight and mail loaded and unloaded)

Rank-ing	NUTS	Region	Airports contributing by NUTS 2 regions	Total freight and mail in 2009 (1 000 tonnes)	Growth rate 2008/09 (%)	Average an-nual growth 2003–08 (%)	Rank-ing 2003
1	DE71	Darmstadt	Frankfurt/Main	1 883	-10.5	5.1	1
2	UKI2	Outer London	London Heathrow	1 349	-9.0	2.7	3
3	NL32	Noord-Holland	Amsterdam/Schiphol	1 317	-17.3	3.3	2
4	FR10	Île de France	Paris-Charles De Gaulle Paris/Orly	1 266	-13.5	2.8	4
5	LU00	Luxembourg	Luxembourg	627	-20.4	5.5	6
6	DEA2	Köln	Köln/Bonn Bonn-Hangelar	549	-4.4	1.6	7
7	DED3	Leipzig	Leipzig/Halle	509	18.4	93.1	58
8	ITC4	Lombardia	Milano/Malpensa Bergamo/Orio Al Serio Milano/Linate Brescia/Montichiari	496	-15.2	4.4	8
9	BE33	Prov. Liège	Liege/Bierset	402	5.2	:	:
10	BE24	Prov. Vlaams Brabant	Bruxelles/National	364	-40.7	0.2	5
11	ES30	Comunidad de Madrid	Madrid/Barajas	330	-7.0	3.7	9
12	UKF2	Leicestershire, Rutland and Northants	Nottingham East Midlands	287	-1.7	4.3	11
13	CH04	Zürich	Zürich	259	-8.2	1.6	10
14	DE21	Oberbayern	München Oberpfaffenhofen	234	-11.7	10.2	15
15	UKH3	Essex	London Stansted Southend	213	-7.4	2.5	13
16	AT12	Niederösterreich	Wien-Schwechat	198	-1.5	9.6	17
17	ITE4	Lazio	Roma/Fiumicino Roma/Ciampino	156	-9.8	-1.1	14
18	DK01	Hovedstaden	Kobenhavn/Kastrup) Bornholm	152	-38.5	:	:
19	FI18	Etelä-Suomi	Helsinki-Vantaa Turku Lappeenranta Utti Helsinki-Malmi Immola	126	-13.7	10.7	20
20	IE02	Southern and Eastern	Dublin Shannon Cork Kerry	112	-11.8	24.8	35

Source: Eurostat (online data code: tran_r_avgo_nm).

Table 14.3: Top 20 NUTS 2 regions with highest number of maritime passengers, 2009
(1 000 passengers carried)

Rank-ing	NUTS	Region	Ports contributing by NUTS 2 regions		Total pas-sengers in 2009 (1 000 passengers)	Growth rate 2008/09 (%)	Average annual growth 2003–08 (%)	Rank-ing 2003
1	GR30	Attiki	Eleusina Lavrio Megara Paloukia Salaminas	Perama Pireus Rio	30 228	-3.9	-4.6	1
2	ITG1	Sicilia	Augusta Catania Gela Lipari Milazzo	Messina Palermo Pozzallo Santa Panagia Trapani	13 816	-7.3	1.4	7
3	SE22	Sydsverige	Helsingborg Karlskrona Karlshamn Malmö	Sölvesborg Trelleborg Ystad	13 304	-11.1	-0.9	3
4	UKJ4	Kent	Dover Medway	Ramsgate	13 238	-5.5	-1.2	4
5	HR03	Jadranska Hrvatska	Bakar Biograd na Moru Bol Cres Dubrovnik - Gruž Hvar - passenger port Jablanac Korcula Krk Makarska Novalja Omišalj Ploce Porec - passenger port Preko - passenger port	Pula Rab Rijeka - basin Raša - Bršica Rabac Rogac Rijeka Stari Grad Šibenik Split Sucuraj - passenger port Supetar Vodice Vis - passenger port Zadar - passenger port	12 964	3.1	:	:
6	FR30	Nord - Pas-de-Calais	Calais	Dunkerque	12 947	-6.2	-0.7	6
7	FI18	Etelä-Suomi	Helsinki Hanko Hamina Inkoo Kotka Koverhar	Loviisa Naantali Parainen Sköldvik Turku Uusikaupunki	12 676	0.7	0.0	8
8	ITF3	Campania	Napoli	Salerno	12 533	5.8	0.7	10
9	SE11	Stockholm	Bergs Oljehamn Kappelskär	Nynäshamn (ports) Stockholm	12 242	3.4	1.9	11
10	DK01	Hovedstaden	Avedøreværkets Havn Københavns Havn Helsingør (Elsinore) Rønne	Frederiskværk Havn (Frederiksværk Stålvalseværk)	12 000	-11.9	-1.3	5

Rank-ing	NUTS	Region	Ports contributing by NUTS 2 regions		Total pas-sengers in 2009 (1 000 passengers)	Growth rate 2008/09 (%)	Average annual growth 2003–08 (%)	Rank-ing 2003
11	DEF0	Schleswig-Holstein	Föhr I. Amrum I. Brunsbüttel Büsum Dagebüll Helgoland I. List/Sylt	Nordstrand, Insel Pellworm I. Flensburg Kiel Lübeck Puttgarden	11 449	-3.1	1.9	12
12	DK02	Sjælland	Asnæsværkets Havn Gedser Kalundborg Køge	Rødby (Færgehavn) Stigsnæsværkets Havn Statoil-Havnen	11 162	-7.1	0.4	9
13	ITF6	Calabria	Gioia Tauro		11 047	9.2	0.8	13
14	ITG2	Sardegna	Cagliari Olbia Porto Foxi	Porto Torres Portovesme Oristano	10 271	3.7	2.8	14
15	ITE1	Toscana	Livorno Marina Di Carrara	Piombino	8 374	-9.2	8.2	17
16	GR42	Notio Aigaio	Milos Island	Rhodes	8 027	-4.4	10.4	20
17	EE00	Eesti	Kunda Miiduranna Pärnu	Tallinn Vene-Balti	6 841	-0.4	5.8	19
18	ES61	Andalucia	Málaga Algeciras Cádiz	Huelva Almería Sevilla	6 078	-5.2	0.4	15
19	DE94	Weser-Ems	Wangerooge I. Bensersiel Brake Borkum I. Baltrum I. Carolinensiel Emden Juist	Langeoog, Insel Nordenham Neuharlingersiel Norddeich Norderney I. Spieckeroog I. Wilhelmshaven	5 677	10.2	3.9	21
20	DK05	Nordjylland	Aalborg Frederikshavn Hirtshals	Aalborg Portland (Cementfabrikken Rordal)	4 879	-6.2	-3.6	16

Source: Eurostat (online data code: tran_r_mapa_nm).

Table 14.4: Top 20 NUTS 2 regions with highest volume of maritime goods, 2009
(1 000 tonnes of total goods loaded and unloaded)

Ranking	NUTS	Region	Ports contributing by NUTS 2 regions	Total goods in 2009 (1 000 tonnes)	Growth rate 2008/09 (%)	Average annual growth 2003–08 (%)	Ranking 2003
1	NL33	Zuid-Holland	Dordrecht Rotterdam Scheveningen Vlaardingen Zwijndrecht	349 303	-10.7	4.4	1
2	BE21	Prov. Antwerpen	Antwerpen	142 116	-17.0	6.3	2
3	DE60	Hamburg	Hamburg	94 762	-20.3	4.9	3
4	FR23	Haute-Normandie	Dieppe Le Havre Rouen	92 213	-7.2	2.0	5
5	ES61	Andalucia	Málaga Algeciras Cádiz Huelva Almería Sevilla	83 366	-14.7	2.8	6
6	NL32	Noord-Holland	Amsterdam Den Helder Velsen/Ijmuiden Zaanstad	82 561	-15.8	10.5	13
7	FR82	Provence-Alpes-Côte d'Azur	Marseille Toulon	80 887	-13.1	0.1	4
8	UKE1	East Yorkshire and Northern Lincolnshire	Trent River River Hull & Humber Goole Hull Immingham	76 676	-15.7	2.4	8
9	ITC3	Liguria	Genova La Spezia Savona - Vado	73 170	-8.2	1.8	10
10	NO05	Vestlandet	Ålesund Bergen, Mongstad, Sture, Ågotnes, Eikefet, Askøy, Modalen Bremanger Florø/Flora Kristiansund N/Grip Måløy	71 023	3.0	-3.0	9
11	ITG1	Sicilia	Augusta Catania Gela Lipari Milazzo Messina Pozzallo Santa Panagia Trapani	69 212	-15.8	-0.4	7
12	ES51	Cataluña	Barcelona Tarragona	68 677	-6.7	4.8	15

Rank-ing	NUTS	Region	Ports contributing by NUTS 2 regions	Total goods in 2009 (1 000 tonnes)	Growth rate 2008/09 (%)	Average an-nual growth 2003–08 (%)	Rank-ing 2003
13	SE23	Västsverige	Brofjorden Preemraff Göteborg Halmstad Stenungsund (Ports) Uddevalla Varberg	64 271	-7.3	3.5	14
14	ES52	Comunidad Valenciana	Alicante Castellón Valencia	61 388	-6.8	8.6	27
15	LV00	Latvia	Liepaja Riga Ventspils	58 569	-2.3	2.2	18
16	FI18	Etelä-Suomi	Helsinki Hanko Hamina Inkoo Kotka Koverhar Loviisa Naantali Parainen Sköldvik Turku Uusikaupunki	56 863	-18.5	1.9	11
17	FR30	Nord - Pas-de-Calais	Calais Dunkerque	56 836	-17.8	2.0	12
18	ITG2	Sardegna	Cagliari Olbia Porto Foxi Porto Torres Portovesme Oristano	54 130	-11.5	5.3	23
19	DE50	Bremen	Bremen, Blumenthal Bremerhaven	53 941	-15.1	8.4	29
20	ITF4	Puglia	Brindisi Barletta Bari Manfredonia Taranto	51 413	-21.3	5.4	21

Source: Eurostat (online data code: tran_r_mago_nm).

Currently, data on maritime transport are collected under Directive 2009/42/EC on statistical returns in respect of carriage of goods and passengers by sea. This directive provides detailed quarterly data for ports handling more than 1 million tonnes of goods or recording more than 200 000 passenger movements a year. The data collected at port level are then aggregated at NUTS 2 regional level.

This section on maritime transport focuses on the total number of passengers and the total number of tonnes loaded and unloaded in NUTS 2 regions in Europe. Tables 14.3 and 14.4 show the top 20 regions with the highest number of sea passengers and highest volume of sea freight in 2009.

Unsurprisingly, maritime passenger transport is dominated by regions with a sea-faring tradition. By far the largest number of passengers transported by sea (30.2 million) is recorded by the Attiki region, where the port of Piraeus is the main gateway for passengers to the Greek islands. The second highest number of passengers was recorded in Sicilia, with 13.8 million passengers; Sicilia services several ferry connections to the mainland of Italy, as well as ferry routes to Malta and Tunisia. The ports of the Sydsverige region in Sweden, counting 13.3 million passenger movements in 2009, service a large number of ferry connections to the other countries around the Baltic Sea. The high passenger counts in Kent (13.2 million) and Nord - Pas-de-Calais (12.9 million) reflect the close ties across the English Channel, with the ports of Dover, Medway and Ramsgate on the English side and Calais and Dunkerque on the French side.

As in previous years, the rise in passenger numbers from 2008 to 2009 varied greatly between the top 20 European regions in terms of maritime passenger transport. In 13 of the 20 top regions, passenger numbers fell, but they increased in the other seven regions. The largest region in terms of maritime passenger transport, Attiki, continued the negative trend seen over the previous five years, with a 3.9 % fall in passenger numbers from 2008 to 2009. The other top regions also recorded declines: Sicilia (– 7.3 %), Sydsverige (– 11.1 %) and Kent (– 5.5 %). By contrast, the Weser-Ems region with its connections to the East Frisian Islands recorded a 10.2% increase from 2008 to 2009, continuing the increase over the previous five-year period. Other regions with notable increases in maritime passenger numbers included Calabria (9.2 %) and Campania (5.8 %).

For maritime freight, Zuid-Holland in the Netherlands with the port of Rotterdam is in the lead by far. It handled 349 million tonnes of freight in 2009, more than twice the volume of the second of the top 20 European regions, Antwerpen in Belgium (142 million tonnes). These two regions were followed by Hamburg in Germany (95 million tonnes) and Haute Normandie (Dieppe, Le Havre, Rouen) in France (92 million tonnes). These volumes are far

higher than those recorded for other modes of transport and illustrate the key role maritime freight plays in the European economy. Maritime transport is characterised by high flexibility, allowing large volumes to be loaded and unloaded close to the main recipients and producers.

From 2008 to 2009, freight volumes fell in all but one of the top 20 regions in terms of maritime freight handled. In nine regions, it fell by more than 15 %. Nevertheless, the magnitude of the decline reflects to a varying extent the global economic crisis and associated fall in international trade from 2008 to 2009. Amongst the top 20 regions, the most dramatic decreases were seen in Puglia in Italy (– 21.3 %) and Hamburg in Germany (– 20.3 %). The only region in the top 20 to record an increase in freight volumes from 2008 to 2009 (+ 3 %) was Vestlandet in Norway, with the Mongstad crude oil terminal. However, freight volumes in Vestlandet had fallen by an annual average of 3 % over the previous five years.

Data sources and availability

Eurostat collects, compiles and disseminates a variety of regional indicators. Data on road and railway infrastructure, inland waterways, vehicle stocks and road accidents are currently collected by Member States and candidate countries on a voluntary basis. Data on road transport of goods and maritime and air transport for passengers and goods are derived directly from data collected under legal acts. Data on journeys made by vehicles are derived from a specific study of road transport data.

Regional transport indicators are available on Eurostat's website under 'Transport' and are mirrored in the 'General and regional statistics'. Full datasets and predefined tables are available, covering infrastructure, the vehicle fleet, journeys by road, rail, sea and air and road safety (numbers of deaths and injuries in road accidents). All data are annual.

The data used in the maps and tables were extracted from Eurostat's website, although not all the derived indicators are directly available there.

Further information can be found in Eurostat's *Statistics in focus* series on transport issues and in CARE, a database managed by the European Commission's Directorate-General for Energy and Transport, which contains detailed data on road accidents collected by the Member States (http://ec.europa.eu/transport/road_safety/specialist/statistics/care_reports_graphics/index_en.htm).

Precise definitions of all the variables used can be found in the *Illustrated glossary for transport statistics* (fourth edition) (http://ec.europa.eu/eurostat/product?code=KS-RA-10-028&mode=view).

Science, technology and innovation

15

Introduction

Based on a number of data sources available at Eurostat, this chapter presents statistical data and indicators designed to illustrate the trends and structure of science, technology and innovation (STI) in European regions and compare them to other regions. The domains covered are research and development (R & D), patents, high technology and human resources in science and technology (HRST). More regional indicators on science, technology and innovation are available on the Eurostat website under 'Science and technology'.

Main statistical findings

Research and development

Twenty-five of the 260 EU regions shown on Map 15.1 spend the equivalent of more than 3 % of their GDP on R & D. These regions exceed the R & D intensity target set by the Barcelona Council in 2002 and maintained in the Europe 2020 strategy.

A cluster of four research-intensive regions can be found in south-western Germany: Stuttgart (5.83 %), Karlsruhe (3.75 %), Tubingen (3.79 %) and Darmstadt (3.11 %). These regions are also very important in absolute terms, as together they generate around 8 % of the total R & D expenditure in the EU. Another leading region in terms of R & D is Oberbayern (4.29 %), to the east of the four-region cluster, which contributes another 3 % to the EU total. Further north, Braunschweig (6.75 %), in the middle of Germany, is the most R & D-intensive region on the map. East of Braunschweig are two more major R & D regions: Dresden (4.08 %) and Berlin (3.31 %).

The two most R & D-intensive regions in the UK are East Anglia (5.93 %), which is the second most R & D-intensive region on the map, and Cheshire in North West England (5.7 %). Together these regions generate around 2 % of the EU total. Other R & D-intensive regions in the UK are Essex (3.24 %), Berkshire, Buckinghamshire and Oxfordshire (3.24 %) and North Eastern Scotland (3.18 %).

Eight of the most R & D-intensive regions are located in the Nordic countries. These regions are, starting from the south, Hovedstaden (the region surrounding the capital København) in Denmark (5.1 %), Sydsverige (4.75 %), Västsverige (3.72 %), Östra Mellansverige (3.74 %) and Stockholm (4.03 %) in Sweden and Etelä-Suomi (3.66 %), Länsi-Suomi (3.91 %) and Pohjois-Suomi (5.87 %) in Finland, the last of which is the third most R & D-intensive region on the map.

In France ([1]), the most R & D-intensive region is Midi-Pyrénées (4.15 %), just north of the Iberian Peninsula. In absolute terms, Île de France (3.11 %), which includes the French capital, is among the leading regions in the EU. Two more regions with relatively high R & D intensity are located in Austria: Steiermark (3.74 %) and Wien (3.61 %).

Map 15.2 provides an overview of the regional distribution of the share of researchers in total employment (measured in headcount). Researchers are the core category directly employed on R & D activities. They are defined as 'professionals engaged in the conception or creation of new knowledge, products, processes, methods and systems and in the management of the projects concerned'. The highest share of researchers out of all persons employed (more than 1.8 %) was found in 25 of the regions shown on Map 15.2. With six regions in this group of front-runners, the United Kingdom was the leading country, followed by Germany with five regions, Finland with three and Sweden and Norway with two each. Austria, Belgium, the Czech Republic, France, Portugal, Slovakia and Iceland each had one top region.

The share, or intensity, of researchers ranged from 1.2 % to 1.8 % in 40 European regions. Again, most were located in the United Kingdom (11), followed by another nine regions in Germany. In the vast majority of European regions, the share of researchers did not exceed 0.6 % of all persons employed. Twenty EU Member States and Norway reported at least one region with an intensity of researchers below 0.6 %.

Looking at national differences, the spread between the regions with the highest and lowest proportions of researchers in total employment was particularly wide in the United Kingdom (4.47 percentage points between North Eastern Scotland and Highlands and Islands) and the Czech Republic (2.91 percentage points between Praha and Severozapad). Ireland had the narrowest regional disparities in intensity of researchers (0.16 percentage points).

Human resources in science and technology

Investment in research, development, education and skills is a key policy area for the European Union, as they are essential to economic growth and to developing a knowledge-based 'smarter' economy. This has led to an increasing interest in the role and measurement of skills of the human resources in science and technology. It is therefore extremely important for policymakers at regional level (and also at EU and national levels) to analyse the stock of highly qualified people who are actively participating in science and technology activities and technological innovation. One way to measure the concentration of highly

([1]) Data for France is from 2004.

qualified people in the regions is to look at human resources in science and technology (HRST). HRST includes persons who have completed tertiary (i.e. university) education (HRSTE) and/or are employed in a science and technology occupation (HRSTO). The stock of HRSTO can be used as an indicator of development of the knowledge-based economy in the EU.

As Map 15.3 shows, HRSTO are mostly concentrated in urban regions, in particular around the capitals. In 2009, 11 of the 25 leading regions were capital regions, where there is often a high concentration of highly qualified jobs, for example due to the presence of head offices of companies and government institutions. Capitals are often big cities with many higher education facilities and a high number of highly educated people. This makes these and the surrounding regions attractive places to open science and technology-related businesses. At the same time, highly skilled people are often attracted to larger cities, as they are more likely to find a job that meets their requirements in a region where there are many companies.

This urban concentration of human resources employed in science and technology can also be seen by looking at two of the three large regional clusters with shares of HRSTO exceeding 35 % in 2009. The first of these clusters stretches from Switzerland into central and south-eastern Germany. In general, the regions in this cluster are very densely populated. This also applies to the regions in the second distinct cluster, which spans the Benelux countries and the western border regions of Germany. The third cluster is in the Scandinavian countries, where regions — apart from the capital regions — are very sparsely populated. The regions with the second, third and fifth highest shares of HRSTO are also in Scandinavia: Stockholm in Sweden (47.4 %), Oslo og Akershus in Norway (46.2 %) and Hovedstaden (København) in Denmark (45.1 %). The highest share, however, is reported in Praha (Czech Republic), where 50.6 % of the labour force are HRSTO.

Based on R & D intensity, sectors of economic activity can be subdivided into more specific subsectors for the purpose of analysing employment in science and technology. For manufacturing industries, four groups have been identified, depending on the level of R & D intensity: high, medium-high, medium-low and low-technology sectors. Services are classified into knowledge-intensive (KIS) and less knowledge-intensive services.

High-tech knowledge-intensive services and high-tech manufacturing are the two subsectors of greatest importance for science and technology in terms of generating relatively high added value, providing new jobs and contributing to competitive growth. Consequently, these two sectors are often analysed jointly as high-tech sectors. The NACE Rev. 2 classification defines high-tech knowledge-intensive services as including motion picture, video and television programme production, sound recording and music

publishing activities, programming and broadcasting, telecommunications, computer programming and related activities, information service activities and research and development.

High-tech manufacturing covers the manufacture of pharmaceutical products and pharmaceutical preparations and of computers and electronic and optical products.

The service sector employed around 69 % of the labour force in the EU in 2009, but only 2.6 % of the labour force was employed in high-tech knowledge-intensive services. The manufacturing sector employed 16.2 %, but only 1.1 % of the labour force was employed in high-tech manufacturing.

Figure 15.1 shows the regional disparities in high-tech sectors (by NACE Rev. 2) as a share of total employment. This figure plots the national average for each country and the regions with the lowest and highest shares of employment in high-tech sectors. At EU level, high-tech sectors (high-tech manufacturing and high-tech KIS) represented 3.7 % of total employment in 2009 with two thirds employed in high-tech knowledge-intensive services and one third occupied in high-tech manufacturing.

As the figure shows, the national and regional highest and lowest shares vary significantly from one country to another and significant disparities can be observed at regional level.

Regarding national averages, 17 out of the 32 observed countries registered values higher than the EU-27 average (3.7 %) with over 5.0 % in Denmark, Malta, Finland, Sweden, Iceland and Switzerland. On the other range of the scale, the lowest national shares of high-tech sectors in total employment below 2.5 % were registered in Greece, Cyprus, Latvia, Lithuania, Portugal, Romania and Turkey. Six European countries (Estonia, Cyprus, Latvia, Lithuania, Luxembourg and Malta) and Iceland are classified at NUTS level 1.

At regional level, urban regions, especially capital regions or regions situated close to capitals, often exhibit high shares of employment in high-tech sectors. Berkshire, Buckinghamshire and Oxfordshire (United Kingdom), situated in close proximity to London, stood out with approximately 10.0 % of the labour force in high-tech sectors. No region exceeded this share, the next closest being Comunidad de Madrid (Spain) with 9.3 %, Hovedstaden (Denmark) with 9.2 % and Province Brabant Wallon (Belgium) (9.1 %). The lowest shares of less than 1 % were registered in Trabzon (Turkey), Sud - Muntenia (Romania) and Centro (Portugal). Spain, the United Kingdom, Denmark, Belgium and Sweden are the countries with the highest regional employment, while Italy and France showed the biggest regional disparities when measured by the ratio of highest share to the lowest share. The lowest discrepancies in employment between regions were observed in Ireland, Greece, the Netherlands, Croatia and Turkey.

Map 15.1: R & D intensity, by NUTS 2 regions, 2008 (¹)
(total R & D expenditure as % of GDP)

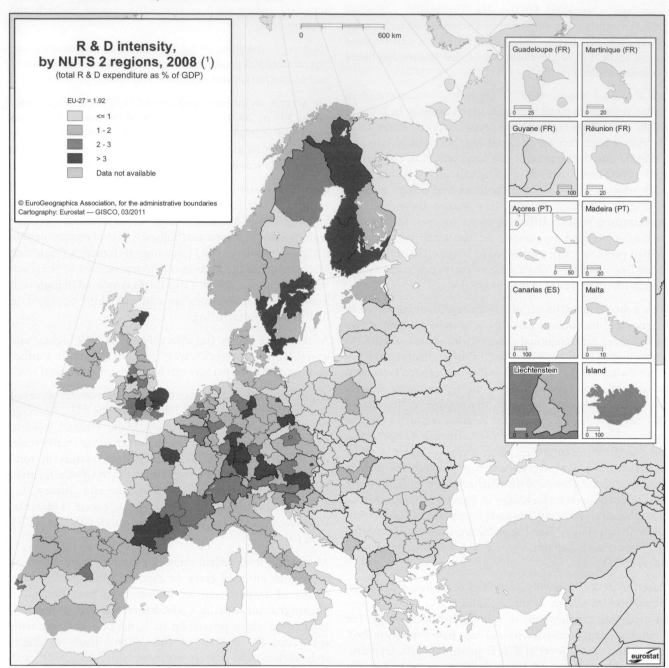

R & D intensity,
by NUTS 2 regions, 2008 (¹)
(total R & D expenditure as % of GDP)

EU-27 = 1.92

<= 1
1 - 2
2 - 3
> 3
Data not available

© EuroGeographics Association, for the administrative boundaries
Cartography: Eurostat — GISCO, 03/2011

0   600 km

Guadeloupe (FR)   Martinique (FR)
0   25   0   20

Guyane (FR)   Réunion (FR)
0   100   0   20

Açores (PT)   Madeira (PT)
0   50   0   20

Canarias (ES)   Malta
0   100   0   10

Liechtenstein   Ísland
0   5   0   100

(¹) EU-27, Eurostat estimate; Belgium, Denmark, Germany, Ireland, Netherlands, Austria and Sweden, 2007; Greece, 2005; France, 2004; Belgium, Départements d'outre-mer (France) and Croatia, by NUTS 1 regions; Norway, Switzerland and Turkey, national level; Niederbayern and Oberpfalz (Germany), confidential data; Estonia, Ireland, Luxembourg and Malta, provisional data; Netherlands, estimate; Sweden, in some cases researchers are allocated to the head office; Denmark, break in series with previous year for which data is available.

Source: Eurostat (online data code: rd_e_gerdreg).

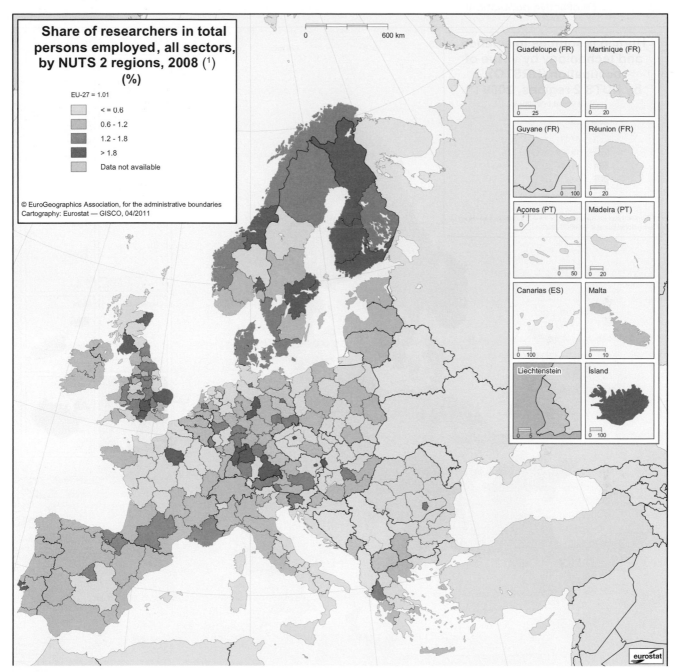

Map 15.2 Share of researchers in total persons employed, all sectors, by NUTS 2 regions, 2008 (¹) (%)

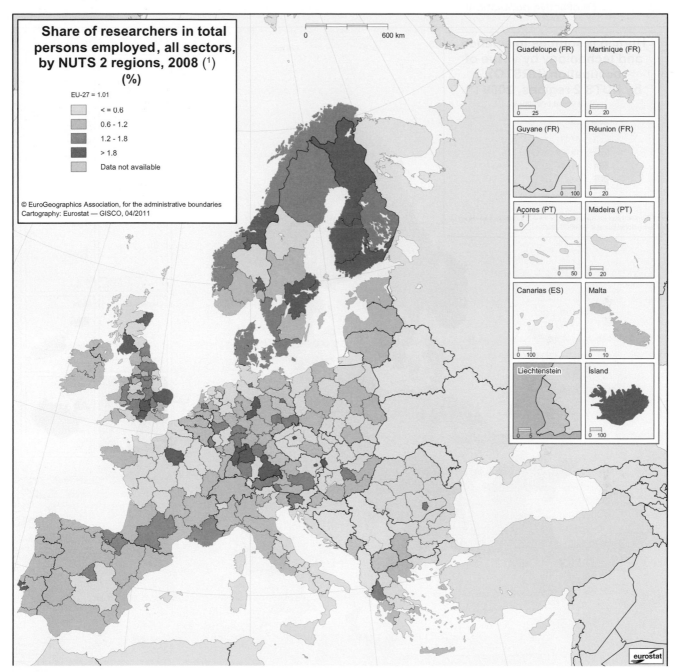

Share of researchers in total persons employed, all sectors, by NUTS 2 regions, 2008 (¹) (%)

EU-27 = 1.01

- < = 0.6
- 0.6 - 1.2
- 1.2 - 1.8
- > 1.8
- Data not available

© EuroGeographics Association, for the administrative boundaries
Cartography: Eurostat — GISCO, 04/2011

Guadeloupe (FR)
Martinique (FR)
Guyane (FR)
Réunion (FR)
Açores (PT)
Madeira (PT)
Canarias (ES)
Malta
Liechtenstein
Ísland

(¹) EU-27, Eurostat estimate; Belgium, Germany, Ireland, Italy, Cyprus, Latvia, Lithuania, Luxembourg, Malta, Netherlands, Austria, Sweden and United Kingdom, 2007; Greece, 2005; France, 2001; Denmark, Switzerland and Turkey, national level; Belgium, Départements d'outre-mer (France) , by NUTS 1 regions; Estonia, Luxembourg, Netherlands and United Kingdom, national estimates; Ireland, provisional data; Niederbayern, Oberpfalz, Brandenburg - Nordost and Brandenburg - Südwest (Germany), confidential data; Sweden, in some cases researchers are allocated to the head office.

Source: Eurostat (online data code: rd_p_persreg).

Map 15.3: Human resources in science and technology by virtue of occupation (HRSTO),
by NUTS 2 regions, 2009 (¹)
(% of active population)

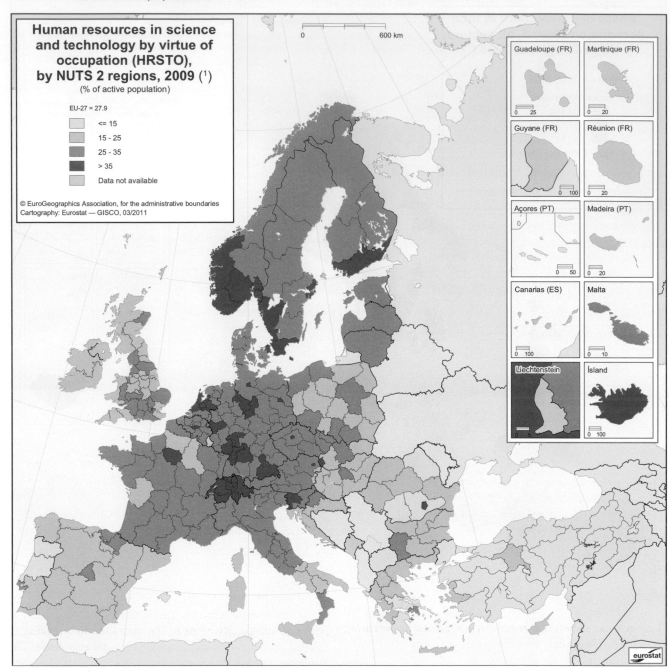

Human resources in science
and technology by virtue of
occupation (HRSTO),
by NUTS 2 regions, 2009 (¹)
(% of active population)

EU-27 = 27.9

<= 15

15 - 25

25 - 35

> 35

Data not available

© EuroGeographics Association, for the administrative boundaries
Cartography: Eurostat — GISCO, 03/2011

(¹) Corse (France) and Åland (Finland), data lack reliability due to reduced sample size, but publishable.

Source: Eurostat (online data code: hrst_st_rcat).

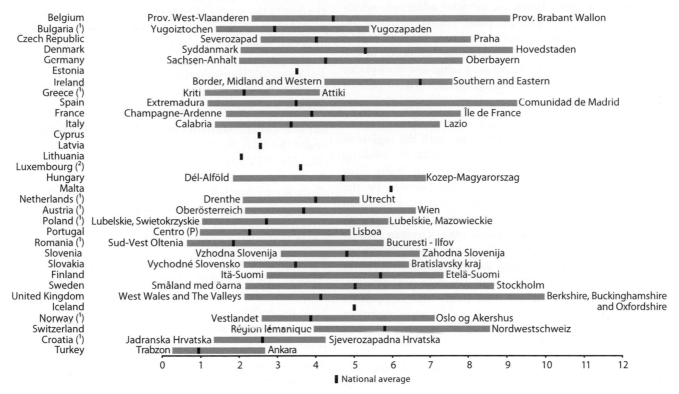

Figure 15.1: Employment in high-tech sectors as a share of total employment, highest and lowest NUTS 2 region within each country, 2009 (¹)

(¹) High-tech sectors = high-technology manufacturing plus high-tech knowledge-intensive services (KIS). Data lack reliability due to small sample size, but are publishable in region with the smallest share in Bulgaria, Greece, Netherlands, Austria, Poland, Romania, Norway and Croatia.
(²) Luxembourg, 2008.

Source: Eurostat (online data code: htec_emp_reg2).

Patents

In today's knowledge-based economy, new knowledge creation and innovation are increasingly important for sustaining and improving the economic welfare and growth of regions and countries. Research and development activities as well as innovation are therefore at the heart of many regional policies, including the Europe 2020 strategy for smart growth. Patent data are an important source of information on the location of technological inventions, and on the organisations and research institutions involved. Research has shown that innovative activities, as measured by patent counts, tend to cluster geographically in a limited number of regions. This is especially true for the high-tech industries.

Regional patent statistics are based on patent applications to the European Patent Office (EPO). Based on the address of the inventors, patents can be linked to a region, as defined in the nomenclature of territorial units for statistics (NUTS). Regional patent statistics have several advantages. First, they give a comparison of the technological performance of regions in Europe. In addition, the trend in the technological performance of regions can be monitored over time. Finally, they give detailed information on the technological

content of patent filings that allow investigation of specific technology fields. However, there are disadvantages to using patents as indicators of technological performance as not all inventions are patented, patent propensities vary across industries and firms and patented inventions vary in technical and economic value.

Regional patents statistics for EPO patent applications build on information from addresses of inventors. Eurostat has developed a methodology that allows postcode and city information to be parsed out from the address fields of inventors and allocates these addresses based on the postcode and/or city name to the corresponding regions as defined by NUTS. Different quality control procedures are built into the allocation process to prevent misallocations from errors in postcodes and city names, historical changes in postal code systems and city homonyms.

In the following figures, the technological performance of regions is calculated as the number patents per population at NUTS level 3 regions in Europe. Reporting technology figures in relation to population allows a comparison to be made of regions of different sizes. However, it also implies that, in some cases, less densely populated regions or regions with a comparatively low number of inhabitants may rank relatively high in terms of patents per population, even

though the region does not perform that well in terms of absolute number of patents. Furthermore, patents have been allocated to regions based on inventor addresses, which may not always tally with the place (region) of invention. Indeed, inventors do not necessarily live in the same region as the one in which they work. The bias introduced by the phenomenon of commuting between home and work places is likely to increase when smaller geographical units (NUTS 3 regions) are used.

Map 15.4 shows that technological activity is very much concentrated in the centre of Europe, with the region of Zuidoost-Noord-Brabant in the Netherlands ranking highest in terms of patents per population (more than 2 000 patents per million population), followed by the regions of Erlangen Kreisfreie Stadt, Erlangen-Höchstadt, Heidenheim, Ludwigsburg and Starnberg (over 1 000 patents per million population) and many other German regions (more than 500 patents per million population). The regions of Pirkanmaa in Finland and Rheintal-Bodenseegebiet in Austria count more than 500 patents per million inhabitants. Important technological activities (more than 250 patents per million inhabitants) are also found in some regions in France, Sweden, Denmark, Italy and Belgium, and others in Austria, Finland and Germany.

In the field of ICT (Map 15.5), the regions of Zuidoost-Noord-Brabant in the Netherlands and Erlangen Kreisfreie Stadt in Germany are the top regions in terms of the number of patents per population (approximately 1 000 patents per million population). The regions of Erlangen-Höchstadt, München Landkreis, Starnberg and Schwarzwald-Baar-Kreis in Germany count more than 400 patents per million population. In the other European countries, the regions of Pirkanmaa, Uusimaa and Pohjois-Pohjanmaa (Finland), Isère (France) and Skåne län (Sweden) can be considered as the leading regions in ICT patenting (more than 200 patents per million population).

Figure 15.2 shows large differences between the top regions of countries in terms of patents per population in the field of biotechnology. With more than 180 biotech patents per million population, the region of Weilheim-Schongau in Germany is by far the top region in Europe. The region of Zuidoost-Noord-Brabant in the Netherlands, Uppsala län in Sweden, the region of Nivelles in Belgium and Hovedstaden in Denmark are top regions in their country in terms of biotechnology patents per population and also among the top-performing regions in Europe in the field of biotechnology (more than 50 patents per million population). Figure 15.2 also illustrates that the average technological performance of regions differs greatly by country. Germany, Denmark, Sweden and the Netherlands, and to a lesser extent Belgium and Austria, have the highest average number of biotech patents per population.

Data sources and availability

The data in the maps and tables in this chapter are, wherever possible, by NUTS 2 and NUTS 3 regions. Data are extracted from the 'Science, technology and innovation' domain and, more specifically, from the subdomains 'Research and development', 'Human resources in science and technology', 'High technology industries and knowledge-intensive services' and 'Patents'.

Eurostat collects **statistics on research and development** under the legal requirements of Commission Regulation (EC) No 753/2004, which determines the dataset, breakdowns, frequency and transmission delays. The methodology for national R & D statistics is laid down in the *Frascati manual: proposed standard practice for surveys on research and experimental development* (OECD 2002), which is also used by many non-European countries.

Statistics on **human resources in science and technology (HRST)** are compiled annually, based on microdata extracted from the EU Labour Force Survey (EU LFS). The basic methodology for these statistics is laid down in the *Canberra manual*, which lists all the HRST concepts.

Data on **high-technology industries and knowledge-intensive services** are compiled annually, based on data collected from a number of official sources (EU LFS, structural business statistics, etc.). The high-technology employment aggregates are defined in terms of R & D intensity, calculated as the ratio of R & D expenditure on the economic activity to its value added, and based on the statistical classification of economic activities in the European Community (NACE). The NACE was revised from Rev. 1.1 to Rev. 2, which led to changes in the high-technology and knowledge-intensive sectors. The statistics in this chapter are based on NACE Rev. 2.

Data on **patent applications to the EPO** are compiled on the basis of microdata from the European Patent Office (EPO). The patent data reported include patent applications filed at the EPO during the reference year, classified by the inventor's region of residence and in accordance with the international patents classification of applications. Patent data are regionalised using procedures linking postcodes and/or place names to NUTS 2 and 3 regions. Patent statistics published by Eurostat are almost exclusively based on the EPO Worldwide Statistical Patent Database, Patstat, developed by the EPO in 2005, using its patent data collection and its knowledge of patent data. The data are largely taken from the EPO's master bibliographic database, DocDB, which is also known as the EPO Patent Information Resource. It includes bibliographic details on patents filed at more then 90 patent offices worldwide and contains more than 50 million documents. It covers a large number

Map 15.4: Patent applications to the EPO, by NUTS 3 regions, 2006 (^{1})
(per million inhabitants)

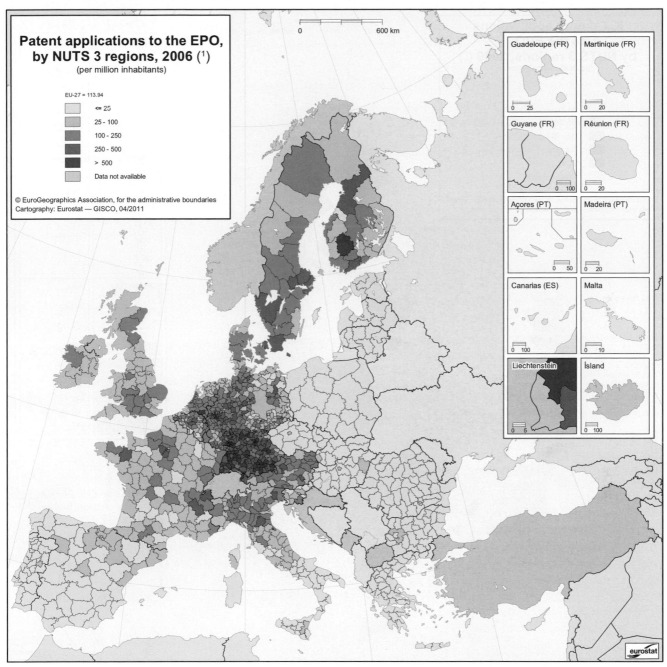

Patent applications to the EPO, by NUTS 3 regions, 2006 (^{1})
(per million inhabitants)

EU-27 = 113.94

- <= 25
- 25 - 100
- 100 - 250
- 250 - 500
- \> 500
- Data not available

© EuroGeographics Association, for the administrative boundaries
Cartography: Eurostat — GISCO, 04/2011

0   600 km

Guadeloupe (FR)   Martinique (FR)   0 25 / 0 20

Guyane (FR)   Réunion (FR)   0 100 / 0 20

Açores (PT)   Madeira (PT)   0 50 / 0 20

Canarias (ES)   Malta   0 100 / 0 10

Liechtenstein   Ísland   0 5 / 0 100

(^{1}) Ireland, Greece and Finland, population data for 2007; London (United Kingdom), by NUTS 1 region; Denmark, Sachsen-Anhalt (Germany), Illes Balears and Canarias (Spain), Sardegna (Italy), Poland and United Kingdom, by NUTS 2 regions.

Source: Eurostat (online data code: pat_ep_rtot).

Map 15.5: ICT patent applications to the EPO, by NUTS 3 regions, 2006 (^{1})
(per million inhabitants)

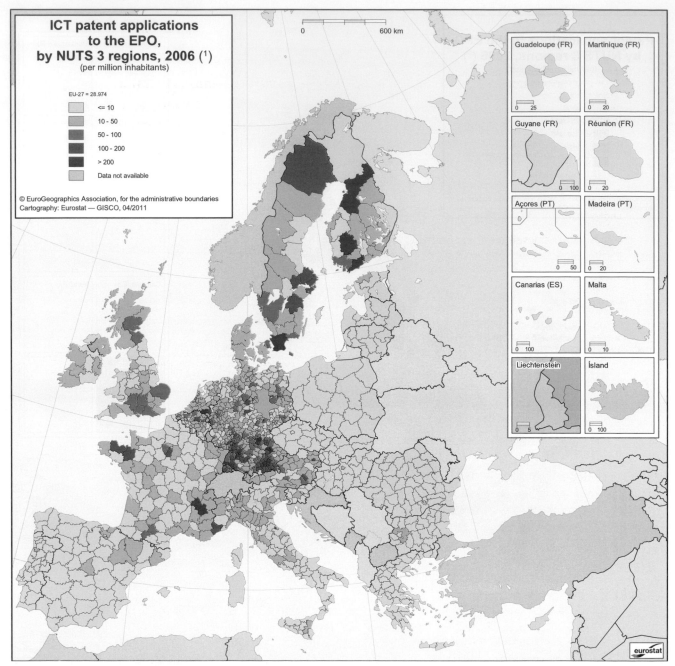

**ICT patent applications
to the EPO,
by NUTS 3 regions, 2006 (^{1})**
(per million inhabitants)

EU-27 = 28.974

- <= 10
- 10 - 50
- 50 - 100
- 100 - 200
- > 200
- Data not available

© EuroGeographics Association, for the administrative boundaries
Cartography: Eurostat — GISCO, 04/2011

0 ——— 600 km

Guadeloupe (FR)   Martinique (FR)
0   25   0   20

Guyane (FR)   Réunion (FR)
0   100   0   20

Açores (PT)   Madeira (PT)
0   50   0   20

Canarias (ES)   Malta
0   100   0   10

Liechtenstein   Ísland
0   5   0   100

(^{1}) Ireland, Greece and Finland, population data for 2007; London (United Kingdom), by NUTS 1 region; Denmark, Sachsen-Anhalt (Germany), Illes Balears and Canarias (Spain), Sardegna (Italy), Poland and United Kingdom, by NUTS 2 regions.

Source: Eurostat (online data code: pat_ep_rtot).

Figure 15.2: Biotechnology patent application to the EPO, highest and lowest region within each country, by NUTS 3 regions, 2006 (^{1})
(per million inhabitants)

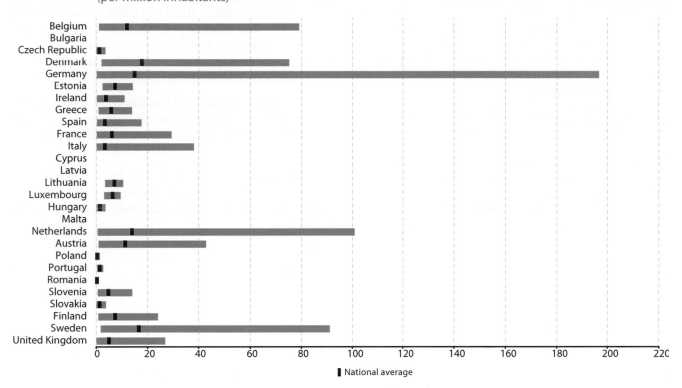

■ National average

(^{1}) Ireland, Greece and Finland, population data for 2007; Denmark, Poland and United Kingdom, by NUTS 2 regions.

Source: Eurostat (online data code: pat_ep_rbio).

of fields included in patent documents, such as application details (claimed priorities, application and publication), technology categories, inventors and applicants, title and abstract, patent citations and non-patent literature.

Context

Since the Lisbon Council in March 2000 and the Barcelona Council in 2002, the European Union and the Member States have spared no effort in turning the EU into the 'most competitive and dynamic knowledge-based economy in the world, capable of sustainable economic growth with more and better jobs and greater social cohesion' by 2010.

These efforts — based on the Lisbon strategy — highlighted the importance of R & D and innovation in the EU. To follow up, the 2005 initiative on 'Working together for growth and jobs' gave new momentum and placed science, technology and innovation back at the heart of EU national and regional policies to deliver targeted action on 'Knowledge and innovation for growth'.

The EU and the Member States fully recognised that science, technology and innovation, together with high-quality education and lifelong learning, are essential to turn Europe into a leading knowledge-based society, thus creating the right conditions for long-term prosperity. To achieve this, building the European research area (ERA) is at the top of the political agenda.

As the Lisbon strategy expired and the recent economic crisis hit, a new strategy for the EU was called for. On the basis of the conclusions of the Spring European Council of March 2010 and of the Commission communication on 'Europe 2020', the European Council agreed on the main pillars of this new strategy, which was formally adopted in 2010. Supported by seven flagship initiatives, Europe 2020 puts forward three mutually reinforcing priorities: **smart growth** (developing an economy based on knowledge and innovation); **sustainable growth** (promoting a more resource-efficient, greener and more competitive economy); and **inclusive growth** (fostering a high-employment economy delivering social and territorial cohesion).

The European Commission's 'Innovation Union' is a flagship initiative under the Europe 2020 strategy. It sets out a strategic approach to innovation, backed at the highest

political level. The Innovation Union will focus Europe's efforts — and cooperation with third countries — on challenges like climate change, energy and food security, health and an ageing population. It will use public-sector intervention to stimulate the private sector and to remove bottlenecks that stop ideas reaching the market. These include lack of finance, fragmented research systems and markets, under-use of public procurement for innovation and slow standard-setting.

Part of the EU's growth potential has been seriously undermined by the economic crisis, which changed the overall perspective dramatically and was largely responsible for steering some European regions off the course to growth and economic sustainability. Overall, the effects of the crisis make the challenges that existed before the crisis, such as globalisation, demographic ageing, lagging productivity and climate change, much harder to handle.

This underlines the need for meaningful indicators on science, technology and innovation. Such indicators are of paramount importance for informing policymakers on where European regions stand and can help them take the necessary measures to bring all regions back on the path to more knowledge and growth. This information also helps to draw a clear comparative picture as to how regions are evolving both at European level and worldwide.

Based on the statistics and indicators, this publication highlights the European regions that are performing well in research and development activities and those that need support.

Data on high-tech industries and knowledge-intensive services, patents and human resources in science and technology were also used extensively to complete the regional picture.

**Trends in densely
and thinly populated areas**

16

Introduction

This chapter looks at the differences between thinly populated areas (or rural areas) and densely populated areas (or urban areas) in European countries. It covers five issues: severe material deprivation; income levels that put people at risk of poverty; difficulty accessing primary healthcare; broadband Internet connectivity; and crime, violence and vandalism. Only three of these show a consistent pattern: in urban areas, broadband connections and people reporting crime, violence and vandalism are more common; in rural areas, access to primary healthcare is more difficult. For the two poverty-related issues, the pattern is more mixed.

Main statistical findings

Severe material deprivation

Romania and Bulgaria have the highest proportions of their populations experiencing severe material deprivation, at 32 % and 42 % respectively. Such deprivation is especially high in rural areas, where the share is 11 and 15 percentage points respectively higher than in urban areas. For the six countries ranked below the top two — Latvia, Hungary, Lithuania, Poland, Slovakia and Greece — deprivation is more prevalent in rural areas than in urban areas, but the gap is significantly smaller.

In 19 out of the 22 remaining countries, severe material deprivation is higher in urban areas than in the country-side ([1]) (see Figure 16.1). In some countries, the difference is quite marked. Both in Belgium and Austria, severe material deprivation is 5 percentage points higher in densely populated areas than elsewhere. In short, for most Member States, especially the more developed ones, severe material deprivation is more of a problem in urban areas than in the countryside.

In the 10 central and eastern Member States, severe material deprivation tends to be higher, sometimes much higher, and the shares are higher in rural areas. This may also explain why these countries still have significant migration from rural to urban areas, which is not the case elsewhere.

At-risk-of-poverty

Although severe material deprivation was concentrated in urban areas in 19 out of the 30 countries examined, the at-risk-of-poverty rate is higher in rural than in urban areas

([1]) In Malta and the Netherlands, densely populated areas were compared with intermediate areas, as none of the population lives in thinly populated areas. In Iceland, intermediate density area was compared with thinly populated areas, as there are no densely populated areas.

in 24 out of 30 countries. However, the overall statistics can give a misleading impression.

While severe material deprivation is influenced by the local cost of living, the at-risk-of-poverty rate is set at the same level for an entire country. So the income of someone living in London is compared to the same threshold as that for someone living in rural Wales, although the cost of living is likely to be far higher in London. Furthermore, housing costs are not factored into disposable income. As housing costs tend to be higher in cities, and more people tend to rent in cities than in rural areas, it is likely that once income has been adjusted to take housing costs into account, a more accurate picture emerges. Other aspects of the cost of living, such as transport costs, also need to be factored in. Transport costs may be higher in rural areas, because of the need for a car, and longer trip distances than in urban areas, but the impact of these costs depends on income levels, as well as on the availability and cost of public transport.

Despite the caveats above, in the two countries where severe material deprivation was much higher in urban than in rural areas, Belgium and Austria, the risk of poverty in urban areas was also higher (see Figure 16.2). The risk of poverty in urban areas in the UK and Luxembourg was also significantly higher than in rural areas. In Romania and Bulgaria, the difference in poverty risk between rural and urban areas is even bigger than that for severe material deprivation.

The risk of poverty is lowest in intermediate density areas. These typically include smaller towns and the suburbs of cities. For example, in Germany, France, Switzerland and Sweden, people living in suburbs and towns were least at risk of poverty.

Access to primary healthcare

This is clearly a rural issue. In all countries, people living in rural areas report more difficulty in gaining access to primary healthcare than their counterparts in urban areas (see Figure 16.3). Rural dwellers have to travel longer distances to general practitioners and primary healthcare centres. Nevertheless, some countries have been able to minimise this problem. In Norway, Sweden and Finland the gap between urban and rural areas is negligible, but the overall share of people reporting difficult access is still quite high (between 12 % and 17 %). In France, the UK and the Netherlands, access is better, with only between 6 % and 9 % reporting problems, and the difference between urban and rural areas is small. In the Netherlands, a small, urbanised country, good access to primary healthcare could be expected, but the UK and particularly France, with large sparsely populated areas, have put in place systems to ensure good access even in relatively remote locations.

At the other end of the spectrum, Latvia, Malta, Italy, Slovakia and Italy score poorly, and more than 30 % of their

Figure 16.1: Share of population severely materially deprived, by degree of urbanisation, 2009 ([1])
(%)

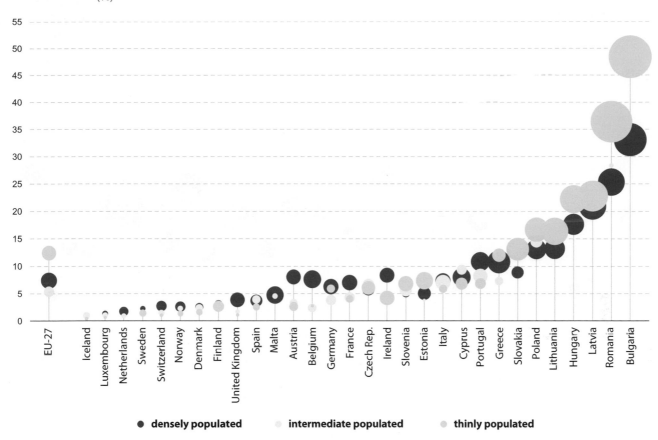

● **densely populated**   ○ **intermediate populated**   ● **thinly populated**

([1]) 'Severely materially deprived' defined as living in a household lacking at least four out of nine important items.
Reading note: Countries ranked by share of total population severely materially deprived. Bubble size is severely materially deprived population in area as % of total population in all areas.
Source: EU-SILC.

population have difficulty accessing primary healthcare services. The gap between urban and rural areas in these countries also tends to be much larger. For example, in Romania, 40 % of the rural population has difficulty with access to primary healthcare services, compared to only 15 % in urban areas. The gap is also wide in Belgium and Malta, but both countries have a very small rural population, so these figures should be interpreted with a certain degree of caution. (The size of the bubbles in the graph is determined by the share of the total population living in these areas, multiplied by the share of population reporting difficulty. As a result, the rural bubbles for Belgium and Malta are quite small, even though a high share of the population in rural areas in both countries reports difficulties.)

Broadband Internet connection

In 28 out of 30 countries, broadband Internet connections are more prevalent in urban than in rural areas (see Figure 16.4). Only in the UK and Luxembourg are broadband Internet

connections more prevalent in rural areas, by 2 percentage points.

The gap between urban and rural areas is over 25 percentage points in Latvia, Romania and, despite its IT industry, Ireland. In Spain, Portugal, Greece, Croatia and Bulgaria, the gap is between 20 and 25 percentage points. In some countries, this gap is partly due to the lack of broadband coverage in rural areas. According to Europe's Digital Competitiveness Report 2010 ([2]), coverage in rural areas in Latvia and Romania is only 67 % and 45 % respectively. Overall, broadband coverage for the EU's rural population is high at 80 %, with shares below 50 % only in Cyprus, Romania and Bulgaria.

In Ireland's rural areas, broadband connections were available to 82 % of the population, but only 42 % actually had a connection. This shows that other issues, such as

([2]) 'Europe's digital competitiveness report 2010', Commission staff working document SEC(2010) 627, Publications Office of the European Union, Luxembourg, 2010 (http://ec.europa.eu/information_society/digital-agenda/documents/edcr.pdf).

Figure 16.2: Share of population at risk of poverty, by degree of urbanisation, 2009
(%)

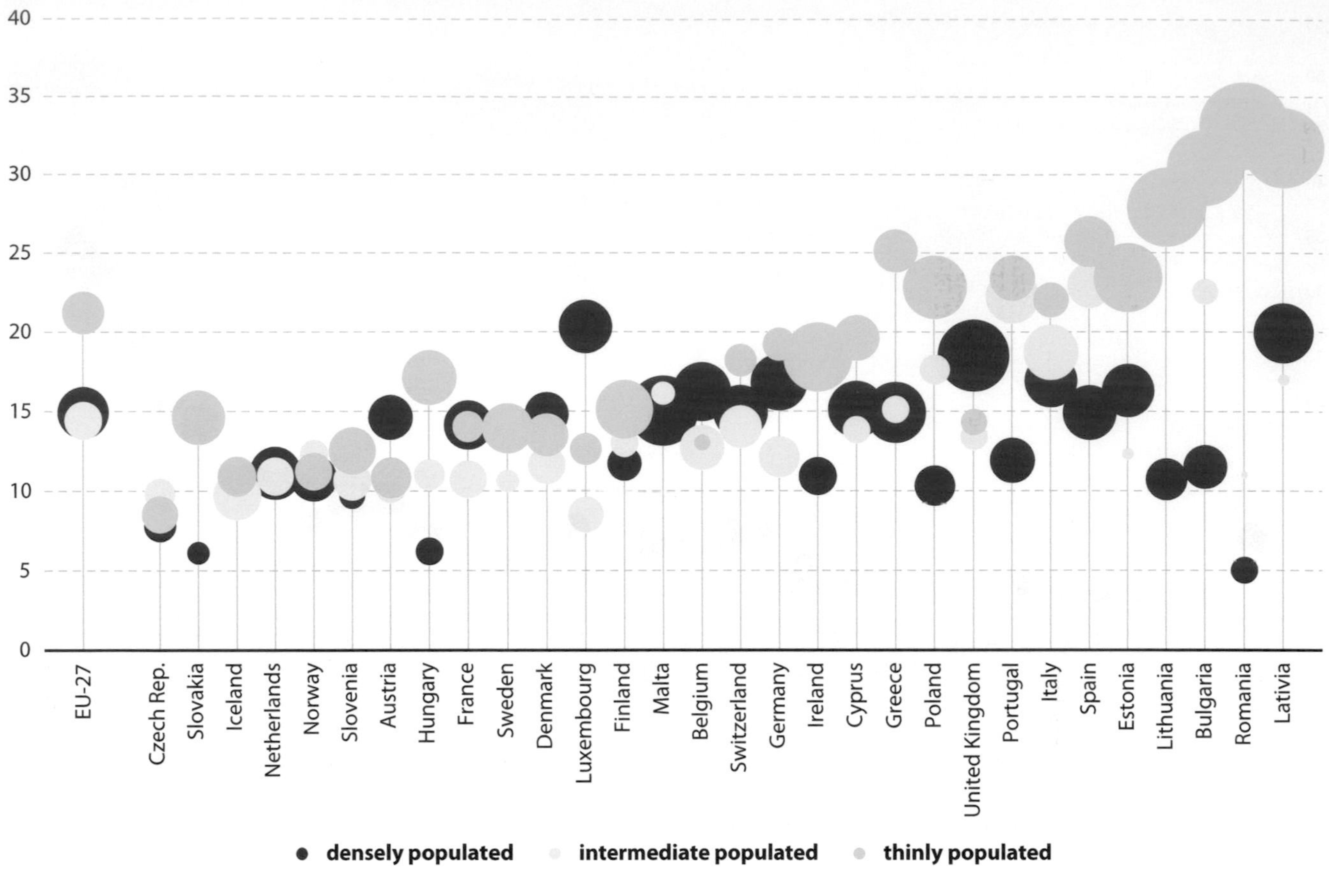

Reading note: Countries ranked by share of population at risk of poverty. Bubble size is population at risk of poverty in area as a % of total population in all areas.
Source: EU-SILC.

differences in broadband costs, disposable income, e-skills or the use to which broadband connections are put, may also differ between urban and rural areas. These differences may also account for the gap between urban and rural areas to a greater extent than broadband coverage.

Crime, violence and vandalism

The urban population tends to have better access to primary healthcare and broadband connections, but it also witnesses more crime, violence and vandalism (see Figure 16.5). In every country, the share of people reporting these problems in their neighbourhoods is highest in urban areas. The EU averages highlight this clearly. In urban areas, 23 % report these issues, compared to only 8 % in rural areas. This is also holds true for environmental concerns, such as grime, air pollution and noise (for data on these issues see the fifth cohesion report).

The four countries where more than 20 % of the population reported crime, violence and vandalism are Bulgaria, Latvia, the United Kingdom and the Netherlands. The four countries where those reporting them accounted for less than 7 % of

the population are Iceland, Norway, Lithuania and Poland. The fact that both the top four and the bottom four are a mix of countries with a high level of GDP per head and others with some of the lowest levels of GDP per head in Europe is significant. It implies either that such issues are completely independent of the level of economic development in a country, or that they take on different meanings, depending on the context and respondents' expectations. The way in which questions have been translated may also influence respondents, as it may be difficult to capture the exact same nuance in all languages.

The political debate can have a strong influence on the number of people reporting these issues. For example, in the Netherlands, the political debate has focused intensely on public safety since the murders of film director Theo van Gogh and politician Pim Fortuyn. This may in part explain why such a high share of people identified crime, violence and vandalism as major concerns in the Netherlands.

In Italy and Portugal, the gap between urban and rural areas is more than 20 percentage points. The gap is the smallest in Cyprus, Iceland and Norway.

Figure 16.3: Share of population with difficult access to primary healthcare, by degree of urbanisation, 2007 (%)

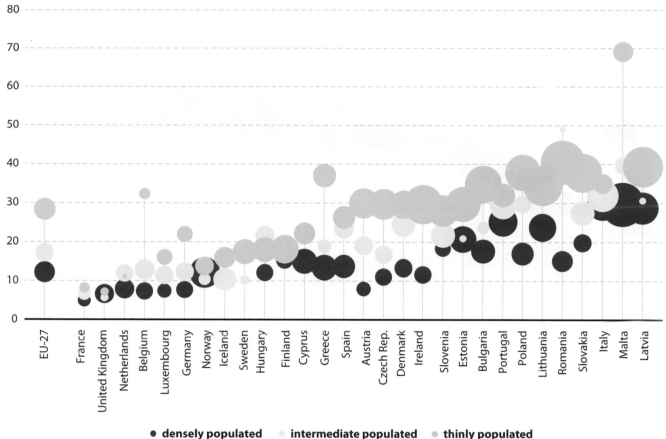

● **densely populated**   ○ **intermediate populated**   ○ **thinly populated**

Reading note: Countries ranked by share of population with difficult access to primary healthcare. Bubble size is population reporting difficult access to primary healthcare in area as % of population in all areas.
Source: EU-SILC.

Data sources and availability

The bubble graphs shown in this chapter have been refined to condense a large amount of information into a single graph. This shows:

- country name (horizontal axis);
- country ranking according to national shares (horizontal axis);
- shares for the three types of areas per country (three colour-coded bubbles);
- the share of the population in the area multiplied by the share of population in the area with the issue (bubble size); for the issues which reflect problems, the bubble size reflects the relative importance of the problem per area in a country.

This type of graph can also be time-animated, so that the bubbles change over time, adding another dimension to a graph which is already rich in data.

The data on broadband access presented in this chapter is derived from annual surveys on ICT usage in households and by individuals. It is published online by Eurostat (table isoc_pibi_hba).

The remaining four graphs are based on custom extractions from the EU Survey on Income and Living Conditions (EU-SILC).

Areas by degree of urbanisation are defined as part of the EU Labour Force Survey (EU-LFS).

The concept of 'degree of urbanisation' was defined in the context of the LFS. Three types of area are defined, using a criterion of geographical contiguity in combination with a minimum population threshold, based on local administrative units level 2 (LAU2) and 2001 census data.

Densely populated area

This is a contiguous set of LAU2s, each of which has a density of more than 500 inhabitants per km², where the total population for the set is at least 50 000 inhabitants.

Figure 16.4: Share of households with broadband connection, by degree of urbanisation, 2009
(%)

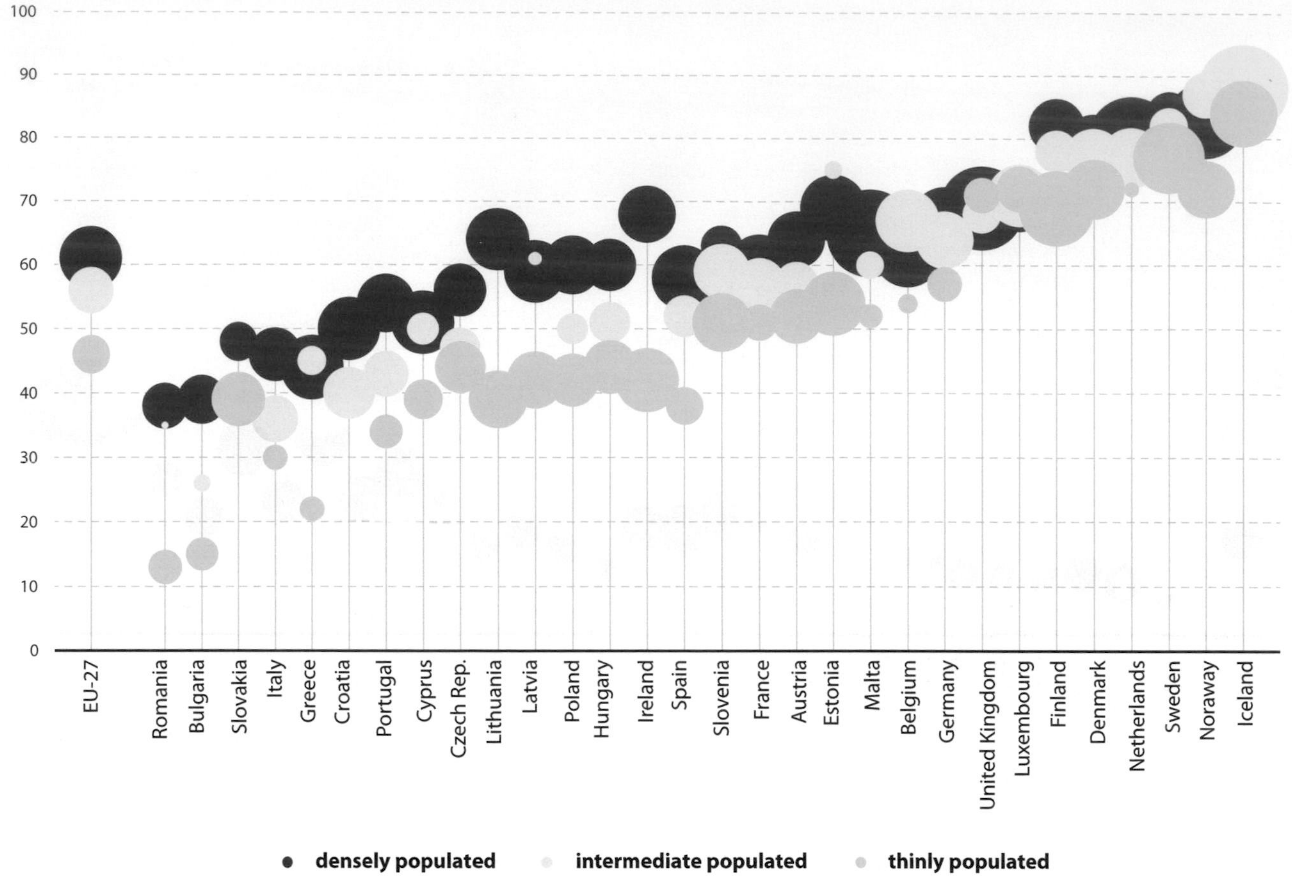

● **densely populated**   ○ **intermediate populated**   ○ **thinly populated**

Reading note: Countries ranked by share of population with access to broadband in total population. Bubble size is % of total population.
Source: EU-SILC.

Intermediate area

This is a contiguous set of LAU2s, not belonging to a densely populated area, each of which has a density superior to 100 inhabitants per km², and either with a total population for the set of at least 50 000 inhabitants or adjacent to a densely populated area.

Thinly populated area

This is a contiguous set of LAU2s belonging neither to a densely populated nor to an intermediate area. A set of LAU2s totalling less than 100 km², not reaching the required density but entirely enclosed within a densely populated or intermediate area, is considered as part of that area. If it is enclosed within a densely populated area and an intermediate area, it is considered to be part of the intermediate area.

A GIS layer with this information can be downloaded here:

http://epp.eurostat.ec.europa.eu/portal/page/portal/gisco_Geographical_information_maps/geodata/reference

Exceptions: France, Greece, Finland and Ireland

A number of countries have opted to use a modified or updated classification. Map 16.1 includes these classifications.

France

The French National Statistical Institute (INSEE) has used a different methodology to define the degree to which its communes are urbanised.

Greece

The definition as described above has been applied to the LAU1 level by Eurostat as it did not have the Greek LAU2 digital boundaries. However, Greece has classified its LAU2 regions according to this methodology.

Finland

Finland has applied this methodology to a more recent set of LAU2 boundaries.

Figure 16.5: Share of population reporting crime, violence or vadalism, by degree of urbanisation, 2009 (%)

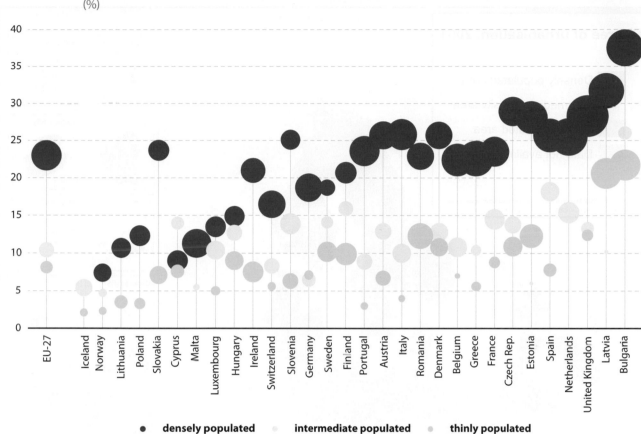

● **densely populated** ○ **intermediate populated** ○ **thinly populated**

Reading note: Countries ranked by share of population having problems. Bubble size is population reporting crime, violence or vandalism in area as % of total population in all areas.
Source: EU-SILC.

Ireland

Ireland has also used an approach which differs from that described above. It has classified LAU1s instead of LAU2s. As a result, the following cities (LAU1) are classified as densely populated: Cork City, Dublin, Galway, Limerick and Waterford. The remainder of the country is thinly populated.

For more information on these exceptions please see: https://circabc.europa.eu/d/d/workspace/SpacesStore/b65ef11a-ade2-40e2-8696-e5224e28b59d/CNTR_DEGURBA.zip

Revision of the degree of urbanisation

The European Commission has revised the original degree of urbanisation, using population grid cells as the main criteria instead of LAU2s. This improves the accuracy and the comparability of this classification. The main criteria in the new methodology are:

(1) Thinly-populated area (alternative name: rural area):

more than 50 % of the population lives in rural grid cells.

(2) Intermediate density area (alternative name: towns and suburbs):

less than 50 % of the population lives in rural grid cells and less than 50 % live in high-density clusters.

(3) Densely populated area (alternative names: cities/urban centres/urban areas):

at least 50 % lives in high-density clusters ([3]).

([3]) In addition, each high-density cluster should have at least 75 % of its population in densely-populated LAU2s. This also ensures that all high-density clusters are represented by at least one densely-populated LAU2, even when this cluster represents less than 50 % of the population of that LAU2.

Map 16.1: Degree of urbanisation, 2001

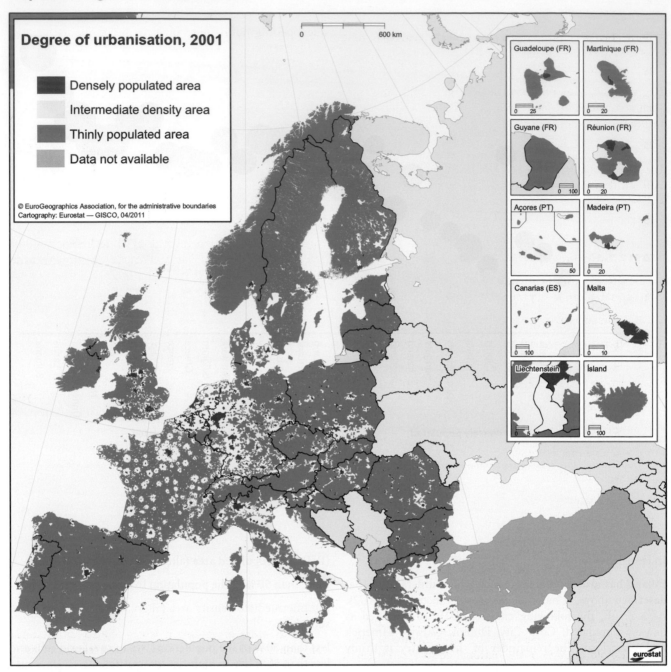

Degree of urbanisation, 2001

- Densely populated area
- Intermediate density area
- Thinly populated area
- Data not available

© EuroGeographics Association, for the administrative boundaries
Cartography: Eurostat — GISCO, 04/2011

0   600 km

Guadeloupe (FR)   Martinique (FR)
0   25   0   20

Guyane (FR)   Réunion (FR)
0   100   0   20

Açores (PT)   Madeira (PT)
0   50   0   20

Canarias (ES)   Malta
0   100   0   10

Liechtenstein   Ísland
0   5   0   100

eurostat

Sources: Eurostat, NSI.

In the above, the following definitions are used.

Rural grid cells: grid cells outside urban clusters.

Urban clusters: clusters of contiguous [4] grid cells of 1 km² with a density of at least 300 inhabitants per km² and a minimum population of 5 000.

High-density cluster: contiguous [5] grid cells of 1 km² with a density of at least 1 500 inhabitants per km² and a minimum population of 50 000.

For more information, see the new Eurostat LFS guidance note on degree of urbanisation. This revised classification will be implemented from reference year 2012 onwards.

Severe material deprivation

The severe material deprivation rate is the share of people who cannot afford to pay for at least four of the following:

- unexpected expenses;
- one week's annual holiday away from home;
- arrears (mortgage or rent, utility bills or hire purchase instalments);
- a meal with meat, chicken or fish every other day;
- heating to keep the home adequately warm;
- a washing machine;
- a colour TV;
- a telephone;
- a personal car.

At-risk-of-poverty

The at-risk-of-poverty rate relies on a relative income definition. A person counts as 'poor' if they live in households where equivalised disposable income is below the threshold of 60 % of the national equivalised median income. Given the nature of the retained threshold, and the fact that having an income below this threshold is neither a necessary nor a sufficient condition of having a low standard of living, this indicator is referred to as a measure of poverty risk.

Access to primary healthcare

Access is assessed in terms of physical and technical access and opening hours, but not in terms of quality, price or similar aspects. Physical access has to be assessed in terms of distance, but also takes into account infrastructure and equipment; for example, if the nearest health provider is far away, so it takes too much time to get there, or if getting there is impossible due to lack of means of transport.

Primary healthcare is understood to mean a general practitioner, primary health centre, or a casualty department or similar where first-aid treatment is available.

Broadband Internet connection

An Internet connection through xDSL-technology, a cable network upgraded for Internet traffic or through other broadband technologies.

Reporting crime, violence or vandalism in the area

The question in EU SILC is:

Do you have any of the following problems with your dwelling/accommodation:

Crime, violence or vandalism in the area? Yes/No

Context

The Lisbon Treaty has included territorial cohesion alongside economic and social cohesion as an objective for the EU. This new concept was presented in a Green Paper in 2008 and the debate has been synthesised in the sixth Progress Report on Cohesion in 2009. The fifth Cohesion Report explains the main issues related to territorial cohesion and how these could be transposed into policy proposals. One of the main issues related to territorial cohesion is the need for data on different territorial levels, particularly for lower levels of geography. The classification of the degree of urbanisation provides a unique insight into trends at the local level, and highlights the differences between urban and rural areas.

---

[4] Contiguity for urban clusters includes the diagonal (i.e. cells with only the corners touching). Gaps in the urban cluster are not filled (i.e. cells surrounded by urban cells).
[5] Contiguity does not include the diagonal (i.e. cells with only the corners touching) and gaps in the cluster are filled (i.e. cells surrounded by a majority of high-density cells).

Annex 1 — NUTS (Nomenclature of territorial units for statistics)

European Union: NUTS 2 regions

Belgium

BE10 Région de Bruxelles-Capitale/ Brussels Hoofdstedelijk Gewest

BE21 Prov. Antwerpen

BE22 Prov. Limburg (B)

BE23 Prov. Oost-Vlaanderen

BE24 Prov. Vlaams-Brabant

BE25 Prov. West-Vlaanderen

BE31 Prov. Brabant Wallon

BE32 Prov. Hainaut

BE33 Prov. Liège

BE34 Prov. Luxembourg (B)

BE35 Prov. Namur

Bulgaria

BG31 Severozapaden

BG32 Severen tsentralen

BG33 Severoiztochen

BG34 Yugoiztochen

BG41 Yugozapaden

BG42 Yuzhen tsentralen

Czech Republic

CZ01 Praha

CZ02 Střední Čechy

CZ03 Jihozápad

CZ04 Severozápad

CZ05 Severovýchod

CZ06 Jihovýchod

CZ07 Střední Morava

CZ08 Moravskoslezsko

Denmark

DK01 Hovedstaden

DK02 Sjælland

DK03 Syddanmark

DK04 Midtjylland

DK05 Nordjylland

Germany

DE11 Stuttgart

DE12 Karlsruhe

DE13 Freiburg

DE14 Tübingen

DE21 Oberbayern

DE22 Niederbayern

DE23 Oberpfalz

DE24 Oberfranken

DE25 Mittelfranken

DE26 Unterfranken

DE27 Schwaben

DE30 Berlin

DE41 Brandenburg - Nordost

DE42 Brandenburg - Südwest

DE50 Bremen

DE60 Hamburg

DE71 Darmstadt

DE72 Gießen

DE73 Kassel

DE80 Mecklenburg-Vorpommern

DE91 Braunschweig

DE92 Hannover

DE93 Lüneburg

DE94 Weser-Ems

DEA1 Düsseldorf

DEA2 Köln

DEA3 Münster

DEA4 Detmold

DEA5 Arnsberg

DEB1 Koblenz

DEB2 Trier

DEB3 Rheinhessen-Pfalz

DEC0 Saarland

DED1 Chemnitz

DED2 Dresden

DED3 Leipzig

DEE0 Sachsen-Anhalt

DEF0 Schleswig-Holstein

DEG0 Thüringen

Estonia

EE00 Eesti

Ireland

IE01 Border, Midland and Western

IE02 Southern and Eastern

Greece

GR11 Anatoliki Makedonia,Thraki

GR12 Kentriki Makedonia

GR13 Dytiki Makedonia

GR14 Thessalia

GR21 Ipeiros

GR22 Ionia Nisia

GR23 Dytiki Ellada

GR24 Sterea Ellada

GR25 Peloponnisos

GR30 Attiki

GR41 Voreio Aigaio

GR42 Notio Aigaio

GR43 Kriti

Spain

ES11 Galicia

ES12 Principado de Asturias

ES13 Cantabria

ES21 País Vasco

ES22 Comunidad Foral de Navarra

ES23 La Rioja

ES24 Aragón

ES30 Comunidad de Madrid

ES41 Castilla y León

ES42 Castilla-La Mancha

ES43 Extremadura

ES51 Cataluña

ES52 Comunidad Valenciana

ES53 Illes Balears

ES61 Andalucía

ES62 Región de Murcia

ES63 Ciudad Autónoma de Ceuta

ES64 Ciudad Autónoma de Melilla

ES70 Canarias

France

FR10 Île-de-France

FR21 Champagne-Ardenne

FR22 Picardie

FR23 Haute-Normandie

FR24 Centre

FR25 Basse-Normandie

FR26 Bourgogne

FR30 Nord - Pas-de-Calais

FR41 Lorraine

FR42 Alsace

FR43 Franche-Comté

FR51 Pays de la Loire

FR52 Bretagne

FR53 Poitou-Charentes

FR61 Aquitaine

FR62 Midi-Pyrénées

FR63 Limousin

FR71 Rhône-Alpes

FR72 Auvergne

FR81 Languedoc-Roussillon

FR82 Provence-Alpes-Côte d'Azur

FR83 Corse

FR91 Guadeloupe

FR92 Martinique

FR93 Guyane

FR94 Réunion

Italy

ITC1 Piemonte

ITC2 Valle d'Aosta/Vallée d'Aoste

ITC3 Liguria

ITC4 Lombardia

ITD1 Provincia Autonoma Bolzano/Bozen

ITD2 Provincia Autonoma Trento

ITD3 Veneto

ITD4 Friuli-Venezia Giulia

ITD5 Emilia-Romagna

ITE1 Toscana

ITE2 Umbria

ITE3 Marche

ITE4 Lazio

ITF1 Abruzzo

ITF2 Molise

ITF3 Campania

ITF4 Puglia

ITF5 Basilicata

ITF6 Calabria

ITG1 Sicilia

ITG2 Sardegna

Cyprus

CY00 Kypros/Kıbrıs

Latvia

LV00 Latvija

Lithuania

LT00 Lietuva

Luxembourg

LU00 Luxembourg (Grand-Duché)

Hungary

HU10 Közép-Magyarország

HU21 Közép-Dunántúl

HU22 Nyugat-Dunántúl

HU23 Dél-Dunántúl

HU31 Észak-Magyarország

HU32 Észak-Alföld

HU33 Dél-Alföld

Malta

MT00 Malta

Netherlands

NL11 Groningen

NL12 Friesland (NL)

NL13 Drenthe

NL21 Overijssel

NL22 Gelderland

NL23 Flevoland

NL31 Utrecht

NL32 Noord-Holland

NL33 Zuid-Holland

NL34 Zeeland

NL41 Noord-Brabant

NL42 Limburg (NL)

Austria

AT11 Burgenland (A)

AT12 Niederösterreich

AT13 Wien

AT21 Kärnten

AT22 Steiermark

AT31 Oberösterreich

AT32 Salzburg

AT33 Tirol

AT34 Vorarlberg

Poland

PL11 Łódzkie

PL12 Mazowieckie

PL21 Małopolskie

PL22 Śląskie

PL31 Lubelskie

PL32 Podkarpackie

PL33 Świętokrzyskie

PL34 Podlaskie

PL41 Wielkopolskie

PL42 Zachodniopomorskie

PL43 Lubuskie

PL51 Dolnośląskie

PL52 Opolskie

PL61 Kujawsko-pomorskie

PL62 Warmińsko-mazurskie

PL63 Pomorskie

Portugal

PT11 Norte

PT15 Algarve

PT16 Centro (P)

PT17 Lisboa

PT18 Alentejo

PT20 Região Autónoma dos Açores

PT30 Região Autónoma da Madeira

Romania

RO11 Nord-Vest

RO12 Centru

RO21 Nord-Est

RO22 Sud-Est

RO31 Sud - Muntenia

RO32 Bucureşti - Ilfov

RO41 Sud-Vest Oltenia

RO42 Vest

Slovenia

SI01 Vzhodna Slovenija

SI02 Zahodna Slovenija

Slovakia

SK01 Bratislavský kraj

SK02 Západné Slovensko

SK03 Stredné Slovensko

SK04 Východné Slovensko

Finland

FI13 Itä-Suomi

FI18 Etelä-Suomi

FI19 Länsi-Suomi

FI1A Pohjois-Suomi

FI20 Åland

Sweden

SE11 Stockholm

SE12 Östra Mellansverige

SE21 Småland med öarna

SE22 Sydsverige

SE23 Västsverige

SE31 Norra Mellansverige

SE32 Mellersta Norrland

SE33 Övre Norrland

United Kingdom

UKC1 Tees Valley and Durham

UKC2 Northumberland and Tyne and Wear

UKD1 Cumbria

UKD2 Cheshire

UKD3 Greater Manchester

UKD4 Lancashire

UKD5 Merseyside

UKE1 East Yorkshire and Northern Lincolnshire

UKE2 North Yorkshire

UKE3 South Yorkshire

UKE4 West Yorkshire

UKF1 Derbyshire and Nottinghamshire

UKF2 Leicestershire, Rutland and Northamptonshire

UKF3 Lincolnshire

UKG1 Herefordshire, Worcestershire and Warwickshire

UKG2 Shropshire and Staffordshire

UKG3 West Midlands

UKH1 East Anglia

UKH2 Bedfordshire and Hertfordshire

UKH3 Essex

UKI1 Inner London

UKI2 Outer London

UKJ1 Berkshire, Buckinghamshire and Oxfordshire

UKJ2 Surrey, East and West Sussex

UKJ3 Hampshire and Isle of Wight

UKJ4 Kent

UKK1 Gloucestershire, Wiltshire and Bristol/Bath area

UKK2 Dorset and Somerset

UKK3 Cornwall and Isles of Scilly

UKK4 Devon

UKL1 West Wales and the Valleys

UKL2 East Wales

UKM2 Eastern Scotland

UKM3 South Western Scotland

UKM5 North Eastern Scotland

UKM6 Highlands and Islands

UKN0 Northern Ireland

EFTA countries: Statistical regions at level 2

Iceland
IS00 Ísland

Liechtenstein
LI00 Liechtenstein

Norway
NO01 Oslo og Akershus
NO02 Hedmark og Oppland
NO03 Sør-Østlandet
NO04 Agder og Rogaland
NO05 Vestlandet
NO06 Trøndelag
NO07 Nord-Norge

Switzerland
CH01 Région lémanique
CH02 Espace Mittelland
CH03 Nordwestschweiz
CH04 Zürich
CH05 Ostschweiz
CH06 Zentralschweiz
CH07 Ticino

Candidate countries: Statistical regions at level 2

Montenegro

ME00 Crna Gora

Croatia

HR01 Sjeverozapadna Hrvatska

HR02 Središnja i Istočna (Panonska) Hrvatska

HR03 Jadranska Hrvatska

The former Yugoslav Republic of Macedonia

MK00 Poranešna jugoslovenska Republika Makedonija

Turkey

TR10 İstanbul

TR21 Tekirdağ

TR22 Balıkesir

TR31 İzmir

TR32 Aydın

TR33 Manisa

TR41 Bursa

TR42 Kocaeli

TR51 Ankara

TR52 Konya

TR61 Antalya

TR62 Adana

TR63 Hatay

TR71 Kırıkkale

TR72 Kayseri

TR81 Zonguldak

TR82 Kastamonu

TR83 Samsun

TR90 Trabzon

TRA1 Erzurum

TRA2 Ağrı

TRB1 Malatya

TRB2 Van

TRC1 Gaziantep

TRC2 Şanlıurfa

TRC3 Mardin

Annex 2 — Cities participating in the Urban Audit data collection (^{1})

European Union: Urban Audit cities

Belgium
BE001C **Bruxelles/Brussel**
BE002C Antwerpen
BE003C Gent
BE004C Charleroi
BE005C Liège
BE006C Brugge
BE007C Namur

Bulgaria
BG001C **Sofia**
BG002C Plovdiv
BG003C Varna
BG004C Burgas
BG005C Pleven
BG006C Ruse
BG007C Vidin
BG008C Stara Zagora

Czech Republic
CZ001C **Praha**
CZ002C Brno
CZ003C Ostrava
CZ004C Plzeň
CZ005C Ústí nad Labem
CZ006C Olomouc
CZ007C Liberec
CZ008C České Budějovice
CZ009C Hradec Králove
CZ010C Pardubice
CZ011C Zlín
CZ012C Kladno

CZ013C Karlovy Vary
CZ014C Jihlava

Denmark
DK001C **København**
DK002C Aarhus
DK003C Odense
DK004C Aalborg

Germany
DE001C **Berlin**
DE002C Hamburg
DE003C München
DE004C Köln
DE005C Frankfurt am Main
DE006C Essen
DE007C Stuttgart
DE008C Leipzig
DE009C Dresden
DE010C Dortmund
DE011C Düsseldorf
DE012C Bremen
DE013C Hannover
DE014C Nürnberg
DE015C Bochum
DE017C Bielefeld
DE018C Halle an der Saale
DE019C Magdeburg
DE020C Wiesbaden
DE021C Göttingen
DE022C Mülheim a. d. Ruhr
DE023C Moers
DE025C Darmstadt

DE026C Trier
DE027C Freiburg im Breisgau
DE028C Regensburg
DE029C Frankfurt (Oder)
DE030C Weimar
DE031C Schwerin
DE032C Erfurt
DE033C Augsburg
DE034C Bonn
DE035C Karlsruhe
DE036C Mönchengladbach
DE037C Mainz
DE039C Kiel
DE040C Saarbrücken
DE041C Potsdam
DE042C Koblenz
DE043C Rostock

Estonia
EE001C **Tallinn**
EE002C Tartu

Ireland
IE001C **Dublin**
IE002C Cork
IE003C Limerick
IE004C Galway
IE005C Waterford

Greece
GR001C **Athina**
GR002C Thessaloniki
GR003C Patra

(^{1}) Cities in bold are capitals.

GR004C Irakleio
GR005C Larisa
GR006C Volos
GR007C Ioannina
GR008C Kavala
GR009C Kalamata

Spain
ES001C **Madrid**
ES002C Barcelona
ES003C Valencia
ES004C Sevilla
ES005C Zaragoza
ES006C Málaga
ES007C Murcia
ES008C Las Palmas
ES009C Valladolid
ES010C Palma de Mallorca
ES011C Santiago de Compostela
ES012C Vitoria/Gasteiz
ES013C Oviedo
ES014C Pamplona/Iruña
ES015C Santander
ES016C Toledo
ES017C Badajoz
ES018C Logroño
ES019C Bilbao
ES020C Córdoba
ES021C Alicante/Alacant
ES022C Vigo
ES023C Gijón
ES024C L'Hospitalet de Llobregat
ES025C Santa Cruz de Tenerife
ES026C Coruña, A

France
FR001C **Paris**
FR203C Marseille
FR003C Lyon

FR004C Toulouse
FR205C Nice
FR006C Strasbourg
FR007C Bordeaux
FR008C Nantes
FR009C Lille
FR010C Montpellier
FR011C Saint-Etienne
FR012C Le Havre
FR013C Rennes
FR014C Amiens
FR015C Rouen
FR016C Nancy
FR017C Metz
FR018C Reims
FR019C Orléans
FR020C Dijon
FR021C Poitiers
FR022C Clermont-Ferrand
FR023C Caen
FR024C Limoges
FR025C Besançon
FR026C Grenoble
FR027C Ajaccio
FR028C Saint Denis
FR029C Pointe-à-Pitre
FR030C Fort-de-France
FR031C Cayenne
FR032C Toulon
FR035C Tours
FR202C Aix-en-Provence
FR207C Lens - Liévin

Italy
IT001C **Roma**
IT002C Milano
IT003C Napoli
IT004C Torino

IT005C Palermo
IT006C Genova
IT007C Firenze
IT008C Bari
IT009C Bologna
IT010C Catania
IT011C Venezia
IT012C Verona
IT013C Cremona
IT014C Trento
IT015C Trieste
IT016C Perugia
IT017C Ancona
IT018C l'Aquila
IT019C Pescara
IT020C Campobasso
IT021C Caserta
IT022C Taranto
IT023C Potenza
IT024C Catanzaro
IT025C Reggio di Calabria
IT026C Sassari
IT027C Cagliari
IT028C Padova
IT029C Brescia
IT030C Modena
IT031C Foggia
IT032C Salerno

Cyprus
CY001C **Lefkosia**

Latvia
LV001C **Rīga**
LV002C Liepāja

Lithuania
LT001C **Vilnius**
LT002C Kaunas
LT003C Panevėžys

Luxembourg

LU001C **Luxembourg**

Hungary

HU001C **Budapest**

HU002C Miskolc

HU003C Nyíregyháza

HU004C Pécs

HU005C Debrecen

HU006C Szeged

HU007C Győr

HU008C Kecskemét

HU009C Székesfehérvár

Malta

MT001C **Valletta**

MT002C Gozo

Netherlands

NL001C **'s-Gravenhage**

NL002C Amsterdam

NL003C Rotterdam

NL004C Utrecht

NL005C Eindhoven

NL006C Tilburg

NL007C Groningen

NL008C Enschede

NL009C Arnhem

NL010C Heerlen

NL011C Almere

NL012C Breda

NL013C Nijmegen

NL014C Apeldoorn

NL015C Leeuwarden

Austria

AT001C **Wien**

AT002C Graz

AT003C Linz

AT004C Salzburg

AT005C Innsbruck

Poland

PL001C **Warszawa**

PL002C Łódź

PL003C Kraków

PL004C Wrocław

PL005C Poznań

PL006C Gdańsk

PL007C Szczecin

PL008C Bydgoszcz

PL009C Lublin

PL010C Katowice

PL011C Białystok

PL012C Kielce

PL013C Toruń

PL014C Olsztyn

PL015C Rzeszów

PL016C Opole

PL017C Gorzów Wielkopolski

PL018C Zielona Góra

PL019C Jelenia Góra

PL020C Nowy Sącz

PL021C Suwałki

PL022C Konin

PL023C Żory

PL024C Częstochowa

PL025C Radom

PL026C Płock

PL027C Kalisz

PL028C Koszalin

Portugal

PT001C **Lisboa**

PT002C Porto

PT003C Braga

PT004C Funchal

PT005C Coimbra

PT006C Setúbal

PT007C Ponta Delgada

PT008C Aveiro

PT009C Faro

Romania

RO001C **Bucureşti**

RO002C Cluj-Napoca

RO003C Timişoara

RO004C Craiova

RO005C Brăila

RO006C Oradea

RO007C Bacău

RO008C Arad

RO009C Sibiu

RO010C Târgu Mureş

RO011C Piatra Neamţ

RO012C Călăraşi

RO013C Giurgiu

RO014C Alba Iulia

Slovenia

I001C **Ljubljana**

SI002C Maribor

Slovakia

SK001C **Bratislava**

SK002C Košice

SK003C Banská Bystrica

SK004C Nitra

SK005C Prešov

SK006C Žilina

SK007C Trnava

SK008C Trenčín

Finland

FI001C **Helsinki**

FI002C Tampere

FI003C Turku

FI004C Oulu

Sweden

SE001C **Stockholm**

SE002C Göteborg

SE003C Malmö

SE004C Jönköping

SE005C Umeå

SE006C Uppsala

SE007C Linköping

SE008C Örebro

United Kingdom

UK001C **London**

UK002C Birmingham

UK003C Leeds

UK004C Glasgow

UK005C Bradford

UK006C Liverpool

UK007C Edinburgh

UK008C Manchester

UK009C Cardiff

UK010C Sheffield

UK011C Bristol

UK012C Belfast

UK013C Newcastle upon Tyne

UK014C Leicester

UK015C Derry

UK016C Aberdeen

UK017C Cambridge

UK018C Exeter

UK019C Lincoln

UK020C Gravesham

UK021C Stevenage

UK022C Wrexham

UK023C Portsmouth

UK024C Worcester

UK025C Coventry

UK026C Kingston-upon-Hull

UK027C Stoke-on-Trent

UK028C Wolverhampton

UK029C Nottingham

UK030C Wirral

EFTA countries: Urban Audit cities

Norway

NO001C **Oslo**

NO002C Bergen

NO003C Trondheim

NO004C Stavanger

NO005C Kristiansand

NO006C Tromsø

Switzerland

CH001C Zürich

CH002C Genève

CH003C Basel

CH004C **Bern**

CH005C Lausanne

CH006C Winterthur

CH007C St Gallen

CH008C Luzern

CH009C Lugano

CH010C Biel/Bienne

Candidate countries: Urban Audit cities

Croatia

HR001C **Zagreb**

HR002C Rijeka

HR003C Slavonski Brod

HR004C Osijek

HR005C Split

Turkey

TR001C **Ankara**

TR002C Adana

TR003C Antalya

TR004C Balıkesir

TR005C Bursa

TR006C Denizli

TR007C Diyarbakır

TR008C Edirne

TR009C Erzurum

TR010C Gaziantep

TR011C Hatay

TR012C İstanbul

TR013C İzmir

TR014C Kars

TR015C Kastamonu

TR016C Kayseri

TR017C Kocaeli

TR018C Konya

TR019C Malatya

TR020C Manisa

TR021C Nevsehir

TR022C Samsun

TR023C Siirt

TR024C Trabzon

TR025C Van

TR026C Zonguldak

European Commission

Eurostat regional yearbook 2011

Luxembourg: Publications Office of the European Union

2011 — 235 pp. — 21 x 29.7 cm

Theme: General and regional statistics
Collection: Statistical books

ISBN 978-92-79-20366-4
ISSN 1830-9674
doi:10.2785/1392
Cat. KS-HA-11-001-EN-C

Price (excluding VAT) in Luxembourg: EUR 20

How to obtain EU publications

Free publications:

- via EU Bookshop (http://bookshop.europa.eu);
- at the European Union's representations or delegations. You can obtain their contact details on the Internet (http://ec.europa.eu) or by sending a fax to +352 2929-42758.

Priced publications:

- via EU Bookshop (http://bookshop.europa.eu).

Priced subscriptions (e.g. annual series of the Official Journal of the European Union and reports of cases before the Court of Justice of the European Union):

- via one of the sales agents of the Publications Office of the European Union (http://publications.europa.eu/others/agents/index_en.htm).